First In, Last Out

*An American Paratrooper in Vietnam
with the 101st and Vietnamese Airborne*

John D. Howard

Brigadier General, U.S. Army Retired

STACKPOLE
BOOKS

Guilford, Connecticut

Published by Stackpole Books
An imprint of Globe Pequot
Trade Division of The Rowman & Littlefield Publishing Group, Inc.
4501 Forbes Boulevard, Suite 200, Lanham, Maryland 20706

Distributed by NATIONAL BOOK NETWORK
800-462-6420

British Library Cataloguing in Publication Information available
Library of Congress Cataloging-in-Publication Data available

ISBN 978-0-8117-1962-9 (hardcover)
ISBN 978-0-8117-6606-7 (e-book)

∞™ The paper used in this publication meets the minimum requirements of American National Standard for Information Sciences—Permanence of Paper for Printed Library Materials, ANSI/NISO Z39.48-1992.

Printed in the United States of America

This book is dedicated to all the soldiers who answered their nation's call in Vietnam and served there under difficult circumstances, especially those who were with me on this odyssey. Two deserve special mention: COL Dave Hackworth and COL Art Taylor. Both men had a huge influence on me during my Vietnam tours. They are in warriors' Valhalla now; it won't be long before I join them . . . but not just yet.

It is also dedicated to my wife, COL Brooke Myers, U.S. Army (Ret.). Without her love, encouragement, and wise counsel, this narrative would have never been written. She too is a combat veteran, having distinguished herself as a battalion commander in Iraq in 2003 and 2004. Between the two of us, we have fifty-seven years of commissioned service in the U.S. Army and seven combat "hash" marks, each symbolizing six months in a war zone. She has borne the burden of Vietnam ghosts throughout our marriage.

Contents

Preface

FROM 1964 TO 1973, ROUGHLY TWENTY-SEVEN MILLION MEN WERE eligible for service in the U.S. armed forces. More than half did not serve. Military duty was avoided by a variety of means, mostly legal. Dick Cheney, the secretary of defense during Desert Storm and former vice president, had five draft deferments. When asked about it, his response was, "I had other priorities in the 60s than military service."[1] Among prominent politicians, Cheney was not alone. Senator, later Vice President, Joe Biden also had five deferments.

Eleven million did answer the nation's call, either by enlisting or being drafted. Two million, less than 8 percent of the eligible population, received sixty-five dollars per month combat pay in Southeast Asia. Most were on the ground in Vietnam; some were offshore aboard ships or in Vietnam's airspace. Fifty-eight thousand died there, 304,000 were wounded, and 74,000 of the wounded were permanently disabled. In 1973 when the last U.S. soldiers left Vietnam, over 2,200 service members were listed as missing in action.[2]

Many myths flourished about those who served. Little of the mythology was complimentary. One of the most prominent and oft repeated was that black soldiers were called to fight a "white man's war" and suffered a disproportionate number of casualties. This litany was common among organizations like the Black Panthers, the Student Nonviolent Coordinating Committee, and the NAACP that were not known for tempering their oratory with facts. The reality was that casualties suffered by black soldiers were the same as the percentage of blacks in the U.S. population. Blacks suffered 7,243 deaths in the Vietnam War; this was 12.4 percent of the total, which was below the proportion of blacks in the U.S. military.[3]

Vietnam veterans also suffered from the inevitable comparison to the "greatest generation," those who had served in World War II. We always came up short and were never deemed quite as good as they were. We stayed away from organizations like Veterans of Foreign Wars and the American Legion because many of the World War II vets were less than welcoming; some were even demeaning of our service. Those who had enjoyed more adulation than any veterans in our nation's history seemed unable or unwilling to share it.

More volunteered for Vietnam than anyone realized. Two-thirds of our World War II veterans were draftees while two-thirds of the Vietnam vets were volunteers. Three-quarters of those who died in Southeast Asia were volunteers. Eighty percent who served in Vietnam were high school graduates, making the wartime force more educated than any previous one.[4]

A small number of Americans—mostly middle class, educated, and white—became actively involved in the antiwar movement, and some of them called us fascists and baby-killers. Men in uniform were their favorite targets and spitting, by both males and females, was their weapon of choice. Their fervor was directed at both the policymakers and those of us who took the orders and executed the policies. The activists' intellect was not sufficient to make the distinction between the two. The press, the clergy, and their faculty advisors cheered them on. They wore the mantle of self-righteousness like a badge of honor. Some managed to convince themselves and others that their courage was equal to or greater than that of combat soldiers. Their commitment, in most cases, did not include the inconvenience of leaving the country, the stigma of going to prison, or the testicular virility to serve as unarmed combat medics. Instead, they played the deferment game or found other angles to keep them out of harm's way. Seminars on Ivy League campuses were offered to ensure students failed their pre-induction medical examinations. Selective Service Category IV-F, "Registrant Not Qualified for Service," became more valuable than a graduate school grant.

When draft calls began shrinking as the United States withdrew from Vietnam, the protestors' moral outrage diminished. By the mid-1970s changing the world seemed less important than moving back into mainstream America. Politics was a favored vocation, and the protestors far outnumbered the Vietnam veterans in government. In January 1993, twenty years after the signing of the Paris Peace Accords, a master manipulator of draft deferments moved into the White House.

—~—

I served in Vietnam in 1965–1966 and again in 1972–1973. My experiences framed America's involvement in that country . . . the beginning and the end. In the summer of 1965, our unit, the 1st Brigade of the 101st Airborne Division, was part of a massive buildup of U.S. forces that ultimately reached a half million U.S. troops. Our knowledge of the country and our enemy was lacking. We fought Viet Cong guerrillas and North Vietnamese soldiers. Even though we never lost a battle, there was little sign of progress. Victory as defined by previous wars was elusive. Today, the men I served with are fond of saying, "We were winning when I left." That statement expresses our pride in service, not reality.

As the commitment dragged on, America grew tired of the war. In 1969 President Nixon started a program of disengagement, called Vietnamization. When I returned to Vietnam in May of 1972, U.S. withdrawal continued in the face of the largest North Vietnamese offensive of the war. The assault known as the Easter Offensive changed the conflict from an insurgency to a conventional war. Equipped and assisted by the USSR and China, the enemy fielded three combined arms corps made up of infantry divisions, armor regiments, and artillery battalions. The only Americans fighting on the ground were a small number of tactical advisors. I was one of them, a battalion advisor in the Vietnamese Airborne Division. Thankfully, President Nixon did not abandon us. The political climate did not allow for the re-introduction of U.S. ground combat troops, but the president reinforced South Vietnam with scores of fighter aircraft and B-52 bombers. Airpower filled the gap and saved the day. The

North Vietnamese Army was decimated, losing 100,000 men, nearly all of its tanks, and most of its large-caliber artillery pieces. The end result was a ceasefire agreement in January 1973 that stopped the fighting long enough for the U.S. POWs to be released and the remaining Americans to depart Vietnam. Washington's policymakers called it peace with honor. Later events proved that there was neither peace nor honor.

—◦—

Over the years, the body of literature about Vietnam has become more balanced and more objective. Pundits and professors became less shrill with the passage of time. Journalists who lauded the "Genius of General Giap" modulated their commentaries as the costs versus the gains of the Tet and Easter Offensives were tallied. It is now all a part of history.

My service in Vietnam was with "Regular, By God" Army volunteers, men of the 101st Airborne Division and Vietnamese Airborne Division advisors. We were there because we had raised our hands to serve when our nation needed us. In 1965, we did not have to be challenged by a dead president about what we could do for our country—our fathers, grandfathers, neighbors, and friends had set an example. To us, following in their footsteps was perfectly normal. We owed our country and this is how we settled accounts. We came from all walks of life, all creeds, all cultures, and all parts of the United States. Most served honorably and returned to civilian life. Those who went back to Main Street U.S.A. did not find a welcoming America. Others, like me, made a lifelong commitment to the profession of arms. To some extent, the Army insulated us from an indifferent and sometimes hostile public. Regardless of our individual experiences in Vietnam and its aftermath, none of us would ever be the same.

Arlington, Virginia
2016

Introduction

If you ain't been, you're goin'; if you've been, you're goin' back.
—An expression heard often at the U.S. Army
Infantry School, Fort Benning, Georgia,
during the Vietnam War

In the mid-late 1960s, the U.S. Army's focus was the war in Vietnam. As a result, the U.S. Army Infantry School at Fort Benning, Georgia, was swarming with officers who were either headed to Vietnam or who had just come back. When I arrived in January 1969, six Infantry Officers' Advanced Courses (IOAC), nine months of instruction, were in session. Two hundred captains and majors were enrolled in each course. All considered it R&R, an interlude between Vietnam tours. As a result, the officers' clubs, the hub of military social life in the '60s, prospered as never before. There was a club in the Custer Terrace housing area, where most of the IOAC students lived. The Custer Terrace O Club was packed, especially on Wednesday and Friday nights. We swilled beer, chain-smoked, and told war stories. It was said that there was only one difference between a fairy tale and a war story; the fairy tales started, "Once upon a time . . ." and a war story started, "This is no shit. . . ."

War stories, unlike Aesop's fables and Grimm's fairy tales, seem to ripen with age and re-telling. Perhaps it is because the works of Aesop and Grimm are committed to writing, while war stories are only in our minds. As a result, war stories are susceptible to embellishment. Over time those embellished details take on a life of their own. Having been told and retold so many times, the story becomes real in the teller's mind.

Some of us conveniently forgot hard or unpleasant truths. We protected ourselves by masking failings. Once vivid memories became clouded and were pushed back into the recesses of the subconscious. Rarely do ugly incidents come to the surface; moments of clarity are few and far between.

In 2012, I was talking with several of my old platoon members about a firefight on September 10, 1965. We were trying to piece together what actually happened in the midst of a monsoon downpour near An Khe, Vietnam. My radio operator (RTO), SP4 Raymond "Rocky" Ryan, was wounded in that action; he almost lost his leg. To the best of my knowledge, SSG Travis Martin was also wounded. Ryan's recollection parallels mine. SSG Billy Robbins, weapons squad leader, swears that Martin was wounded another time. Robbins also cited Sergeant Wolfe as being wounded in action (WIA) that day. I have no memory of Wolfe being hit. SP4 Charlie Lostaunau, who was in Sergeant Wolfe's squad, remembered the day well; he said Wolfe was wounded later. For the 3rd Platoon, A Company, 1-327th Infantry (Airborne), it was the first action after our arrival in Vietnam. Fifty years later, the contradictions have not been resolved. Time, embellishment, and the chaos of the moment have tinted our memories. With me, that September afternoon is only one of many that may have become distorted over time.

What follows is my attempt to strip away some distortion; however, there are no guarantees. It is with this caveat that I begin my war story . . . and this is no shit!!

The War We Came to Fight

The life or death of a hundred, a thousand, or even tens of thousands of human beings, even if they are our own compatriots, represents really very little.

—GEN VO NGUYEN GIAP[1]

SOUTH VIETNAM'S JOINT GENERAL STAFF (JGS) CALLED THE counter-offensive *Lam Son 72*. On June 28, 1972, an operation was launched to drive the North Vietnamese Army (NVA) out of the Republic of Vietnam's (RVN) northern-most province, Quang Tri. After being battered for three months by conventional attacks, Lam Son 72 was South Vietnam's first large-scale attempt to regain the initiative. Quang Tri City was the only provincial capital in enemy hands, a lingering symbol of North Vietnam's earlier military successes. Nguyen Van Thieu, the South's president, was adamant that the city be retaken even though it had no strategic or military value. The mission was assigned to RVN's best units and best commander.

In the spring of 1972, North Vietnam, officially the Democratic Republic of Vietnam (DRV), initiated the largest offensive of the war. The Politburo's Central Military Committee gave it the code name *Nguyen Hue*, in honor of the eighteenth-century ruler who unified the northern and southern portions of the country. The combined arms assault was a three-phase operation designed to defeat the Army of the Republic of Vietnam (ARVN) and unseat President Thieu. Communist success on the battlefield might snap any remaining U.S. resolve and thwart President Nixon's reelection bid. Hanoi's decision to abandon the protracted conflict in favor of a conventional invasion was only a change in means to the ultimate end . . . unification of Vietnam under its rule. The first attack hit Quang Tri Province; a week later three divisions struck 60 miles from Saigon, surrounding the town of An Loc; on April 14 NVA troops moved on Kontum in the Central Highlands (see Map 1-1).

Phase I of Nguyen Hue kicked off when the NVA rolled across the demilitarized zone (DMZ) on Thursday, March 30, 1972. The U.S. press named it the Easter Offensive because Holy Thursday was the beginning of Easter celebrations for Vietnam's Catholic population. The "new face of war" ushered in full-fledged conventional operations employing three infantry divisions, 200 tanks, artillery of all calibers, and mobile air defense batteries. Forty thousand combat soldiers were supported by a sophisticated logistical system that included new road networks and a petroleum pipeline. The M46 130mm field gun, SA 7 Strela heat-seeking antiaircraft missile, AT-3 Sagger antitank missile, and the T54 tank with 100mm main gun were employed in quantities not previously seen. The NVA juggernaut was opposed by two brigades of the Vietnamese Marine Corps (VNMC) and the newly organized 3rd Infantry Division. Vietnamese Marines and ARVN soldiers, only 10,000, occupied a line of former U.S. Marine Corps (USMC) firebases that extended from the coastal plains to the western foothills. They were no match for the overwhelming number of veteran enemy troops.

The command of I Corps, covering five provinces of South Vietnam, was in the hands of an inept officer, LTG Hoang Xuan Lam. He was a staunch supporter of President Thieu who overlooked the general's incompetence. Lam disregarded intelligence indicators

Map 1-1

showing a large NVA buildup across the DMZ, not believing the enemy would openly violate the demilitarized zone. Americans were no more perceptive than their Vietnamese counterparts. All seemed more focused on the enemy's intentions than his capabilities, resulting in the North Vietnamese achieving tactical surprise. Nowhere was this more apparent than in the 3rd Infantry Division's area of operations (AO). The lack of awareness was so acute that two regiments were rotating between firebases as the attack commenced. Totally demoralized, the commander of the 56th ARVN Regiment, LTC Pham Van Dinh, surrendered his unit and Camp Carroll, a former USMC firebase, without a fight. Two regimental advisors, LTC William Camper and MAJ Joseph Brown, escaped rather than being taken captive. The loss of Camp Carroll put enemy forces behind the VNMC occupying Fire Support Base (FSB) Mai Loc and Sarge, forcing the defenders to withdraw eastward. The Marines' resolve and discipline under fire stiffened the remainder of the 3rd Division and allowed a new defensive line to be established along the Cua Viet River, providing temporary respite for the hard-hit South Vietnamese.[2]

As both armies regrouped and resupplied, the NVA continued to engage the ARVN with artillery and mortars. For the defenders, it was the first time they had been under sustained shelling by Soviet 130mm field guns. The impact of the heavy fire was compounded by the loss of a significant amount of friendly artillery when the firebases along the DMZ were abandoned. Now the captured artillery pieces were added to the North Vietnamese arsenal and turned on their former owners. There was little relief from the air because few B-52 bombers were in the theater and heavy cloud cover limited the effectiveness of U.S. tactical aircraft.

The situation became worse when Lieutenant General Lam altered the defensive plan by giving conflicting orders, hastily reversing decisions, and skirting the chain of command by communicating directly with subordinate units. Since the corps headquarters normally served as an administrative office in Da Nang, the general and his staff had no concept how to operate as a field headquarters. It was high-stress, unfamiliar territory where standard operating procedures were lacking and coordination was poor. Contingency planning was nonexistent and orders were dispatched haphazardly. Nor was General Lam one to report bad news. Consequently, President Thieu and the JGS were slow to grasp the seriousness of the situation. Lam maintained a "business-as-usual" attitude, commuting from Da Nang aboard a U.S. helicopter to his forward command post in Hue. He was usually home for an afternoon tennis match and dinner. One U.S. advisor called him an absentee warlord.[3]

BG Vu Van Giai, the 3rd Division commander, found himself in an untenable situation. By mid-April, he was commanding the equivalent of nine brigades consisting of twenty-three battalions, plus regional militia forces. MG Frederick Kroesen, I Corps senior advisor, recommended another operational headquarters be established to alleviate some of Giai's command and control issues but General Lam waved the suggestion off as too difficult. Thus Giai's span of supervision far exceeded all doctrinal standards at a time his authority was undermined by the corps commander. When Lam was present for duty, he could not resist the temptation to issue a flurry of directives that, due to poor coordination, left the division commander uninformed of the changes. When the corps commander unilaterally moved the 20th Tank Regiment, a battalion-size unit with fifty new M48 tanks, ARVN morale broke and troops began streaming south.[4] Soldiers were joined by thousands of refugees who were fleeing in the face of the enemy advance. Men who were expected to form a new defensive line at Quang Tri City continued south toward Hue. Unable to stem the retreat, Giai was forced to abandon Quang Tri City on May 1. As the rabble of soldiers and civilians fled, the North Vietnamese attacked them, creating havoc and inflicting terrible carnage. Equipment was abandoned, and wounded and dead were left where they fell. Luckily, the VNMC brigades executed a fighting withdrawal and established strong defensive positions along the My Chanh River, just 30 kilometers outside of Hue. The Marines stopped the overextended NVA and the river became the forward edge of the battle area.

South of the My Chanh, disorganized soldiers straggled into Hue's old city. Leaderless, they turned into a mob and began a drunken rampage of looting and burning. Destruction was widespread as law and order dissolved. Most of the affluent citizens packed what they could and fled south to safety in Da Nang. The riots, widely publicized at home and abroad, added to the malaise created by the Easter Offensive.[5]

The debacle in Quang Tri Province and the loss of control in Hue forced President Thieu to make a change. He assigned Lieutenant General Lam to the Ministry of Defense and replaced him with the IV Corps commander, LTG Ngo Quang Truong, RVN's most competent soldier. Highly regarded, he was nonpolitical and not tainted by rampant corruption that infected the army's senior ranks. His task was to stabilize the situation, then take the offensive and recover lost territory.[6] Truong received some welcomed reinforcements. In May two brigades of the Airborne Division were sent to I Corps; another brigade would follow in late June. He now controlled five of RVN's thirteen fighting divisions. Two were apportioned to the provinces in the southern part of the corps area while the 1st Infantry Division, the Airborne Division, and the Marine Division spearheaded the counter-offensive. A tough operation was about to begin.

Lam Son 72 was the war's last ground campaign involving U.S. personnel. Our assistance and support in Vietnam, products of the Cold War, spanned almost a quarter-century, beginning in 1950 when France requested $94 million in U.S. arms and equipment for Indochina. The government in Paris had been struggling since 1946 to reassert control over its former colonies, Vietnam, Cambodia, and Laos. French officials stated that their government would be unable to meet its North Atlantic Treaty Organization (NATO) commitments if the war continued to drain its resources.[7] The alliance was the Free World's first line of defense against Soviet expansionism, thus NATO could not be allowed to fail. The threat of communism in Western Europe was greater than U.S. empathy for Asian people subjugated by colonialism. Ho Chi Minh's fight was viewed as a subset of the "Red assault." Mao Tse-tung's victory in the Chinese civil war, the conflict in Indochina, and the invasion of South Korea were believed to be global initiatives orchestrated by the Kremlin. The United States was obligated to assist the French to maintain a united front against the USSR.

An influx of U.S. aid necessitated the formation of the Military Assistance Advisory Group (MAAG) in Vietnam. The French, like many aid recipients, resented having to rely on the United States. Gallic pride, already wounded by World War II, was further battered. They needed American equipment and money but wanted no input or constraints on their use. Relations were further strained by the insatiable demand for more assistance. As the Indochina War dragged on, the United States picked up an ever-increasing share of its cost, but paying the bills did not give Americans any meaningful influence. Government-to-government requests to prepare Vietnam for independence were largely ignored and the French Expeditionary Corps dragged its feet on the U.S. MAAG chief's offer to assist in creation of a national army with a well-trained officer and noncommissioned officer (NCO) corps.

By 1954, France's days in Indochina were numbered as the major powers began talks in Geneva to craft a peace accord. French defeat at Dien Bien Phu on May 7 hastened the process and precipitated an agreement. Ho Chi Minh, a strong nationalist leader, was unhappy with the partition of North and South Vietnam but was pressured to accept it by his Soviet and Chinese allies. One of the provisions of the Geneva Accords was the requirement for a 1956 plebiscite to determine if the people wanted unification. Ho was confident he would become the leader of all of Vietnam after the '56 elections. His plans to expand communist rule in the south were upset by the emergence of Ngo Dinh Diem, a staunch anticommunist who enjoyed strong support from the United States. Knowing he would lose the 1956 referendum, Diem disregarded it, eliminated opposition from urban gangsters and religious sects, ordered remaining French troops out and, at the request of his new benefactor, began revamping his armed forces.

With no hope of uniting Vietnam through the ballot box, Hanoi's leadership began fanning discontent in the South. President Diem never enjoyed total support of the people, so it was not difficult to generate opposition. His government was unable to cope with all the requirements of a developing nation. Heavy-handed policies, coupled with the French legacy of colonial misrule, created intractable problems in the form of inequitable land distribution, excessive taxation, and overwhelming poverty. Conditions were ripe for revolutionary action.

Cadres from the North returned to assist the resistance, augmenting hardcore communist cells that remained in the South after the Geneva Accords were signed. These groups, collectively known as the Viet Cong (VC), were able to start a viable insurgency against the Diem regime. By 1961, communist successes were causing grave concern. John F. Kennedy's administration viewed South Vietnam through the same Cold War lens as South Korea and Berlin; it was another place to stop aggression and stand firm with Free World allies. Nikita Khrushchev, Soviet premier, added to Cold War tensions when he vowed to "bury the United States" and support wars of national liberation. His words and actions were a direct challenge to the new U.S. president.

By January 1962, 3,200 Americans were in Vietnam, U.S. aircraft supported combat operations, and advisors accompanied ARVN units as they hunted the VC. A new headquarters, Military Assistance Command Vietnam (MACV), was established to coordinate the expanding American presence and the influx of U.S. equipment.[8] American aid and advice did not appear to be making headway as South Vietnamese forces suffered military setbacks and communist control in rural areas expanded. Diem's answer was more repressive measures on individual freedom and increased insularity, relying on the counsel of his brother, Nhu, and Nhu's wife, described in the U.S. press as the "Dragon Lady."

Domestic opposition to President Diem was an unexpected ally of the resistance. Buddhist riots in June 1963 drew attention to the disproportionate number of senior government officials, including the president and his family, who were Roman Catholic. They were accused of corruption and being out of touch with the people. The Viet Cong took advantage of the urban unrest and went on the offensive. President Kennedy and his advisors believed significant reforms were needed if South Vietnam was to survive, but Diem was incapable or unwilling to make them. By the summer of 1963, JFK was committed to a leadership change. His inner circle, considered America's best and brightest, thought they could control events and craft a post-coup regime more acceptable to the U.S. government. They had no idea that the plotters intended to eliminate Diem and his brother and chart their own course into the future. All, including President Kennedy, were shocked on November 2, 1963 when Diem and Nhu were murdered. This callous act underminded U.S. support of the new junta and caused critics of American policy to question its legitimacy. Several weeks later, John F. Kennedy was assassinated in Dallas.

Lyndon B. Johnson, Kennedy's successor, inherited the shambles of Vietnam. A series of coups by South Vietnamese generals added to the instability. A frustrated chief executive was forced to dispatch an emissary to RVN with the crude message that "this coup shit has to cease." Johnson's threat had little impact on the revolving door of lackluster governments or ARVN's performance in the field. His leverage changed on the night of August 2, 1964, when North Vietnamese patrol boats attacked a U.S. destroyer in the Gulf of Tonkin. Enraged over such a flagrant incident in international waters, the U.S. Congress passed a resolution giving President Johnson authority to use any force deemed necessary in Vietnam. Even though he had a *carte blanche* congressional mandate, Johnson was careful; 1964 was an election year and his opponent was Arizona senator Barry Goldwater, a vocal interventionist who wanted to use U.S. power to quash the communist insurgency. LBJ, as he was now referred to in the press, made a campaign pledge not to send U.S. troops to join the fight in Vietnam. The intervention issue became one of the center-pieces of the '64 election.

When the results were tallied, Lyndon Johnson won more than 60 percent of the popular vote and carried forty-four states, a stunning victory. Hanoi's Politburo, always a close observer of the American political scene, took the president's campaign pledges as the articulation of the administration's new foreign policy, ruling out intervention by U.S. ground troops. Intent on discrediting South Vietnamese security forces, NVA sappers raided a U.S. compound in Pleiku, killing Americans and destroying helicopters. Instead of causing LBJ to question the continuing commitment to South Viet-nam, the attack strengthened his resolve. Invoking the provisions of the Gulf of Tonkin Resolution, he initiated a bombing campaign against the DRV and a month later ordered two U.S. Marine battal-ions to Vietnam. Army units, including the 173rd Airborne Brigade, 1st Infantry Division, and the 1st Brigade, 101st Airborne Division, soon followed. Facility security was the rationale provided for public consumption, but the troops were combat soldiers who could and would fight. Initiation of offensive action against the VC raised few concerns in the United States.

America was becoming totally immersed in Vietnam. Before 1965 ended, 200,000 Americans were "in country," requiring a logis-tical effort that consumed billions of dollars. U.S. Marines and Army soldiers were fighting insurgents and NVA regulars. The American-ization of the war continued as more troops poured in, ultimately exceeding a half million. American combat units became the domi-nant presence in Vietnam's four military regions. As draft calls and U.S. casualties increased, opposition at home mounted. As 1967 came to a close, U.S. forces had been fighting for more than two years without appreciable signs of progress. Civilian and military leaders assured the American public success was not far off. No statement got more press coverage than the reference to the "light at the end of the tunnel."[9]

These assurances were dashed when the VC and North Vietnamese launched an offensive coinciding with the lunar New Year celebration, Tet. Shortly after midnight on January 30, 1968, well-orchestrated enemy attacks broke out all over the country targeting provincial capitals and military installations. In Saigon, a detachment of sappers hit the U.S. Embassy and a multi-battalion attack was launched against Tan Son Nhut Air Base. U.S. and South Vietnamese forces responded aggressively and quickly gained the upper hand. Only in Hue did the VC/NVA hold captured ground. It took U.S. Marines and the ARVN nearly a month to clear the city. While the communist forces sustained a massive military defeat with catastrophic losses in men and materiel, they gained a huge psychological victory. The U.S. home front was inundated with TV footage showing vicious combat. The small attack on the U.S. Embassy in Saigon received a disproportionate amount of airtime and flew in the face of previous assessments of progress. The credibility gap widened on February 18, 1968 when weekly casualties were announced; 543 U.S. soldiers were killed in action, the highest death toll of the war. The following week 470 were killed and 2,675 wounded.[10] Following a short visit to observe the fighting, America's most respected media personality, Walter Cronkite, opined that the war was stalemated and it was time to negotiate an end to the conflict. It was the turning point of the war.

The Tet Offensive caused LBJ to withdraw from the 1968 presidential race, halt bombing of North Vietnam, and make multiple concessions to the National Liberation Front (NLF) and the Politburo to start peace negotiations. Talks began in Paris but delays over procedural matters, such as table arrangements, frustrated U.S. negotiators and disappointed President Johnson. Richard Nixon, the 1968 Republican presidential nominee, declared that he would end the war in Vietnam, although he did not disclose many details of his plan. He narrowly defeated his Democratic opponent, Vice President Hubert Humphrey, and in 1969 began withdrawing American personnel from the war zone. Nixon's initiative, called

"Vietnamization," was a phased troop reduction while providing the South Vietnamese enough equipment and training to stand alone against a skilled enemy.

Still the war dragged on. Spoiling attacks were launched into Cambodia in 1970 and Laos in 1971. These preventative strikes, meant to disrupt NVA offensive capability, stoked antiwar sentiments on college campuses and in the U.S. Congress. Negative public opinion appeared to limit President Nixon's future options, including the opportunity to strike hard at North Vietnam. When U.S. strength was projected to drop below 100,000, Politburo leaders decided the time was right to settle the unification issue by massive force. Operation Nguyen Hue was their solution. On March 30, 1972, North Vietnamese forces attacked across the DMZ causing South Vietnam to fight for its life.

My tour with the Vietnamese Airborne Division began in May 1972; it was the second time I had served in RVN. I was a U.S. Army major assigned as the advisor to the 6th Airborne Battalion, reconstituting after being mauled near An Loc. Sixth Battalion had been part of an airborne task force dispatched in mid-April to reinforce the beleaguered garrison. The battalion was nearly destroyed in multiple attacks by NVA regiments. The remnants of two companies evaded capture by infiltrating into An Loc while eighty others retreated southward. The small group was saved from annihilation by U.S. airstrikes directed by a U.S. Army first lieutenant.

After replacing men and equipment, the 6th Airborne Battalion returned to the battle on June 4 and fought its way into An Loc. U.S. airpower allowed the 6th to be the first ARVN unit to break through the enemy encirclement. The tide turned and President Thieu declared the siege lifted. There was great rejoicing throughout RVN because it was the first victory since the Easter Offensive began. With Saigon no longer at risk, national priorities shifted and Quang Tri was now the priority theater. The paratroopers who defended An Loc fought their way out of the town and were transferred to I Corps for the counter-offensive.

Lam Son 72 incorporated several diversions and feints to draw North Vietnamese attention away from Quang Tri City. The 1st Infantry Division attacked west of Hue and two seaborne demonstrations simulated amphibious landings along the coast, north of the provincial capital. The main attack kicked off on June 28 when a VNMC brigade and three battalions of the 3rd Airborne Brigade conducted a night river crossing, routing the NVA on the north bank of the My Chanh. After breaching the enemy defenses, two airborne battalions, the 9th and 11th, and two VNMC battalions launched an air assault 10 kilometers behind the main line of fighting. Helicopter landings in their rear unhinged the NVA defense. With their lines of communication and logistics endangered, the North Vietnamese hastily withdrew to Quang Tri City. They had lost a battle but they were far from defeated (see Map 1-2).

When Lam Son 72 kicked off, the 6th Airborne Battalion occupied an assembly area awaiting orders. My counterpart, LTC Nguyen Van Dinh, was fully apprised of success of the river crossing and the air assault but he chose not to share the information with me. It was one of many traits that made our relationship tenuous. Dinh's surly attitude surfaced in April when his battalion was nearly destroyed outside An Loc and LT Ross Kelly, the deputy advisor, saved the day. During the chaotic retreat Kelly became the de facto commander, orchestrating a B-52 strike and multiple tactical air sorties, all the while encouraging the troops to keep moving when the battalion commander was ready to give up. Colonel Dinh's lackluster performance in a life or death situation was a significant loss of face, a devastating failure. Now Americans, personified by Ross Kelly, joined the North Vietnamese as Nguyen Van Dinh's adversaries.

I was unable to establish even a modest level of rapport with Dinh. Since I controlled U.S. air support, we maintained a modicum of civility as we fought our way into An Loc, but it dissolved when the

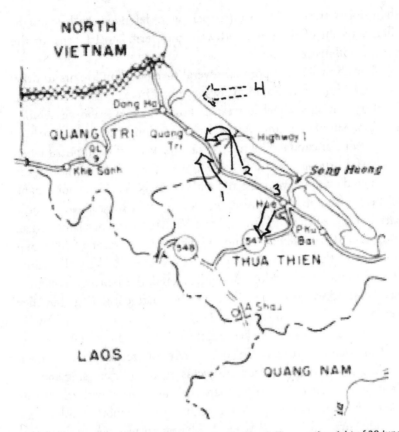

1. 3rd Brigade, Airborne Division attacked across the My Chanh River on the night of 28 June 1972.
2. Two airborne battalions and two VNMC battalions air assaulted behind the North Vietnamese main defenses after the attack across the river.
3. 1st ARVN Division attacked west from Hue toward the former US fire bases, Bastogne and Birmingham.
4. VNMC, supported by the US Navy, conducted an amphibious feint along the coast to draw NVA attention away from the primary objective of *LAM SON 72*, Quang Tri City.

Map 1-2

battle ended. Typical of ARVN-U.S. relations throughout the war, no senior officers, Vietnamese or American, made an issue of it. Dinh was not held accountable for his actions, notwithstanding the negative impact on the battalion. There were many U.S. apologists for the 6th Airborne Battalion commander and those of his ilk. Some in the Airborne Division intimated I did not understand the advisory business and perhaps was being hypercritical. I heard their comments: "We lack cultural understanding," "They're worn out," or "They have been fighting far longer than we have." The NVA had been fighting tenaciously for a long time too, and their casualty rates far exceeded those of ARVN. The North Vietnamese lacked the allies' massive firepower, quality medical care, and the "creature comforts" supplied by the U.S. military. Enemy hardships did not enter the discussions.

When I questioned Colonel Dinh about when the battalion would be committed, he feigned ignorance of future plans. Two months with the man conditioned me to his behavior. SSG Bill Phelps, the light weapons advisor (LWA), and I needed to find out what was going on and the best way to do it was to see for ourselves. Through advisor channels, I obtained the locations of friendly units and a brief situation report. We grabbed our weapons and drove a jeep up the main road, Quoc Lo 1 (QL 1, National Highway 1).

The scene on the north side of the My Chanh River defied description. Equipment from the May retreat littered QL 1 for miles. There were burned-out hulks of every vehicle in the ARVN inventory—tanks, personnel carriers, jeeps, wreckers, trucks, and ambulances. Several of the tanks were the newly issued M48s. The one we inspected had plenty of fuel and was not hit by enemy fire. The crew abandoned it in the rush to flee from the North Vietnamese.

The wreckage along the highway reminded me of pictures of the debris left by the retreating German army during the latter stages of World War II. Most disconcerting were the bodies, soldiers and refugees, which had been there since the May debacle. Blackened from the harsh summer sun, they lay along the road and in the vehicles. There were even corpses on the stretchers in the ambulances. In the panic, the wounded were abandoned to die agonizing deaths. Wild animals had grown fat feasting off the carrion. Some of the bodies were totally consumed with only tattered clothing and bleached bones left. The dry season's hot wind added to the sense of desolation.

Neither Phelps nor I spoke as we moved through the charnel house. Eventually we arrived at the 11th Airborne Battalion command post (CP) and were met by the U.S. advisor, CPT Gail "Woody" Furrow. Woody was on his third tour in Vietnam, had been wounded several times, and was recommended for the Distinguished Service Cross (DSC), America's second highest award for valor. When attacked by a tank regiment on June 22, he exposed himself several times directing airstrikes that turned back the NVA. Furrow had a great relationship with MAJ Le Van Me, the battalion commander, whose reputation was on par with Woody's. U.S. advisors lauded Me's leadership and his selflessness. My counterpart, Colonel Dinh, was never described in such glowing terms.

It was refreshing to talk to a battalion commander and be treated as a fellow professional, not one of the auxiliaries. Very fluent in English, Me stated the Easter Offensive was a new war for the Airborne Division. While not openly critical of his bosses, he sensed some in the chain of command did not grasp how much the nature of fighting had changed. Mid-intensity warfare against an army equipped with tanks and heavy artillery did not accommodate establishing firebases to serve as a hub for operations. If friendly forces remained in one location too long, they were targeted and pounded with artillery and mortars. There was still a tendency in the Airborne Division to split an infantry battalion into two task forces of two rifle companies each. This tactic was fine for combating smaller forces, but it courted disaster facing full-strength North Vietnamese regiments. Major Me said he would keep his battalion together and resist any attempts by higher headquarters to dictate obsolete tactics that dispersed his soldiers. His candor was out of character for a Vietnamese commander. In an aside, Furrow told me that the brigade commander still called on the radio and ordered Me to move single platoons around. "Old habits die hard. Put a platoon here . . . a platoon there and pretty soon you won't have any platoons," was the way Woody described it. This level of micromanagement was a carryover from the era when brigade commanders circled the battlefield in helicopters and told unit commanders on the ground how to fight the enemy. It was a bad habit picked up from some American units.

Eleventh Battalion was the division's forward-most unit, "leaving our ass exposed," is what Woody called it. The day before, Major Me was ordered to halt in place, dig in, and consolidate the gains. This pause gave the enemy a much-needed reprieve and time to fortify the Citadel, the dominant structure in Quang Tri City. The directive to stop came from Lieutenant General Truong, the corps commander who chose not to exploit the enemy's disorganization or initiate a pursuit. Woody said: "We had 'em on the run! We should've gone around this shit hole," pointing toward Quang Tri City. The NVA established a new defensive line, brought in reinforcements, and resupplied its battered units. The communists did not disengage or limp back to a sanctuary in Laos to lick their wounds. For the first time we were facing a modern, combined arms enemy with an extensive logistical infrastructure. While the U.S. press made much to-do about bicycles carrying supplies along the Ho Chi Minh Trail, those days were long past. Members of the Fourth Estate who lionized our pajama-clad adversaries were more than a day late and a dollar short; it was not the first time journalists got it all wrong. North Vietnam's forces were as mechanized and modern as our NATO allies. Such armies are not sustained by bicycle pushers, nor do they fade away after a single battle. Failure to maintain the pressure when the adversary was reeling would have near-fatal consequences for the Airborne Division. Paratroopers would become bogged down in Quang Tri City when it could have been isolated and bypassed, allowing the recovery of more territory. Casualties sustained during the July 1972 battles would plague the Airborne Division throughout my tour as an advisor.

＿＿～＿＿

As Phelps and I returned to the 6th Battalion's assembly, I was struck by how the Vietnam conflict had changed. When the first U.S. ground troops arrived in Vietnam in 1965, Americans were fighting an insurgency; big battles were the exception, rather than the rule. Now, in 1972, the war had evolved into a conventional one where large attacks were a daily occurrence and enemy ground troops were supported by armor and artillery. The Easter Offensive was a different war.

I deployed to Vietnam in June 1965 as an infantry second lieutenant in the 1st Battalion (Airborne), 327th Infantry. Our parent unit, 1st Brigade, 101st Airborne Division, part of the U.S. buildup that summer, was schooled in the tactics of World War II and Korea. We were prepared to fight that kind of war rather than one against dedicated guerrillas who had perfected hit and run operations and only fought when it was to their advantage. Counter-insurgency training prior to our deployment was minimal and our knowledge of the theater of operations was sorely lacking. One of our NCOs put the problem in more earthy terms: "We don't know shit about this fuckin' place." Our battalion was no different from any other American unit that was sent to Vietnam in 1965. Despite these shortfalls, the United States took over the fighting and focused on "killing 'em til they quit." U.S. confidence in its force of arms and a can do spirit would surely prevail. The lowest ranking private was convinced we would quickly defeat the Viet Cong and make a short war of it. Everyone underestimated our adversary and the complexities of counter-insurgency warfare. America's leaders, civilian and military, had no concept of the enemy's resolve, patience, and capacity for suffering. Ho Chi Minh warned the French: "If we must fight, we will fight. You will kill ten of our men, and we will kill one of yours. Yet in the end, it is you who will tire."[11] U.S. planners considered Ho's admonition to be standard communist rhetoric and disregarded it.

U.S. combat battalions launched countless "search and destroy" operations where body count became a measure of effectiveness. When America took over the war in the fall of 1965, no serious attempts were made to operate with the South Vietnamese or upgrade their capabilities. The U.S. high command was perfectly happy for the ARVN to focus on area security, pacification, and its own campaigns. Allowing Vietnamese military operations to be an adjunct to the American war was a major strategic flaw and remained in effect far too long. There was no unified command so our ally, fully funded by the U.S. government, was left to his own devices. GEN Creighton Abrams, who replaced GEN William C. Westmoreland as MACV commander in 1968, implemented the "One War" concept and began integrating allied operations. After three years of the United States fighting the big war, refocusing on improving the ARVN was a difficult challenge.

U.S. recommendations, major and minor, often went unheeded. Since U.S. resources were not used as an incentive, there was little need for the Vietnamese to make important changes, particularly those involving ARVN leaders. The American military overlooked inappropriate conduct and when it happened, wrote it off as cultural differences. At the battalion level, it was the U.S. advisor's job to make the counterpart relationship work. Commanders like Colonel Dinh could act with impunity since there were no consequences for intemperate behavior.

Vietnamization, a term coined by President Nixon's secretary of defense, was a strategy for disengagement, to "de-Americanize" the war, bring the troops and POWs home, and improve South Vietnam's armed forces so they could continue the fight after U.S. forces departed. A huge monetary and training effort expanded the ARVN from 770,000 to over a million soldiers. The 3rd ARVN Division was a product of accelerated growth. It had only been operational for three months when the NVA stormed across the DMZ.

Drawdown of U.S. personnel diluted the advisory effort. As American combat and support units were withdrawn, MACV was forced to eliminate advisor positions. However, the pace was slower and more measured than in U.S. units. By the end of 1971 overall U.S. strength had declined by 66 percent, whereas advisory authorizations only dropped 22 percent, leaving 3,880 in the field.[12] To reduce the American footprint, infantry battalion advisors were eliminated in June 1971. ARVN infantry regiments were still assisted by a U.S. lieutenant colonel and a major.[13]

The Airborne Division and the Marine Division were exceptions, part of the JGS strategic reserve projected to be in the thick of future fighting. In spite of Vietnamization, MACV planners retained a three-man advisory team, a major, captain, and sergeant, in each of the nine airborne battalions. Authorizations and actual U.S. boots-on-the-ground were two different issues because rarely were three Americans present. When Lam Son 72 began, it was not unusual for a single U.S. officer, a captain or major, to be with an airborne battalion. Even one advisor's presence made a difference, a symbol that the United States was still in the fight. The departure of so many U.S. troops had fostered the perception that the Vietnamese were being left in the lurch. One advisor explained, "ARVN always knew they could count on us as long as our guys were down in the trenches with them."[14]

At the half-year mark, June 30, 1972, 49,000 Americans remained in Vietnam, a far cry from the days when U.S. strength was ten times that number. Only two U.S. brigades were in country, guarding airfields at Da Nang and Bien Hoa. Guidance from Washington made it very clear: Neither of these units would be committed to stem the North Vietnamese offensive. Both brigades continued deactivation planning as the enemy overran Quang Tri and threatened An Loc and Kontum. Hence, aviators and a small group of field advisors defined U.S. combat participation. This was ironic, because in the spring and summer of 1972, the South Vietnamese were in the war we came to fight.[15]

CHAPTER 2

Education, the Army Way

WEST POINT (1960–1964)

Let every nation know . . . that we shall pay any price, bear any burden, meet any hardship, support any friend, oppose any foe, in order to assure the survival and the success of liberty. . . . And so, my fellow Americans, ask not what your country can do for you—ask what you can do for your country.
—JOHN F. KENNEDY—INAUGURAL ADDRESS,
JANUARY 20, 1961

I HAVE HAD ONLY TWO AMBITIONS IN MY LIFE. INITIALLY I ASPIRED to be a garbageman. The big truck, the clanking of the cans, and the sound of the compactor impressed me. As soon as I got that idea out of my head at age six, I wanted to be a soldier. My quest was nearly snuffed out before it got started, because my adjustment to the rigors of being a plebe, a freshman, at the U.S. Military Academy (USMA) was very difficult. My first-year academic performance put me in the middle of the pack, but military aptitude was another issue. Each plebe was rated on deportment by his peers and the three upper classes. In the spring of my first year, I was at the bottom of the pile. Neither my classmates nor the upperclassmen thought I was cut out to be an Army officer. As a result, I was ordered to appear before a board of officers who would determine if I should remain at the Academy. The board ruled, in the Academy's words, that I was proficient in aptitude, probably barely so. It was a very traumatic event that made me question the wisdom of attending West Point. Not wanting to let my family and friends down, I made the commitment to improve. Throughout my time at the USMA, my parents were a bastion of support and encouragement; I would not have made it without them.

Dalton and Louise Howard were thirty-seven years old when I was born. Both were high school teachers in Salisbury on Maryland's Delmarva Peninsula. They worked hard, focused on family, and only bought what they could pay for. Mom and Dad were married in 1932 when the Depression was in its third year. They waited until they could buy a house before starting a family. I grew up in the home they purchased for $5,000—cash, no mortgage—no small feat during the Depression. My mother stopped teaching when my sister, Susan, was born in February 1940; in July 1942, I came along.

Susan and I were blessed to have parents whose *raison d'etre* was our well-being. It was no surprise that academic work was the number one priority and going to college was a given, not unusual for teachers' children. What was unusual was that my dad had gone to college at all, because he was the first in his family to complete high school. His mother was a widow who lost her husband and her oldest son. My grandmother made ends meet by taking in laundry and Dad supplemented the family income with an after-school job. They were not below the poverty line but probably right on it. That my father overcame the hardships of growing up impoverished and without a father and persevered to graduate from college was a source of great inspiration to me during my tough days at West Point.

As far back as I can remember, Susan wanted to be a doctor. In the 1950s that was considered a nontraditional job for women. She was a much better student than I was and never lost sight of medicine as her career. When admitted to University of Maryland Medical

School in 1961, she was one of seven women who made up less than 10 percent of the class.

My choice of career paths was almost as unconventional as my sister's, since our family tree had no professional military men. Neither my mother nor my father sought to dissuade me from my aspiration to be an Army officer. My teetotaler mother voiced one concern: "Army folks are a hard-drinking lot!" During my junior year of high school, I set my sights on attending West Point, and with the assistance of many people, I received an appointment from the U.S. representative from Maryland's First District to become a member of the USMA Class of 1964.

In 1960, the U.S. Corps of Cadets (USCC) numbered 2,400 men. Women would not enter the Academy until 1976. The Corps was divided into two regiments, each with twelve 100-man companies. The USCC's size would remain the same throughout my four years at the Academy. Expansion began in the summer of 1965 when West Point started a building program to increase the size of USCC to 4,200, the strength of the Brigade of Midshipmen at the Naval Academy.

I knew the first year at West Point was going to be tough—however, I had no idea how tough. No amount of research prepared me for the shock of "Beast Barracks." Training in July and August was officially known as New Cadet Barracks but called Beast by everyone. It took a young man from the civilian world and made him into a cadet by teaching him how to follow in preparation for learning to lead. The bulk of us were right out of high school, but some had attended a year or so of college and a few had prior military service. Classmates who had served in the Army had a distinct advantage during our first year.

Issuing uniforms, getting a "buzz" haircut, and learning the rudiments of marching were crammed into the carefully choreographed first day. In the late afternoon of July 5, 1960, 802 of us were marched to Trophy Point overlooking the Hudson River and sworn in as new cadets. By taking the oath we incurred a four-year service obligation and were on the U.S. Army's payroll. Cadet pay was set at half of a second lieutenant's base salary, a princely sum of $111.15 a month.

An oft-heard expression was that West Point was not the real Army. The emphasis on an Academy-unique style of marching was an example of learning something that took an inordinate amount of time but had no relation to what we would be doing four years hence. The Corps used a nineteenth-century "Infantry Squad Drill," a carryover from the era when soldiers used volley fire; after the front rank fired, it would kneel to allow the second rank to fire. That method of fighting became obsolete during the Civil War when the U.S. Army realized that fire and maneuver were battlefield imperatives. Tradition won out over reality, and no one seemed to question why if something had been discarded by the Army long ago, West Point insisted on still doing it.

We became full-fledged cadets at the end of Beast Barracks. The academic year started after Labor Day and Plebe Year began in earnest. The Fourth Class System, "Plebe System," was a ritualized program primarily administered by first classmen, seniors, called Firsties, and second classmen, juniors known as Cows. It was a rite of passage, although much of the system had outlived its usefulness. At the core was the requirement for plebes to be at an exaggerated position of attention, called bracing, whenever in the presence of upperclassmen. Posture improvement was the rationale. Bracing carried over into the mess hall, where some upperclassmen took delight in denying food to plebes. Not being a sterling cadet, I stayed hungry most of my first year. Misery was enforced by other traditions: plebes remained at West Point at Christmas, plebes were only allowed to attend the second movie show on Saturday night, and plebes were not permitted to use the soda fountain. Plebes could have visitors, but a myriad of restrictions applied. It was meant to be an unpleasant year.

Hazing was officially banned but it went on, particularly when a fourth classman got a poor reputation. The man became a prime candidate for being "run out of the Corps." Clothing calls were one method to force a cadet into resigning. The offending plebe would be told to report to a certain upperclassman in specific uniform, such as Full Dress, and then be given a minute or two to change into another uniform. You could not win this fixed game and in the process wrecked your room trying to keep up with the uniform changes. Part of the harassment was being awarded demerits for your room being messed up. Once you were branded as a screw-up, recovery was very difficult. The experience caused me to wonder if the men who enjoyed administering the Plebe System, yelling, eroding another individual's dignity, and foolishness like clothing calls, used similar behavior after graduation when they interacted with their Army subordinates. By tacitly condoning even moderate hazing, West Point officials allowed some martinets to join the officer corps.

The Class of '64 was the beneficiary of one modest change. We were the first plebes who did not march to class. Allowing first-year students to walk, while bracing and at a brisk pace, was viewed by upperclassmen and Old Grads, the vocal traditionalists, as a sure sign that the Academy had gone to hell. Even with that change, we continued to follow the same curriculum endured by our forebears in the Long Gray Line. Everyone pursed an engineering degree; there were no majors. Although the focus was on math and science, cadets studied English literature and took two years of a foreign language. I chose Russian over Spanish, German, Portuguese, or French because Russian students had a higher pass rate than those taking other languages.

During our first year, the Class of 1964 lost 177 men from the original 802, an attrition rate of 22 percent. The majority, ninety-one, resigned when they found that West Point was not their cup of tea. Sixty-nine were dismissed for academic deficiencies with a few leaving for other administrative reasons.[1] When Plebe Year ended in June 1961, we were sent on thirty days leave, the first time we had been away from West Point for more than twenty-four hours. The remainder of the summer was spent in the field at nearby Camp Buckner learning the rudiments of soldiering. I found traction there and started to thrive. From then on, my academic and military performance improved. As my comfort level at the Academy increased, so did my grades. Far more important, I was no longer plagued by a potential deficiency in military aptitude and was not looking over my shoulder at the specter of failure.

Most members of the Corps made an art-form out of indifference. Being too gung ho carried the label of a "Gray Hog," a pejorative term. A positive outlook was not cool and it was far more common to hear a cadet say, "I hate this fucking place," versus something even moderately complimentary. If you were not a candidate for the top 5 percent of the class, coasting along was perfectly acceptable.

Each cadet went on Army Orientation Training (AOT) prior to his junior or senior year. In the summer of 1962, I was assigned to a mechanized infantry battalion in Munich, Germany. Western Europe was the epicenter of the Cold War, so the United States maintained over a quarter of a million military personnel there. Berlin, behind the Iron Curtain and technically occupied by France, Britain, the U.S.A., and the USSR, was a flashpoint. The Soviet premier, Nikita Khrushchev, threatened to deny the Allies access to West Berlin and increased the pressure in August 1961 by erecting the Berlin Wall. A few months later a standoff occurred between U.S. and Soviet tanks at Checkpoint Charlie, one of the entryways into East Berlin. The United States stood firm, mobilized 100,000 troops, and upped Defense spending by $3 billion; Khrushchev backed down. A crisis was averted, but tensions were still high a year later when USMA cadets arrived in Germany. My experience serving in the real Army in Europe convinced me I was on the right career path.

The reality of the profession of arms hit us in mid-October 1962. A U2 reconnaissance aircraft discovered Soviet intermediate range ballistic missiles being emplaced in Cuba, a direct threat to the continental United States. As the crisis progressed, the world was on the verge of nuclear war. On the night of October 22, President Kennedy addressed the nation, announcing a naval quarantine of Cuba to prevent Soviet ships from bringing additional missile components to the island. The entire Corps of Cadets was assembled to hear the president's speech. Cadets, usually an irreverent group, were totally focused on John F. Kennedy. Within a week, the crisis was resolved and the USSR removed its offensive weapons from Cuba.

The Cuban Missile Crisis promoted an uncommon level of seriousness at West Point. We were living in a dangerous world and had to prepare for it. In the fall of 1962, the Academy authorities made another rule concession: lights did not have to be turned off at Taps, 10:00 P.M. Prior to that time, cadets who wanted to study later were relegated to using a flashlight or sitting in the hall. Another silly rule was set aside and the Academy edged closer to the twentieth century.

President Kennedy's assassination was the low point of our four years at the Academy. That Friday afternoon, November 22, 1963, I was in the library. One of my classmates told me the president had been shot. Both of us went to an auditorium where a large TV screen was showing a special CBS news program. As the theater was filling up, Walter Cronkite, the network's anchorman, stated that the president was dead. All of us were stunned. Friday night supper in the Cadet Mess, Washington Hall, was a hushed affair. In keeping with West Point's tradition of carrying on in the face of adversity, Saturday classes were still held.

By Christmas, the end was in sight. Relatively speaking, we had more privileges, were taking a few electives, and periodically left West Point for a weekend in New York City. The year was punctuated by the car show and purchasing officer uniforms. I ordered a black '64 Chevrolet Impala with red interior, setting me back $2,500, almost a lieutenant's annual salary. None of the vehicles were delivered until May, a month before graduation, because the authorities did not want us to have too much freedom.

When 1964 began, service selections, branch choices, and postgraduation assignments were the center of our universe. Twelve and a half percent of Academy graduates could opt for commissions in other services. The U.S. Air Force was very popular and some classmates, who were not flight qualified, voted with their feet when it was announced all who were commissioned in the Army would go through Ranger School. Along with the new Ranger requirement, basic branch school attendance, an eight-week course aimed at teaching the fundamentals of our new profession, was eliminated. We were the first graduates not to attend since members of the Class of 1950 were rushed to Korea when war started. Problems with the training base accommodating all the new lieutenants caused the change. The Department of the Army determined that 500 new West Point graduates were better able to skip the course than those recently commissioned through ROTC.

Future Army officers made branch choices based on the Order of Merit List, the cadet's class standing that included grade-point average and aptitude rankings. We were offered commissions in the combat arms: Infantry; Armor; Artillery (included both Field Artillery and Air Defense Artillery); Engineers; or Signal Corps. Floor and ceiling quotas were established for each branch. In accordance with Academy tradition, the Corps of Engineers (CE) was the popular choice among the top-ranked cadets. Of the first twenty men in the class, twelve chose CE, two opted for the Infantry, and six went into the Air Force, most into non-pilot specialties. There were plenty of vacancies for Infantry, my choice, which was far less popular then than it is today. Some who were near the bottom of the class, affectionately called Goats, were not given a choice and told that they would be commissioned in the Infantry. To meet the ground-pounder floor quota, many Goats involuntarily became Grunts.

My selection for assignment was the 101st Airborne Division at Fort Campbell, Kentucky. North of Nashville, Fort Campbell was not as modern as Fort Bragg, home of the 82nd Airborne Division. I selected the 101st because I thought the Screaming Eagle patch was the best in the Army. My knowledge of my new profession was clearly lacking. Sometimes things work out regardless of a faulty decision-making process. Hopefully my thirty-two class-mates who also opted for the 101st Airborne Division made more informed choices.

We graduated on Wednesday, June 3, 1964. Relief, more than anything else, described my emotions. We received our diploma in accordance with our class standing. My cumulative rank of 196 out of 565 indicated my grades and aptitude scores had improved significantly since my dismal first year. If the course had been five years long, I might have actually distinguished myself!

Graduation leave was followed by Airborne and Ranger School at Fort Benning, Georgia. Three weeks of parachute training were followed by nine weeks in the Ranger course. Throughout four years at West Point, we had heard stories about how tough Ranger School would be. Sleep deprivation and testing the limits of one's stamina were its hallmarks. Training was conducted at three locations, initially at Fort Benning, a mountain phase near Dahlonega, Georgia, and finally in the swamps of Eglin Air Force Base (AFB), Florida, located along Florida's panhandle. Leadership under stress and small unit tactics were the focus of instruction. The anticipation of attending Ranger School was worse than its reality. It was like jumping into cold water . . . it wasn't so bad once you got in it.

The 1964 presidential election occurred while we were in the mountains of north Georgia, but the Johnson-Goldwater race was hardly noticed. An instructor told us that President Johnson won by a large margin. His promise not to go to war in Southeast Asia swayed many voters. We were nonplussed because successfully negotiating the Ranger course consumed all our mental and physical energy. Little did we know the election results would have a lasting effect on our future.

We pinned on our Ranger tabs just before Christmas, enjoyed a short holiday leave, and then were off to our first assignments. It was an exciting time. After four years at West Point and five months at Fort Benning, I was ready to get on with it. Combat in Vietnam was not on anyone's radar screen.

FORT CAMPBELL AND THE SCREAMING EAGLES (JANUARY–JUNE 1965)

"We are not about to send American boys nine or ten thousand miles away from home to do what Asian boys ought to be doing for themselves."

—PRESIDENT LYNDON B. JOHNSON DURING
THE 1964 ELECTION CAMPAIGN[2]

Black smoke from coal-burning furnaces shrouded Fort Campbell on the January morning I reported for duty. First Battalion (Airborne), 327th Infantry, one of three battalions in the 1st Brigade, was my designated unit. The adjutant gave a short briefing and assigned me to A Company, known as "ABU." A meeting was scheduled with the battalion commander, LTC James Wilson, who received a direct commission and the Distinguished Service Cross for bravery during the Korean War. The battalion executive officer was MAJ Marcus W. Hansen, an enlisted infantryman during World War II who used the GI Bill to attend Virginia Military Institute. MAJ Arthur E. Taylor Jr. was the battalion operations officer, the S3. He graduated from West Point in 1952 and went to Korea before the 1953 armistice was signed. The combat records of all three men were impressive. In 1972, I would again serve with Marc Hansen and Art Taylor.

My new boss was CPT Donald C. Hilbert, ABU commander. His first concern was that I should make a parachute jump so airborne pay would start. A unit jump was scheduled in a few days; after that I would draw an additional $110 per month jump pay, a 50 percent increase in my second lieutenant salary. He also wanted me to get settled, so he took me to the billeting office where I signed for a place in the bachelor officer quarters (BOQ). Living in the BOQ was close to work and the price was right; you forfeited your $85.20 housing allowance for a small apartment consisting of a living room, bath, kitchenette, and bedroom. It seemed very spacious compared to the barracks at West Point.

The next day I was introduced to the 3rd Platoon as their new leader. The platoon sergeant was a short, stocky sergeant first class, John T. Humphries. He was a veteran of the Korean War who made two combat parachute jumps with the 187th Regimental Combat Team (RCT). Sergeant First Class Humphries proved to be a steady hand at the tiller and a source of sage advice. He was a bachelor, did not own a car, and lived in the barracks. I later found out that he had a wife and son in Japan, where the 187th RCT was billeted in the 1950s. He was a great teacher and I grew under his tutelage.

The 3rd Platoon had a special spirit, and even had its own flag. The platoon members, known as the Kamikazes, walked with a swagger unmatched by the others in the company. The squad leaders were all longtime airborne veterans. SSG Otto Borden had the 1st Squad, SSG Travis Martin ran the 2nd Squad, SSG Bill Bowlin the 3rd, and SSG Billy Robbins was the Weapons Squad leader. The buck sergeants included Robert Turner, Paul Wolfe, Gerald Douglas, Frank Trzebuckowski, Joe Vigil, and Clio Johnson. They were an impressive group. In the field, their strengths became readily identifiable.

The enlisted men were tough guys. Many of them had hardscrabble upbringings and joined the paratroopers to get away from broken homes, dirt-poor rural communities, or inner-city mean streets. Rocky Ryan, the RTO, epitomized them. He was from upstate New York where he learned to use his fists, a tradition he continued at Fort Campbell. Ryan held court in a small beer garden next to the barracks, appropriately named the Bastogne Club in honor of the 101st's epic World War II battle. The place provided a venue for paratrooper aggressions fueled by cheap beer and testosterone.

Duane E. Finley, our hard-as-nails first sergeant (1SG), was the quintessential senior NCO. A glare from him instilled fear in the strongest of men. I tried to steer clear of him, but over time developed unbounded admiration and affection for him. Finley's gruff exterior masked a special place in his heart for the wild ways of young paratroopers. He tried to keep them out of trouble but for some, trouble seemed to follow. Shortly after my arrival a half-dozen troopers got into a melee with combat engineers from the 937th Engineer Group, a non-airborne unit whose soldiers were called "legs," a derisive term. Our guys ended up on the short end of the donnybrook. The next morning at reveille Finley looked at the bandaged troops, shook his head, and said, "I told you people not to fuck with them leg engineers."

Part of my indoctrination was learning about the ABU lineage and its connection with the 187th RCT. When the RCT was part of the occupation force in Japan, I Company created an animal, an "IBU," with the body of a gorilla, the head of a lion, and the antlers of a moose. Parachute jump boots and an alligator tail completed the design. Attachment to the IBU grew so strong that some paratroopers had it tattooed on their left calf. John Humphries was one of the originals who sported the brand. After the 187th RCT was deactivated, many IBU soldiers were transferred to A Company, 327th Infantry in the newly formed 101st Airborne Division. They succeeded in convincing the commander that A Company should be known as ABU, keeping the heraldry of their beloved mystical monster alive. The ABU logo was painted on anything that did not move.

The U.S. Army in 1965 worked Monday through Friday and a half-day on Saturday. A conscientious officer did not get out of the company area until 2:00 or 3:00 on Saturday afternoon. Saturday's requirements limited your Friday night social life . . . since reveille was at 0600 hours (6:00 A.M.) the following morning. Bachelor lieutenants hung out at the officers' club annex, commonly known as the Little Club, located in the hospital complex. Being a club member was mandatory and all officers were expected to participate. It was an era before the Army deglamorized alcohol and drunk driving became a serious offense. Liquor and cigarettes were staples of Army life.

One Friday night in the Little Club, I met a group of Air Force F100 pilots who were at Campbell for close air support training. I helped them close the bar as beer and loud conversation flowed. The price of excess was missing 6:00 A.M. reveille formation. When I arrived at work looking the worse for wear, it did not take long for 1SG Finley to tell me that the company commander wanted to see me. Don Hilbert fixed me in a steely gaze and said: "Young lieutenant, when you drink with the big boys, you have to get up with them!" It was the first of many life lessons learned in the 101st Airborne Division.

Since few enlisted men had cars, they stayed at Fort Campbell and patronized the Bastogne Club where beer was twenty-five cents a can. Right after payday, the place became a battlefield. Officers did not get involved with the happenings at the Bastogne Club; that was NCO business. Following field training, an officer who performed to the NCO's expectation might be invited to have a beer there. The protocol was to drink no more than two and depart. To stay longer might provoke an uncomfortable situation with someone like SGT Johnnie K. Rogers. Rogers had been promoted and demoted multiple times, busted for alcohol-related problems. Ruddy-faced, Johnnie K. symbolized the Old Army NCO: he smoked too much, drank too much, and was often missing in action (MIA) after payday, but in the field he could soldier with the best of them. Overstaying your welcome at the Bastogne Club might subject you to Rogers's observations on the officer corps. For Johnnie K. Rogers, "fuckin' officer" was one word.

A major field training exercise (FTX), Eagle Jump, began in early March. First and 2nd Brigades were pitted against the 3rd Brigade. Like our previous training, we parachuted in, secured the airhead, defended and attacked, a by-the-book airborne operation similar to those conducted in World War II. During the FTX, my platoon was given the mission to conduct a raid on the opposing force's command post (CP). We were directed to load three helicopters, fly to a landing zone (LZ), and move cross-country and attack the CP. SSG Billy Robbins was assigned to be the assistant patrol leader. Everything went according to plan as we lifted off, flew to a landing zone, and moved by a concealed route to the objective. As usually happens, the plan started to come apart. Crawling forward on a recon, I was dismayed by the number of troops in the area and expressed this concern to Billy Robbins. We had the option of attacking the CP or withdrawing in the face of a larger force than the intelligence report had estimated. When I went over the situation with Robbins, he gave me a serious look and said: "What's the mission?" It was a statement, not a question, a method good NCOs used to contribute to a young officer's education. Billy clarified things for me in one sentence and reinforced the age-old axiom that the mission is always first. Over the years, when faced with a vexing situation, I repeated Billy Robbins's rhetorical question. We attacked the target! Before the opposing force could react, we faded into the woods, moved to the designated pickup zone (PZ), and flew back to the battalion.

A debriefing at brigade headquarters was required, so I reported to the brigade S3, MAJ David H. Hackworth. His reputation as a tough, unyielding "hard ass" preceded him. Standing at a map board, I explained our mission, how we accomplished it, and gave him a small sketch of the objective area. To my surprise, Hackworth was extremely professional, asking pointed questions and making cogent observations. That day marked the beginning of a professional relationship that evolved into a forty-year friendship.

Major Hackworth said we needed to apprise the brigade commander, COL James S. Timothy. Timothy was a World War II platoon leader and company commander who fought with the 79th Infantry Division in Europe. He was one of a handful of 79th soldiers to be awarded both the Distinguished Service Cross and the Silver Star.[3] Fluent in French and urbane in manner, he personified the phrase "an officer and a gentleman." Hackworth introduced me, gave an overview of our mission, and told me to debrief the brigade commander. Colonel Timothy's first comment was, "Before we get started, join me for breakfast." It was a gesture that I never forgot and one that I tried to replicate when I became a senior officer. Afterwards, Colonel Timothy said he was very pleased and passed on his compliments to Captain Hilbert and the members of the patrol. I left the brigade Tactical Operations Center (TOC), a field command post, with a spring in my step and a smile on my face.

Throughout the winter and spring, our training continued to orient on conventional warfare. We were woefully unprepared to face an insurgency. Our battalion, brigade, and division exercises had little relation to the conflict heating up in Southeast Asia. Yet there were constant reminders of Vietnam. Weekly articles in the post newspaper, *The Shield and Circle*, highlighted officers' and NCO's recent service there. At the same time, lieutenants and captains who had completed their tours in the 101st were getting orders to serve as advisors with the South Vietnamese. Little good news was coming out of the region, because the ARVN had few successes against the Viet Cong. It appeared that it would only be a matter of time before the communist forces prevailed and RVN would become the first in a series of falling dominos. The attack on the U.S. base at Pleiku on February 7, 1965 was a huge wake-up call. Eight Americans were killed and ten helicopters were destroyed. President Johnson initiated bombing of North Vietnam and dispatched 3,500 U.S. Marines to protect U.S. facilities. The war was expanding without any of us really understanding what was happening.

Major Hackworth prevailed upon the brigade commander to change the training focus. A counter-guerrilla FTX was planned in western Tennessee's Natchez Trace State Park. In the scenario, U.S. forces had to find and defeat the guerrillas, roles played by other paratroopers, and win the support of the "civilians," Special Forces (SF) soldiers who occupied four mock villages scattered over the 48,000-acre park. It was a first in the 101st Airborne Division.[4]

We knew something was amiss when the FTX was terminated on the second day. While awaiting trucks to take us back to Fort Campbell, Captain Hilbert said President Johnson had just ordered Marines and the 82nd Airborne Division to the Dominican Republic to quell a leftist rebellion. The president was concerned that communists were about to create a second Cuba near U.S. shores. Since the 82nd and the 101st were part of the Army's strategic reserve, commitment of one division required the other be placed on a heightened state of alert. The common assumption was that we would be deploying soon. We would . . . but not to the Dominican Republic.

Rumors began to circulate that we were being sent to Vietnam. The whispers were validated when we received a movement order for the 1st Brigade, 101st Airborne Division to deploy to an unnamed, "classified destination." With the Marine regimental landing team already in Vietnam and the 173rd Airborne Brigade headed there from Okinawa, it did not take much deductive reasoning to figure out where we were going. The classified destination was the worst kept secret of 1965.

There were a myriad of deployment issues to address. One was whether this would be a TDY (Temporary Duty) move or a PCS (Permanent Change of Station). The answer determined if families living in government quarters, the military terminology for family housing, remained at Fort Campbell or would have to resettle. If the deployment was a PCS, families were not permitted to remain on the installation. With the TDY/PCS dilemma unresolved, bachelors were sent on leave first. I packed my belongings and drove to my parents' house in Salisbury, Maryland.

Prior to anyone going on leave, First Sergeant Finley gave the single soldiers a little homespun advice. He told them that they didn't have to marry or sign over their $10,000 life insurance policy to the first woman who showered them with her intimate favors. His description of men doing crazy things before they go to war was very graphic. I thought about the first sergeant's admonition when I became serious about the woman I was seeing. Judy Lasley was a Salisbury girl who was attending the local college. We had dated several times during Christmas, so the majority of my leave was spent courting her. We developed a serious relationship, but following Finley's guidance, I didn't sign over my GI insurance.

A week later I was back at Fort Campbell. The decision was made that our move would be a PCS, probably for a year, so many men were on leave taking care of their families. Our vehicles and equipment were already headed by rail to the port at Galveston, Texas. We were issued two sets of jungle fatigues and apprised that jungle boots would be provided once we arrived at our destination. To bring all deploying units up to 110 percent strength, officers and enlisted men from across the division volunteered to join the brigade. ABU received three new officers and a score of enlisted men. Only the old soldiers realized that our numbers were being increased because early casualties were inevitable.

All our efforts were consumed getting out of Fort Campbell; no time was allocated for what we were going to do upon arrival in Vietnam. The appropriate color for dyeing our white T-shirts consumed hours of discussions. There were no country orientations, no lectures on local customs, and not even a rudimentary introduction to the Vietnamese language. We were incapable of winning over the local population because we knew nothing about them. In 1-327th Infantry, there was a cocky attitude that we would persevere where the French had failed. Their early surrender to the Germans in 1940 did not help their military reputation. One soldier voiced the sentiments of the majority of the men in ABU when he said, "We are goin' over there, kick the VC's asses and then be back here by Christmas."

On Sunday after returning from leave, I received a telephone call from Major Hansen, the Battalion XO. He asked if I could be at the battalion commander's quarters in an hour. It was an order, not a request. Second lieutenants were not summoned to Colonel Wilson's house for social calls on Sunday mornings. I was in a state of high anxiety. The CO and XO put me at ease and once we were seated Wilson asked me point-blank: "How soon can you be ready to go to the target area?" Authorities were still calling Vietnam the target area. I did not hesitate and replied: "This afternoon, sir." Lieutenant Colonel Wilson explained that each battalion was sending an officer to Vietnam as a member of a liaison party. We would join units already in country and observe how they were conducting operations. I was to correlate my observations and send them to the battalion commander. I returned to the BOQ and packed my gear.

Our liaison party consisted of three lieutenants from the infantry battalions, a lieutenant from the direct support artillery battalion, and a captain from the provisional support battalion. We would leave for Vietnam within the week and join the 173rd Airborne Brigade, operating just north of Saigon. In the meantime the brigade S3 instructed us to learn more about the country. My preparation was limited to studying the encyclopedia in the post library and reading a battered 1961 edition of Bernard Fall's book, *Street Without Joy*, the only book I could find about fighting in Indochina. If there were any official publications on insurgencies or counter-guerrilla operations, they were not available to members of the liaison party.

Five days later, our departure mirrored events all over the Army as the U.S. military geared up for war. The commitment in Vietnam was as ambiguous to us as it was to the American public. Lack of national dialogue about the mission was of no concern to the men of the 101st, for we went where we were ordered. No one in the 1st Brigade thought it was unusual, out of the ordinary, or asked why. Instinctively, everyone knew we were going to fight. President Johnson's pre-election pledge not to send U.S. boys to fight for Asian boys would go unfulfilled. The American War was starting.

CHAPTER 3

A Far Country

I lie in my tent
Thanking God of free rent
While outside the rain pours
And inside my buddy snores
Muddy floors and a wet cot
But still thanking God a lot.
Got hot chow every day
Rain or shine come what may,
Got a dog 'bout two weeks old
Eats C-rations hot or cold.
Special Forces all around
Keeping safe the hallowed ground.
1st Cav in the air
Landing, fighting here and there.
Ain't got much but could be worse
Just ask the men in the 101st.

—POEM BY A SIGNAL CORPS SOLDIER IN NHA TRANG[1]

OUR FLIGHT TO VIETNAM WAS COURTESY OF THE U.S. AIR FORCE, bucket seats and box lunches. The upside to flying the friendly skies of the USAF was you could carry a loaded gun on board and enjoy an unscheduled maintenance layover in Hawaii. We made the most of our twenty-four hours in Honolulu and then it was on to Vietnam, landing at Saigon's Tan Son Nhut Air Base in the morning. Later, passenger flights came in at night to minimize the possibility of drawing ground fire.

The bustling airport was a window on the Americanization of the war. U.S. airplanes, fighters and transports, were arriving and taking off one after the other. Ramp space was being expanded to accommodate offloading more cargo aircraft. Construction crews were building additional half-moon concrete revetments to protect U.S. fighter-bombers from mortar and rocket attacks. As we walked into the terminal, a soldier asked, "What's that smell?" An NCO who was returning from emergency leave said, "It's just Vietnam . . . you'll get used to it."

Bien Hoa, a dozen miles north of Saigon, was our destination. The 173rd Airborne Brigade base camp was adjacent to the expanding U.S. air base. Nearby was a jungle area known as War Zone D, a thickly forested sanctuary controlled by the VC. A 173rd officer called it "Indian Country," the first time I heard that term.

In the month since their arrival the paratroopers had dug in, strung barbed wire, cleared fields of fire, and constructed bunkers around the perimeter. The newly established base was a tent city; creature comforts, permanent buildings, and recreational facilities would come later. Because the brigade only had two infantry battalions, 1st Battalion and 2nd Battalion, 503rd Infantry, the 1st Battalion, Royal Australian Regiment (RAR) was attached. I was seconded to the Aussies.

The RAR battalion commander, LTC I. R. W. "Lou" Brumfield, was an articulate World War II veteran. Colonel Brumfield cited the battalion's time in Malaya and said that many of his soldiers were veterans of the campaign. He was proud of Aussie accomplishments in that conflict. From 1959 to 1961, the 1st Battalion, Royal Australian Regiment was part of the Commonwealth task force that ultimately defeated the Malayan National Liberation Army, the military arm of the Malayan Communist Party. That success gave the Aussies a sense of confidence in their ability to handle the VC. Counter-insurgency was considered their area of expertise and they were prepared to show the Americans how it was done. Brumfield said the 173rd Airborne Brigade and the RAR were learning to work together, but there were some differences in methodology. These differences, primarily over the use of firepower, would be a source of friction as time went on.

The Australian platoon leaders, who referred to themselves as "lef-tenants," were as interested in the 101st Airborne Division as I was the RAR. My "kit," Aussie terminology for individual equipment, was the source of envy. Their uniforms and load-bearing gear were not nearly as good as ours. They particularly liked our multi-pocket jungle fatigues, made of material that dried quickly. A lieutenant helped me get settled and asked if I wanted a brew. I thought I was getting a cold beer but was handed a canteen cup of hot, sweet tea with milk curdling on the surface. Welcome to the RAR!

The first Aussie casualties were caused by an accident, a mistake a recruit would make. When a soldier jumped off a truck, the pin securing the striker on his grenade pulled out. The explosion killed him and two nearby soldiers. I was shocked to hear the Australian government would not pay to have the bodies of their soldiers flown home; instead, the policy was for remains to be interred in the nearest Commonwealth cemetery, which was in Malaya. When a private businessman stepped in and paid the cost to have the soldiers returned home, the Australian government relented and changed the policy. I told my lieutenant counterparts that the American people would not stand for that. At the end of World War II, next of kin of those U.S. soldiers killed in action had the option to bring their loved ones back to the United States or be buried in centralized overseas cemeteries. Under the policy of concurrent return established in January 1951, all U.S. soldiers who died during the Korean War were brought home. No sane politician in the United States would attempt to change that arrangement.

A War Zone D offensive began on June 28, the first time allied forces had been in the area. Enemy mortars in War Zone D were within range of the air base and there was a continuing concern that the VC would mount raids from the sanctuary. The joint incursion was unique: It was the largest helicopter troop lift to date but more importantly, it was the first multi-battalion operation conducted by U.S. forces. General Westmoreland's offensive ushered in a major change in America's commitment in Southeast Asia; it was no longer a defensive mission. No one sensed anything unusual about it. Combat soldiers expected to take the fight to the enemy.

The Aussies were comfortable in the jungle, moving quietly and methodically searching for the enemy. Their field discipline was impressive. Every soldier in the battalion participated in "stand to." They were 100 percent alert in full uniform manning their fighting positions one hour before dark and one hour prior to sunrise. But the operation produced little contact other than occasional sniper fire. Colonel Brumfield remarked the VC were in the area but did not want to fight.

Aussie soldiers were known by several names. The older NCOs referred to themselves as "Pommies." When Australia was first colonized in the late eighteenth century, British criminals were sent there as punishment. Their clothing was stenciled with the abbreviation, POME . . . Prisoner of Mother England. Troops were also called "Diggers," an expression that originated in Gallipoli during World War I. In 1915, Aussies burrowed into the Dardanelles hills to keep Turkish artillery from decimating their ranks. Now, when the unit stopped moving, everyone dug waist-deep fighting positions, cursing more than any U.S. paratrooper. While the men were laboring with shovels and moving lots of dirt, one looked at me and said, "Sir, it's fuckin' cunt of a day, ain't it?" I had never heard hot, humid weather described that way.

At the conclusion of the operation, I sent a long list of observations to Lieutenant Colonel Wilson. Field craft and stealthy movement received effusive praise, but there were also significant shortfalls. While at home in the jungle, the Australians were not used to operating near other friendly units. Coordination with the 173rd Airborne Brigade was a problem and almost resulted in several friendly fire incidents. Helicopter support created confusion because loading and offloading took too long. Maybe the RAR could learn a few things from the Americans.

We made another foray into War Zone D on July 7 and 8. This time the VC wanted to fight. Sharp engagements from well-concealed positions inflicted casualties before the VC broke contact. Diggers did not have armament like our M79 40mm grenade launcher, a shoulder-fired weapon that resembled a sawed-off shotgun. It could have suppressed VC machine guns before the artillery was brought to bear. Several opportunities to hit the VC hard were missed because the supporting New Zealand artillery battery did not get rounds on the target quickly. U.S. units used artillery extensively and called it as soon as contact was made. RAR did not have that tradition or training. I heard criticism that the 173rd was too quick to use artillery. The Aussies would have been more successful in War Zone D if they picked up the indirect fire pace. Malaya and Vietnam were proving to be two different wars.

When the operation concluded, our liaison group flew north to join the U.S. Marines in I Corps. Third Battalion, 3rd Marines, "3/3," was our new host. Third Battalion left Camp Pendleton in January 1965 expecting a thirteen-month rotation on Okinawa. Because 3/3 was already in the Pacific, it was added to the growing troop list. The battalion arrived in May and was assigned to protect a new airfield being constructed at Chu Lai. The field was needed because Da Nang Air Base to the north was operating at capacity, another sign of increased American presence.

Lieutenant Colonel Muir, the battalion commander, assigned each of us to a rifle company. One of the Marine lieutenants in L Company asked if I knew Doug Wauchope when I was at West Point. Doug was two years ahead of me and had been my plebe squad leader, so I knew him well, better than I would have liked. Doug accepted a commission in the Marine Corps when he graduated in June 1962. "He was killed on June 29," was the Marine's matter-of-fact comment. The war now had a familiar face.

The Marines lived on a shoestring and took joy in it. Their amphibious equipment took a beating on the primitive roads around Chu Lai. The primary command vehicle was a smaller version of the M151 jeep; it was called a Mighty Mite. Most Marines said it was a maintenance nightmare or more commonly, "a piece of shit." AMTRACs (amphibious tractors) substituted as trucks, but compared to the Army's venerable two and a half ton truck, the "deuce & a half," were less durable and more susceptible to catching on fire if hit by a large-caliber weapon. Marines had not received the M16 5.56mm rifle; instead they carried the heavier M14 weapon with a 7.62mm cartridge. Their radios were a generation older with less range and capability than the AN/PRC 25 used by the Army. Their back-packed radios came into the inventory in 1951. A Marine colleague laughingly told me the USMC leadership believed that their gear was good enough for the Korean War so it was good enough for this one too.

Where the Aussies were characterized as stealthy operators, the Marines were heavy-fisted. The USMC motto was "If in doubt, shoot!" After my first firefight with them, I decided I would rather be with the Marines, particularly if North Vietnamese regulars were encountered. They brought everything to bear on the enemy, including jet fighters from their supporting air wing. If they encountered opposition from a village, they burned it down once the shooting stopped. Support of the people was not high on the USMC priority list. Marine battalions and regiments, like Army units deploying to Vietnam in 1965, were not schooled in counter-insurgency warfare. Even if time had been available, there was little doctrine on counter-guerrilla operations. U.S. combat units learned by on-the-job training or as the troops said, by MSU, Making Shit Up.

Starting on July 6, men of the 1st Brigade, 101st Airborne Division left Fort Campbell, flew to California, and boarded a troopship at Oakland Army Terminal. The ship, USNS *Leroy S. Eltinge*, was a World War II transport recently pulled out of mothballs. Configured to carry 2,800 soldiers, the *Eltinge* departed Oakland on July 9 with more than 4,000 paratroopers crammed aboard. The brigade's ultimate destination in Vietnam had not been finalized when the ship sailed, which delayed the arrival of Vietnam-bound equipment that had to be loaded on other vessels departing later.

Conditions aboard the ship were difficult since there was very little room in the troop compartments. Close quarters and overcrowding made tempers flare. Feeding 4,000 souls was a logistical headache. Breakfast was hardly completed when the soldiers were instructed to line up for lunch. To make matters worse, the ship broke down in the middle of the Pacific and had to be towed to the Philippines for repairs. By the time the *Eltinge* docked in Cam Ranh Bay on July 29, 1965, the troops were ready to fight . . . each other or the enemy. The 1st Brigade's arrival brought the number of U.S. personnel serving in Vietnam to 79,000.[2]

I met the 3rd Platoon when the soldiers were trucked from the debarkation pier to an assembly area at Dong Ba Thin, a few miles north of Cam Ranh. On the short truck ride, soldiers got their first immersion in the Vietnamese culture. A farmer working in his field stopped to defecate in full view of the passing convoy. ABU paratroopers were embarrassed by his lack of Western modesty.

First Brigade was welcomed by GEN William C. Westmoreland, the commanding general of MACV, and the U.S. ambassador to Vietnam, GEN (Retired) Maxwell Taylor. One could tell from Westmoreland's remarks that he was not planning on using us as airfield guards.[3] Personnel changes followed the arrival ceremony. LTC Joseph Rogers, the brigade executive officer, switched places with Lieutenant Colonel Wilson. Don Hilbert, our company commander, was promoted to major and became the battalion S3, and CPT George Shevlin, who commanded Headquarters Company at Fort Campbell, assumed command of ABU. These changes were a microcosm of the leadership churn every six months that would plague the U.S. Army throughout the war.

Dong Ba Thin, a U.S. Army Special Forces camp, was our designated training and acclimatization area. It was an ideal location because there was little enemy activity and few local people. The oppressive heat would prepare us for what was ahead. Salt tablets were consumed to replace electrolytes lost by profuse sweating, streaking our jungle fatigues with the white sodium chloride residue. We dug bunkers, calibrated all weapons, and practiced helicopter operations. The UH1 Bell helicopter, the "Huey," was an integral part of daily life. When we loaded the choppers, troops sat on the floor with their legs dangling outside; no safety straps were used. Years would pass before I learned helicopters actually had seats. Hueys were stripped of seats to increase interior capacity. Captain Shevlin, our new company commander, was a terrific trainer and great leader. All in ABU knew we had a winner.

The company's lieutenants got to know each other at Dong Ba Thin. George Reynolds had the 1st Platoon; Harry Godwin led the 2nd; I had the 3rd and Charles "Chuck" Littnan was the weapons platoon leader. George and Harry volunteered at Fort Campbell to fill the ranks of the 1st Brigade and arrived just prior to departure for Vietnam. George Reynolds was African-American in an era when there were few black officers in the Army. He had a tougher row to hoe than the rest of us simply because of his race. George overcame institutional discrimination by demonstrating competence and grace. Harry Godwin was older than the rest of us because he had enlisted in the Marine Corps out of high school. When discharged, he attended Henderson State College in Arkansas and was commissioned through ROTC. Chuck Littnan, a Marquette University grad, was in A Company when I reported for duty in January.

As the battalion prepared for combat, we were oblivious to events outside our area. Riots in the Watts neighborhood of Los Angeles went unnoticed. Thirty-four people were killed in the August 1965 turmoil, a precursor to the convulsions that would rack America as racial discord increased and the Vietnam War expanded.

Some of our equipment was supposed to be delivered in the assembly area. The company mess hall was one of the items that got waylaid. So much cargo was coming into Vietnam that misdirection was common. The initial indecision on where the brigade was to land contributed to the problem. U.S. forces were building up at a rapid rate and the logistical system could not keep up with it. Items we took for granted—cigarettes, sodas, sundry items, and ice—were unknown luxuries. SFC John Humphries was far more perceptive about our supply situation than the rest of us. When word came that some of our equipment would be delayed, John T. told the troops there would be no complaining about C-rations because we would probably subsist on them for the next few months.

A case of C-rations had twelve canned, individual meals, most of which were not very good. "Ham & Limas" and "Ham, Sliced" set records for salt content and were the least palatable. Judging from the dates on the cases, the rations were taken out of war reserve stocks and had been on the shelf since the late 1950s. Each C-ration meal had an accessory packet containing salt, pepper, sugar, instant coffee, and five cigarettes. Most of the cigarettes, Lucky Strikes, Camels, and Pall Malls, were unfiltered, another indication of the rations' age. Sergeant Humphries saved them all because smokes would be scarce after a few weeks. Cigarettes were one leg of the John Humphries Soldiers' Triad of Needs; the other two were women and whiskey, which were nonexistent.

The battalion's graduation exercise was conducted in the mountains separating Dong Ba Thin and Nha Trang. While it was a "walk in the sun," the soldiers' expression for little or no enemy contact, the operation was over difficult terrain. The mountains, where temperature and humidity were in the high 90s, tested us. SGT Gerald Douglas lost his footing on one of the precarious trails and went tumbling off the side of a cliff. SSG Travis Martin, his squad leader, looked down the ravine, disregarded the fact that Douglas might be hurt and yelled, "Get up, Goddamn it!" There was no mercy in the 3rd Platoon. After four days, we were exhausted and even though no one was shooting at us all the men said the operation was a "motherfucker."

We left the mountains and loaded large World War II amphibious ships, called LST's (Landing Ship, Tank), bound for the port city of Qui Nhon. Our final destination was the Central Highlands to provide security for the arrival of the 1st Cavalry Division (Airmobile). On July 28, President Johnson announced he was sending the new airmobile division to Vietnam. The decision was made to station the Cav astride QL 19, halfway between Pleiku and Qui Nhon so it would foil enemy attempts to cut South Vietnam in half.

The LST voyage was a welcomed respite from our recent experience in the mountains. We camped on the deck, smoked cigarettes, and consumed some contraband booze. The overnight trip ended and we headed west to An Khe, the first village in the highlands. Clearing Highway 19 was the initial task, followed by manning outposts in the mountain pass that led to the plateau where the 1st Cav would establish its main camp. A know-it-all staff captain said a French armored column, Mobile Group 100, had been ambushed in the pass. Actually, the 1954 ambush occurred farther west along QL 19. I read about it in Bernard Fall's book but chose not to be a know-it-all too and correct the man. Nothing could be gained by interjecting my newfound knowledge into the conversation with an officer two grades senior to me.

A Company was relieved of duty in the pass and sent to the west. On September 10, 3rd Platoon was ordered to conduct a daytime patrol in an area where the VC were operating and storing supplies. There were no specific intelligence indicators other than no "friendlies" were in the area. Information provided by the battalion S2 (intelligence officer) failed to note the area was inhabited by Montagnards, tribal people who lived throughout the Central Highlands. A few days earlier, Sergeant Humphries departed on reenlistment leave to Japan, an opportunity for him to see his wife and son. Staff Sergeant

Martin, an extremely competent NCO, replaced Humphries as platoon sergeant.

The platoon left the company perimeter at first light. Thick jungle and elephant grass, razor-sharp stalks that grew 10 feet high, dominated the route. Because of the terrain, we moved in a column formation. I was behind the point man and his #2, called a "slack man," with an M60 machine-gun crew and the weapons squad leader, Bill Robbins, directly behind me. Sergeant Martin was farther back in the column with the other M60. If we made contact, Robbins would have the machine gun lay down a base of fire, allowing the platoon to maneuver and attack the enemy from the flank.

In late afternoon, a monsoon storm hit. We were 2 kilometers, a little more than a mile, from the company's night defensive position (NDP). Suddenly the point man froze and gave the signal to stop. He whispered there were voices to our front. Both of us crawled forward to verify the sound. Even in heavy rain we could tell the voices were not Americans. That eliminated my initial concern that a U.S. unit might have wandered into our AO. Elephant grass was so thick we could not see who was there, but we estimated there were at least a dozen individuals speaking what we thought was Vietnamese. Captain Shevlin had emphasized we were the only friendlies in the area, so I assumed it was not an ARVN patrol. If the voices were Vietnamese, they weren't on our side and we needed to attack them.

Crawling back to the platoon, I decided to hit them before they could do the same to us. Instructions were given in whispers and hand gestures. Men were shifted so all our firepower could be brought to bear on the target. I lobbed a fragmentation grenade, our prearranged signal to attack, over the elephant grass into the sound of the voices; the platoon opened up with M16s, both M60 machine guns and M79 grenade launchers. We sustained fire for at least thirty seconds. None of us had been in combat before, so we were unprepared for the noise, smell, and the chaos. When ceasefire was ordered, there were moans from the target area. Rocky Ryan

screamed he was hit and was writhing on the ground, his leg horri-
bly mangled. As SP4 Karl Sunkett, platoon medic, moved to Rocky's
aid, I gave the command to open up again. Within a minute or so
the squad leaders and I managed to get the men to stop shooting.
Someone shouted that Sergeant Martin was on the ground with a
wound in his buttocks. Sunkett went to Martin when he stabilized
Ryan. I grabbed the radio, led a platoon sweep through the area, and
set up a 360-degree perimeter.

The beaten zone was an awful sight with dead and dying Montagnards, men, women and children, spread across a tree-covered
knoll. Blood and body parts were spattered all around. Several families must have been moving through the area and had no idea that
they should not be there. The horror of what had happened did not
immediately register. The men of ABU Company heard the firing,
so the radio net was jammed with requests for situation reports
(SITREPs). Security had to be checked, ammo redistributed, and
the wounded cared for. Bill Robbins took over as the platoon sergeant and made sure everyone had sufficient ammunition to ward off
any counterattacks. It was hard to count the bodies of the people we
had killed and maimed because the scene was so repulsive. I radioed
a SITREP to Captain Shevlin and was told to return to the NDP
ASAP. We had to carry the wounded because the jungle was too
thick to land a medical evacuation (med evac) helicopter. The image
of PFC Pedro Jamie holding an injured child remains with me to
this day.

It was well after dark by the time we got Martin, Ryan, and several of the wounded Montagnards back to the company perimeter.
We dropped Rocky Ryan's makeshift stretcher more than once as we
made our way through the vegetation. Since it was the first contact
in the battalion, higher headquarters wanted all sorts of information,
friendly casualties, body count, ammo expended, VC weapons captured, etc. Captain Shevlin put me on the radio to talk to the battalion commander, Lieutenant Colonel Rogers. My explanation that we
hit an indigenous group of civilians did not sit well. After a lengthy

conversation, I was told that my platoon had intercepted a VC supply party, definitely an enemy unit. Higher headquarters made an assessment and that was that.

The following morning, I briefed the platoon and relayed the battalion's version of the incident. I told the men that we did exactly what we were supposed to do and the shoe could have been on the other foot. I emphasized it was my responsibility and mine alone. The men listened in silence but their eyes told me the incident weighed heavily on them. I did not know it then, but some troops in the other platoons called my guys "baby-killers." No one contradicted the official version of events, but we all knew that something terribly wrong happened.

We never talked about that rainy afternoon. We chose not to question how Rocky Ryan and Travis Martin were hit when the "enemy" was armed with a few crossbows. Could either of them have stepped on a mine? Most likely, they were wounded by friendly fire. Senior officers did not want to sully the battalion's first engagement with the unpleasantness of a rifle platoon mistakenly killing innocent civilians. Poor intelligence, not knowing we were in a Montagnard home range, was part of the problem. It was a function of our lack of preparation for this kind of war. If area studies on that part of Vietnam had been produced, we did not have them. The contact was written off as an unfortunate incident because local people were in the wrong place at the wrong time. In today's terminology, the Montagnards were collateral damage.

I was bothered by my complicity in the official version of events. It would not have happened if I had visually confirmed the target. Captain Shevlin emphasized you never have all the information you need and split-second decisions have to be made; his counsel provided little solace. Later, the battalion's new executive officer, MAJ Dave Hackworth, reviewed the action and recommended me for an award. I lacked the moral courage to refuse it, to say that the citation was incorrect and that I did not deserve any commendation for killing innocent civilians. I regret it to this day.

In mid-September, a jungle boot shortage became a major flap. Our deployment packing list specified bringing two pairs of boots. They would suffice until jungle boots were issued. Most of us had sturdy boots produced by the U.S. Army Quartermaster Corps. A few men packed Corcoran "jump boots" that were great for spit shining but not durable. The soles started to pull apart after several weeks of wet weather. We used tape to keep them together. Several men threw away their Corcoran boots and wore tennis shoes.

An AP reporter, Rick Merron, brought the issue to a head. His photographs of the sorry state of boots in the 101st Airborne Division appeared in multiple U.S. newspapers. A *New York Times* article caused great consternation when it contrasted our footgear with that of troops stationed in Saigon who were wearing new jungle boots. General officers got involved and arranged for an emergency order of boots to be flown directly from the manufacturer to RVN.[4] Every paratrooper soon had two pairs. For his role helping rectify the situation Rick Merron was welcomed on our operations. He was a former Army enlisted man who stayed in the field for extended periods. Other journalists and reporters seemed to clamber aboard the resupply choppers that arrived late in the afternoon. They were day-trippers who sought the comfort and safety of rear areas when darkness came. Not Rick . . . he was there for the duration and probably was the first embedded reporter. A few months later, Ward Just, who would win acclaim as a novelist, joined us and followed Rick's example, making a name for himself as a first-rate journalist.

The days of the VC sitting on the sidelines and watching us ended on September 18. Our sister battalion got into a big fight at An Ninh, a small hamlet east of An Khe. Because of an intelligence oversight, 2nd Battalion, 502nd Infantry unwittingly conducted an air assault into the middle of an enemy training camp. The first choppers landed and were immediately sprayed with automatic weapons fire. All three company commanders were hit in the first minutes. CPT Bob Rawls of C Company was killed and the battalion executive officer, MAJ Herb Dexter, died moving from position to position urging the men to hold the perimeter. Strong leadership by the battalion's junior officers and NCOs saved the day, although thirteen paratroopers were killed and forty were WIA. The enemy body count was 257. Second Battalion, 502nd Infantry was awarded the Presidential Unit Citation, the first in the 101st Airborne Division since World War II.[5]

ABU Company lost a soldier a few days later. PFC Manuel Fernandez, from the 1st Platoon, was killed on September 21 when he stepped on a mine. He was felled by a "Bouncing Betty," a mine that launched out of the ground and detonated at waist-level, spraying shrapnel in all directions. The effects were lethal for those in the immediate vicinity. We never ascertained if the mine was emplaced by the VC or left by the French. The threat of mines had been reported, and we had been cautioned about leaving the well-worn paths. Some controversy emerged about why Fernandez was off the trail. Did he wander off on his own, or was he ordered to move into the bush? Troops were inclined to speculate on everything and tried to find a reason events happened. SFC Robert A. Press, 1st Platoon sergeant, said an unmarked minefield is neither friendly nor enemy, "It is to whom it may concern, so be careful."

The company continued to search for the VC but we only found old men, women, and children in the villages. Military-age males were not seen; however they had to be in the area because there were always pregnant women around. On the second day of the operation, September 27, Captain Shevlin stopped the company outside at a small hamlet and called the platoon leaders forward. A loud explosion, either a booby trap or a mine, engulfed the column. Our company clerk, SP4 Thaddeus Zajac, was killed instantly and others were hit. I found LT Jim Kelly, the artillery forward observer (FO), sitting on the ground with a dazed expression on his face. He was wounded but waved me off saying he was OK; his injuries were far more serious than they appeared. A few minutes later, I saw SP4 Charlie Loustaunau was holding a dying Jim Kelly. His artillery RTO, PFC Halford Logan, was already dead. James Patrick Kelly's death hit me hard, because we were friends going back to our Fort Campbell days. He had been the ABU FO since January 1965.

Other ABU paratroopers, including Loustaunau, were wounded in the blast. By the time casualties were sorted out and first aid rendered it was dark and raining. First Cavalry Division aviators denied our request for a med evac, citing visibility issues. As these conversations were going back and forth, a voice came over the company radio net. "This is Outlaw 6, what's your problem, boys?" An independent aviation company, whose call sign was "Outlaw," was in the air and monitoring our frequency. They heard the radio traffic about wounded American soldiers and wanted to help. The commander of A Company, 502nd Aviation Battalion led two UH1s into a small clearing in the midst of a downpour guided only by flashlights. They took out our dead and wounded soldiers. Captain Shevlin expressed our gratitude as the helicopters lifted off and later recommended Outlaw 6 and his men for Distinguished Flying Crosses.

The Cav assumed responsibility for An Khe at the end of September. Airborne troops pulled up stakes and moved to the coastal area just north of Qui Nhon. The city was becoming a major logistical hub and needed ground combat forces in the vicinity. Qui Nhon was the capital of Binh Dinh Province, a stronghold of the National Liberation Front (NLF) and VC. The province had a history of rebellion dating back to colonial times. ARVN units stayed in their garrisons, so the insurgents had a free run of the countryside. First Brigade was tasked to perform another security mission, code-named *Sayonara*. The Republic of Korea (ROK) was sending its accomplished Capital

Division to Vietnam. We needed to keep a lid on things until the Koreans took over the sector in late October.

Rain defined our Qui Nhon experience because the monsoon season was in full force. Rivers broke their banks and the paddies flooded. Since we patrolled in waist-deep water, immersion foot was a major medical concern. If boots were not given a chance to dry and socks changed regularly, skin would peel off men's feet and incapacitate them. Our company set up on the only high ground in the area, a village along a flooded river, an island in the sea of brown water that was a breeding ground for leeches. After each patrol, we stripped down and carefully examined each other to ensure that none were on us. Mosquito repellent was the best way to remove a leech; otherwise, if they were torn off, the mouth of the leech remained in the skin and caused infection. If you did not have any "bug juice," a lighted cigarette would do. During one patrol debriefing with Captain Shevlin, I scratched an apparent groin itch, not unusual in Vietnam. Blood oozed out and stained my trousers. A leech had clamped on me and my scratching crushed it. Everyone thought it was perfectly normal and did not bat an eye. I finished the debriefing and the medics removed the leech's head, using an antiseptic swab on the open wound. It was all part of a day's work.

Rising water proved to be dangerous and patrols were cancelled. Villagers were used to the monsoon flooding and kept basket boats outside their homes. The circular craft were made of woven bamboo and could hold two or three people. A paratrooper could always find a source of recreation so boat races were organized. The villagers thought that it was great sport and joined in the cheering and wagering. A boat tipping over added to the fun. The boat races, medical treatment, and shared rations with the local residents were the basis for our embryonic people-to-people program. The contests were terminated when an order came from Captain Shevlin, "Stop fooling around in the damn boats; somebody is going to drown."

Operations around Qui Nhon were concluded in early-November. After-action reports cited contact during Operation Sayonara as "light." But two more ABU soldiers, PFC Michael Campbell and PFC Dan Allum, were killed. Like Fernandez and Zajac, they had been with the company at Fort Campbell and had arrived on the *Eltinge*. ABU casualties now numbered four dead and over a dozen wounded. None of the wounded had returned to duty and no replacements had arrived. Casualties and disease were eroding the company's manpower, reinforcing the wisdom of deploying 10 percent over-strength.

The Koreans were ready to take over the AO and the 1st Brigade prepared to move on. We were finally getting a base camp and a short stand-down, a rest period. The news was tempered when Captain Shevlin told me both of us were leaving ABU Company. Shevlin had been selected to be the aide for a two-star general and I was to be assistant S3, working for my old company commander, MAJ Don Hilbert. When I voiced objection, George Shevlin reminded me that we go where the Army sends us. The change would be effective when we arrived at our new base camp area at Phan Rang, a coastal city south of Cam Ranh Bay (see Map 3-1).

As we were preparing to depart Qui Nhon, I received the highest accolade of my short career. First Sergeant Finley was holding a late night meeting with the NCOs. I was standing on the fringe of the group and overheard some of his instructions. His ending comment was, "Things are goin' to be all fucked up around here for a while 'cause Captain Shevlin and Lieutenant Howard are leaving." His words were a source of pride throughout my twenty-eight-plus years in the Army and remain so today.

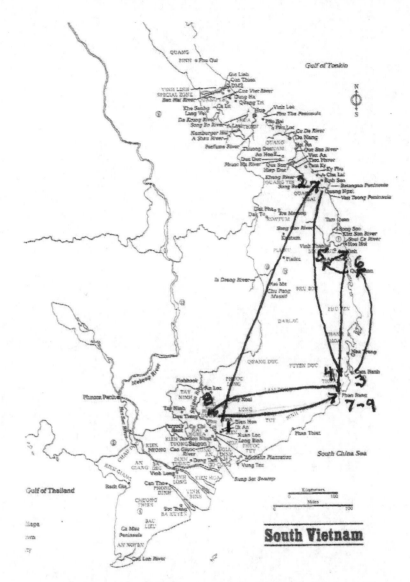

1. June 1965: Service with 1st Battalion, Royal Australian Regiment.
2. July 1965: Service with 3rd Battalion, 3rd Marines.
3. 29 July 1965: 1st Brigade, 101st Airborne Division arrives at Cam Ranh Bay aboard *USNS Eltigne*.
4. August 1965: In-country training at Dong Ba Thin.
5. August-September 1965: OPERATION *HIGHLAND* in An Khe securing AO for 1st Cavalry Division.
6. October 1965: OPERATION *SAYONARA* near Qui Nhon.
7. November 1965: Arrival at the Brigade's permanent base camp, Phan Rang.
8. December 1965: OPERATION *CHECKERBOARD* near Lai Khe.
9. 25 December 1965: "Home for Christmas" at Phan Rang base camp.

Map 3-1: 1965 Vietnam "World Tour"

CHAPTER 4

Steel 5

A hero is a man too afraid to run away.
—DAVE HACKWORTH, 1966

THE EXECUTIVE OFFICER (XO) OF AN INFANTRY BATTALION WORE two hats: He was the chief of staff and served as the deputy commander, the #2. Our new XO, MAJ David Haskell Hackworth, wore both with great aplomb but he favored the second role. Lieutenant Colonel Rogers liked the arrangement and prospered having a strong deputy. Hackworth had swagger, personal charisma, and an innate sense of the battlefield. Most of the officers were in awe of him and some of us even tried to emulate him.

Dave Hackworth's journey to the 1st Battalion (Airborne), 327th Infantry was a remarkable one. Born on Armistice Day, 1930, he dropped out of high school and enlisted in the U.S. Army at sixteen. He came of age as a young private in the occupation forces in Italy, first with a tank battalion in the Po River Valley and then with Trieste U.S. Troops (TRUST). Following World War II, Trieste was an independent city-state on the Adriatic Sea claimed by both Italy and neighboring Yugoslavia. TRUST soldiers were under a UN mandate to maintain order and prevent a shooting war between the two adversaries. Trieste in the late 1940s was on the front lines of the Cold War. Dave Hackworth developed his love of soldiering there and never looked back. When the Korean War started, he volunteered for combat duty, serving with the 27th Infantry Regiment, 25th Infantry Division where he received a battlefield commission in 1951. First Lieutenant Hackworth returned home with several Silver Stars and a number of Purple Hearts. It was the beginning of the Hackworth legend.

He preferred to be known as "Hack" and sometimes referred to himself in the third person, usually a boorish trait but one that made Dave more interesting. I met him during the 101st Airborne Division FTX in March 1965 and was impressed with the man. Stories about him abounded. A common one was that Hackworth had an air of personal infallibility that put off some of his peers. But he was a fighter, in more ways than one. The most recent Hackworth episode was that he had decked the S3 of the 2nd Battalion, 327th Infantry, MAJ Bill Dyke. Dyke had a reputation as being rampantly ambitious, earning him the label, "Dyke the Dick." During a meeting of S3s at the 1st Brigade TOC, Major Hackworth stated, "Well, Dyke, we finally have your fucking battalion taken care of." Major Dyke rushed Hackworth yelling, "Don't call my unit a 'fucking battalion'!" Not one to let a man intimidate him, Hackworth coldcocked Dyke, knocking him to the ground. Only one punch was thrown and the lopsided fight was quickly broken up. However, one field grade officer hitting another was unheard of even in the 101st Airborne Division.

Major Hackworth's arrival in the "Above the Rest" battalion coincided with the 1st Brigade's relocation to a permanent base camp. We had been in country three months and were still nomadic, living out of our packs. Other combat units operated out of fixed sites upon arrival in the theater. The 173rd Airborne Brigade was at Bien Hoa, 1st Infantry Division at Di An, not far from Saigon, and the 1st Cavalry Division was in An Khe. In November, an advanced party went to Phan Rang to lay out our new home. Everyone was excited about it.

Effective with the move to the new base camp, personnel changes were made. I joined MAJ Don Hilbert as his assistant and ABU had a new company commander, CPT Hal S. Eaton. The man acted as if he were Christ coming to cleanse the temple, which did little to engender confidence. An unspoken rule was new guys let their actions, not words, be their credentials. When Eaton first addressed ABU soldiers, he stood on the hood of a jeep and continually used the singular personal pronoun, "I." He implied the company would have been more successful if he had taken the reins earlier. It was a strange litany from someone who had never heard a shot fired in anger. The word circulated that the new commander's middle initial stood for Simon, Simon Legree, the evil overseer in *Uncle Tom's Cabin*. Dave Hackworth got wind of the problems, paid Captain Eaton a visit, and did a little foot locker counseling. Eaton was perceptive enough to know it was best to heed the Hack's advice. A disconnect between the captain's bravado and his tactical acumen would become apparent later.

While Eaton was ostracizing the men of ABU, several new lieutenants arrived. One of them, a Citadel graduate, was slated to take over my former spot in the 3rd Platoon. Dave Hackworth interviewed the man asking him what he wanted to do, expecting an aggressive response. The new officer replied that he would like any job other than being a rifle platoon leader, the most dangerous assignment for an infantry lieutenant. His response was the kiss of death; 101st Airborne was a "no shirker zone," so the man's nascent military career plummeted. He was given some "make work" and a requisition was placed for another officer. Before long, he was gone.

Phan Rang was located on the coast, south of Cam Ranh Bay, 175 miles from Saigon. The Japanese established a small air base there during World War II that the French used until they left Indochina in 1954. Now, the American forces needed a bigger facility so the

U.S. construction giant, RMK, was building a huge airfield with two parallel 10,000-foot runways. The 101st camp was several kilometers from the new air base. The brigade headquarters commandant, who selected the site, had bulldozers scrape off all the topsoil so we moved into a dustbowl, but a dustbowl devoid of VC and NVA. Regardless, we were glad to have a permanent camp, although we would spend very little time there.

The area was the home of the Cham people, an ethnic minority who had settled in Vietnam centuries ago. Many were practicing Hindus, while others were Muslims. Their distinct red brick buildings with spiral roof decorations made their settlements easy to recognize. Cham structures were miniature versions of Cambodia's famous monument, Angkor Wat. We were as ignorant of the Cham as we were of the rest of the Vietnamese people. The culture we embraced was the line of brothels and beer joints that sprang up along the road between the 101st base camp and the airfield. The Vietnamese were natural entrepreneurs and knew an opportunity when they saw one. Made of tin sheets, these shanties flourished. Some went under the guise of steam baths and massage parlors. Paratroopers flocked to them. We had been in the field for more than three months so the establishments made a fortune. SFC Humphries's triad of soldier needs—cigarettes, whiskey, and women—were finally fulfilled on the Phan Rang "Strip."

The pleasures found on the strip amplified the continuing need for good medical care. First Battalion, 327th Infantry found it and more with the arrival of CPT (Dr.) Raphiel Jacques Benjamin, Medical Corps. Doc Benjamin deployed to Vietnam as the surgeon with the 70th Engineer Battalion. He left a wife, Karen, and two young sons back in the States. Despite not being airborne-qualified, he volunteered for the 101st. Leaving the good life of an engineer battalion to join an infantry unit spoke volumes about the man. A native of Baton Rouge and a graduate of Louisiana State University, Doc proved to be a peerless combat surgeon and cool head under fire. His competence, demeanor, and acceptance of hard living endeared him to all of us. He ultimately became our resident philosopher and confidant. Major Hackworth was his #1 fan, so Doc was able to provide an effective counter-balance when Dave got off on a tangent.

Hackworth did not take long to make his imprint on the battalion. His mantra was "More Sweat on the Training Field, Less Blood on the Battlefield." Even though the soldiers were getting some rest, Hack did not want the men sitting around all day. Information on customs of the Vietnamese people was sorely needed and now was a good time to have some classes. Phan Rang was the capital of Ninh Thuan Province, so U.S. advisors were available to provide some cultural insights. Every soldier knew that our lack of knowledge was a major hindrance. One paratrooper remarked that his platoon mistakenly thought Buddhist ceremonial flags were those of the enemy and accused the village people of being VC. After three-plus months in combat, the men of the 101st were getting a country orientation.

———

Not long after arrival at Phan Rang, two officer R&R quotas for Bangkok were sent to the battalion. No one was interested in taking R&R early in their tours so Johnnie Adams, 4.2" mortar platoon leader, and I grabbed them. Johnnie said that you might as well take R&R now since you might get killed before you got a chance to go.

Bangkok was terrific. We saw the sights, hired several ladies of the evening to keep us company, and drank more than our share of the great Thai beer, Singha. Thailand was a welcome respite from Vietnam because the people were warm and friendly and the city was totally secure. Not all our time was spent enjoying feminine companionship. We hired a car and driver, Tru, who was available twenty-four hours a day. Tru was a full-time chauffeur, part-time pimp, and first-rate tour guide. He took us to the more famous sites: the Grand Palace, the National Museum, and several large Buddhist temples. The Floating Market and a cobra farm were also stops. We splurged one night and had dinner at Nick's #1 Hungarian Inn, which was famous for its Kobe beef. The restaurant was in an old mansion and had the reputation of being Bangkok's best. Johnnie and I could have been served well-aged water buffalo, because we would not have known the difference. We finished off Kobe beef with sides of lobster thermidor, then wolfed down baked Alaska. Five days in civilization went very quickly; our money was the only thing that went faster.

Returning to Phan Rang, we caught up on the latest news about the 1st Cav Division and the "ROKs" (pronounced *Rocks*), GI slang for Republic of Korea soldiers. The Cav had been in a big fight near the Cambodian border. We did not know there were actually two battles, one at LZ X-Ray and the other at LZ Albany. The only information was there were hundreds of American casualties. Years later, the battle became famous as a result of the book and movie, *We Were Soldiers Once . . . And Young*. The Koreans were also making a name for themselves with their "take no prisoners" mentality. One of our NCOs had recently returned from Qui Nhon. His assessment was, "the ROKs don't take no shit from anyone." He added, "If you kill everyone who looks at you cross-eyed, you don't have to worry about winning their hearts and minds. VC think twice before they fuck with them ROKs."

Immediately after Thanksgiving, November 25, the 1st Brigade was alerted for an operation in III Corps, the military region that bounded the capital. The 101st was tasked to join the 1st Infantry Division and the 173rd Airborne Brigade near Lai Khe, 40 miles north of Saigon. Earlier, the 9th VC Division had mauled an ARVN regiment, nearly wiping it out. That was followed by a U.S. battalion, 2nd Battalion, 2nd Infantry from the 1st Infantry Division, being attacked by the same enemy force.[1] A major offensive, Operation *Checkerboard*, was organized to search for and eliminate the 9th VC Division. The operation was part of General Westmoreland's big war strategy fought by U.S. units.

Before Checkerboard began, each battalion commander was given a permanent radio call sign. Lieutenant Colonel Rogers was "Silver Sheik" and LTC Henry "Hank" Emerson, the commander of 2-502nd Infantry, was "Gunfighter." We were always competing with the "Five-0-Deuce" and this time they one upped us. The Gunfighter call sign was cool, but Silver Sheik sounded like a prophylactic. Not to be outdone, Hackworth decided he needed a personal call sign too. He became "Steel 5," the number five being the suffix for the second in command. It was a good complement to Gunfighter.

We were airlifted from Phan Rang to the expanding U.S. complex at Bien Hoa. From there, the battalion convoyed north on QL 13 to Lai Khe, the base camp of the 3rd Brigade, 1st Infantry Division. Later in the war, the entire division relocated there. The 101st had its first encounter with command-detonated mines on the highway. First Battalion, 327th Infantry lost five paratroopers on the December 9 motor march with a dozen more wounded. A mine destroyed a 2½-ton truck carrying soldiers from B Company and Headquarters Company. The enemy's preferred mine munitions were dud 105mm and 155mm artillery rounds. The VC collected and buried the unexploded ordnance in the road with wires running to a detonator. As a convoy passed, a concealed observer hit the plunger and destroyed one or more of our vehicles. Because of this, the highway between Lai Khe and Saigon, QL 13, became known as Thunder Road; its bad reputation increased as more Americans began using it. Those rudimentary explosive devices were the forerunners to the improvised explosive devices (IEDs) that caused so many U.S. casualties in Iraq and Afghanistan.

Operation Checkerboard was launched the following day. I was in the field when Major Hackworth told me a liaison officer was needed at the 3rd Brigade Headquarters. Colonel Timothy wanted the 1st Infantry Division kept abreast of our operations and I got the nod. Their TOC was in the laboratory of a defunct French rubber plantation, complete with tile floors, glass windows, overhead fans, and electricity. The contrast between accommodations for the Big Red One and the 1st Brigade, 101st Airborne Division was startling.

The communist forces did not fight since most of the 9th VC Division had slipped back into Cambodia to recover from earlier battles. It suffered 300 KIA in the attack on the 2nd Battalion, 2nd Infantry. Large swaths of Cambodian jungle allowed them to recover without fear of being pursued by U.S. forces. They could rest, rearm, and retrain knowing that the U.S. government abided by international boundaries. They abandoned several caches containing documents, ammo, and tons of rice but there was no body count, disappointing General Westmoreland and his staff who were using that metric as a gauge of success.

The brigade staged out of Bien Hoa Air Base for return to Phan Rang. C-130 aircraft were scrambled to get us back, but the airlift dragged over several days. Troops hunkered down beside the runway, C-rations were issued, and ponchos were put up to shade the sun. We looked like Coxey's Army. U.S. personnel permanently stationed at Bien Hoa did not offer much help, nor did our airborne brothers in the 173rd show any generosity. As usual we were on our own, biding time until enough aircraft were mustered to take us back to our base camp.

Dave Hackworth always made the best of a bad situation. On our second day by the airstrip, SP4 Daryl Nunnally, Hack's driver, flagged me down saying, "Sir, Major Hackworth desires your presence." My first thought was what crisis do we have now? I got in Nunnally's vehicle and he headed off the air base and into the town. We ended up at a two-story house that turned out to be the best brothel in Bien Hoa. The battalion operations sergeant, SFC Charlie Musselwhite, found the place and passed the timely info to the executive officer. Inside, Hack and several of his guys were sitting around a table drinking beer with the ladies. He said, "Johnny, we waited to choose until you got here." He was the only man in the battalion to call me Johnny. I grabbed a beer, made my selection, and off we went. Later, when we finished our business, we assembled at the bar, all filled with a great sense of well-being. After some spirited conversation about the ladies, it was decided we needed another round. There was only one problem . . . we had spent all our money with the first set of partners. I happened to have a new transistor radio that the house madame coveted, so it was determined to be sufficient barter material for Round #2. Greater love hath no man than to give up his new radio for the good of his fellow men.

Our battalion closed into Phan Rang just in time for Christmas. Everyone was in a festive mood because our stand-down would last several weeks, General Westmoreland's holiday gift to the 1st Brigade, 101st Airborne Division. While we were away, the base camp had significantly improved. Large tents were erected, cots were provided, and the battalion CP had a wooden floor. A tent served as the officers' dining facility and club; it even had a plywood bar. By 101st standards, which were not very high, we were living large. The mess tent became the center of the evening social scene. After supper a poker game started which continued long into the night. I wasn't good at cards so I stayed out of them. Considerable sums of money passed across the table, usually in Dave Hackworth's direction. The poker games were a catalyst for great philosophical discussions where Hack held court. My contributions were reciting a little poetry, hoping to enhance the quality of the conversation. Kipling was a group favorite and as the night wore on, I was asked to quote "Tommy," "Gunga Din," or "Mandalay." I acquired the moniker of "Gentleman John" during one of those long evenings, a handle that would stay with me for the rest of our tour.

CPT Ben Willis was one of the mainstays in the holiday poker tournaments. Ben, a West Point grad from the class of 1961, joined the battalion after requesting a transfer from MACV advisory duty. By December of 1965, it was evident that duty with US combat units was viewed as an important station of the cross for advancement. Willis wanted to command a rifle company but had to get in the queue, paying his penance with a stint on the battalion staff. He was taciturn by nature and was one of the few officers who could match Dave Hackworth in poker.

The 1st Brigade got a PX (post exchange—military equivalent of a department store) during the stand-down. The Far East Exchange System based out of Tokyo did not catch up with us until Christmas. Most units arriving in Vietnam in the summer and fall of 1965 had a PX from the outset. For the 101st paratroopers it was a whole new experience and a great diversion. You could buy cigarettes, toilet articles, and snacks. Mail order service was also available. Soldiers were able to order merchandise from an extensive catalog and have it sent directly to a U.S. address. Component stereo systems, with a reel-to-reel tape recorder, a mega-watt amplifier, and speakers 3 feet high, were at the top of everyone's wish list. Lots of money was spent ordering stereos and other items unavailable in stateside PXs. For most of us, it was the first time we could afford such things. I yielded to temptation and ordered a fancy stereo even though I had no ear for music. On one occasion the PX received a shipment of watches. They did not last long because everyone wanted a good wristwatch. I purchased one and showed it to my buddy, Harry Godwin. I was very proud of my new timepiece. Harry said, "Hey, if you get killed, can I have it?"

Anything purchased at a U.S. facility, including the PX, was "cash and carry." Credit cards were not yet a gleam in a greedy banker's eye. Military Payment Certificates (MPC), usually called script or funny money, became the coin of the realm. In September all U.S. personnel were required to convert their US dollars for MPC. Designed by the Bureau of Printing and Engraving, MPC looked like Monopoly money, with small notes for fractional dollars, five cents through fifty cents, and larger notes for one-dollar, five-dollar, and ten-dollar denominations. The colors were loud shades of pink and green. Some of the ladies featured on the bills looked like June Cleaver, the idealized mother in the TV show *Leave It to Beaver*. Script was introduced when the buildup started to prevent currency manipulation. The Vietnamese piaster was fragile, so a large influx of U.S. dollars would undermine its value and threaten economic stability. If a GI wanted to buy Vietnamese currency, he exchanged MPC for piasters at the official rate. A "greenback" U.S. dollar could be changed on the black market for many more piasters than the going rate at a U.S. disbursing office. We were briefed that profits from such transactions usually made their way into enemy coffers. Combat infantrymen did not need much cash so U.S. dollars, MPC, or piasters made very little difference to us. MPC was just another aspect of war.

As civilization caught up with us, so did some new equipment. The most coveted among the grunts was the "Australian shower." I had seen them when I was with the RAR. The device was a collapsible canvas bag with a handle and shower head attached. The bag held several gallons of water. When attached to a rope, it could be thrown over a tree limb or beam, filled, and then hoisted up. You stood under it, opened the head, and enjoyed an instant shower. When not in use, the bag folded up and was easily carried. We were provided enough Aussie showers to provide one per squad. The soldiers thought we now had the comforts of home. Since arriving in Vietnam, we had washed using our steel helmets as a basin, taking what was affectionately known as a "whore's bath." Now that the U.S. logistical system in Vietnam was operating at full capacity, Army supply people contracted for a variety of equipment and distributed it in record time. Major Hackworth reminded us that we were the best-supplied army in the world.

During our Christmas stand-down, camaraderie among the junior officers reached a high point. Some of us developed a special relationship with the battalion XO. We became the recipients of "war and life according to Dave Hackworth." He regaled us with stories about occupation duty in Trieste, being a platoon leader in Korea, and his service in Germany during the 1961 Berlin Crisis. One that stuck with us was his philosophy on courage. Hack opined that courage was like a bottle of liquid with each man's bottle having a different volume. Every time you went on a combat mission, you poured out some of the contents. Over time, the bottle would empty and your courage would run out. It was important to periodically recharge those bottles; that was what we were doing at our base camp. He thought that we had come close to emptying some before we had our stand-down. One paratrooper became a victim of the empty bottle syndrome, committing suicide the day after Christmas. The man had not exhibited any outward signs of depression, nor had he indicated he was considering harming himself. The incident increased our awareness of potential mental health issues and required leaders to become more vigilant.

Dave Hackworth cautioned us about immoderation. He was concerned that the officers would spend too much time on the strip and get into alcohol-fueled disputes with the troops. "You can't have the officers fighting with the troops over the whores," he stated. As a result, most of us stayed in the camp and confined our entertainment to the mess tent. When we strayed from there, trouble ensued.

The Brigade Officers' Club steward announced upcoming live entertainment, a big deal since we were not on the USO circuit. Hence, a Korean or Filipino band was considered big stuff. Several of us made a big mistake when we decided to attend; we failed to invite Dave Hackworth. The evening got ugly; we overindulged and stayed until the club closed. Then we returned to the battalion area, went to the mess tent, and opened the liquor locker. In the course of our revelry, some chairs and a table were broken. The fun ended at dawn but our sleep did not last long. An enlisted man came into our tent and informed us that Major Hackworth wanted us in a formation in ten minutes. In various states of disarray, we stood in the hot morning sun as Hack proceeded to rip us apart. He stated that "this drinking to excess has to cease" and that "we were a disgrace to the Above the Rest battalion." He said if it continued he would send the lot of us to the 173rd. After the tongue lashing, we decided it would be prudent to take a break for a few evenings.

I was on duty in the battalion TOC that night so cooling it was not a problem. After making my checks, I tried to get some sleep. I was awakened by Hackworth and the same group of lieutenants I had been with the previous evening. All of them were roaring drunk. They grabbed me, took me outside, and tied me on the hood of a jeep.

Dave drove around the battalion area, blowing the horn like a hunter showing off a trophy. When they grew tired of that, I was taken back to the TOC. My comment was that it appeared the new era of moderation was short-lived.

As the assistant S3, my days were spent in the TOC. Normal business was conducted, reports rendered, and plans developed. The latter consumed my time. Since the XO was running things, we did not see much of the battalion commander. One morning, Major Hackworth told me to get the Old Man's signature on a document that required expediting. I went to the CO's tent and found Lieutenant Colonel Rogers pouring Johnny Walker into a canteen cup. I cleared my throat, saluted, and said there was an important document for him to sign. He looked up and said, "Good morning, John, you caught me . . . first one today. Leave the paper here and I'll look at it soon." When I returned to the TOC, I told the XO that the boss would sign the paper later. Hack said, "Was he drinking already?" I hesitated and said, "Well, Sir, I didn't see him drinking but he was pouring one." Major Hackworth smiled and said, "My God, don't mention it to anyone. We don't want the Five-O-Deuce to know that the Old Man is a morning drinker!"

One of the advisory teams in Phan Rang requested our assistance training an ARVN infantry battalion in airmobile operations. Harry Godwin, the most experienced platoon leader in the battalion, and a team of NCOs were tapped to help with the instruction. Dave Hackworth asked me to accompany him to the training site where Harry met us and explained that they had conducted multiple rehearsals but the ARVN just did not grasp the concept of loading helicopters in an orderly manner. Discipline broke down on the PZ and soldiers milled around while the helicopters were trying to land. The U.S. advisor and Harry explained over and over, through an interpreter, that each helicopter load was limited to nine Vietnamese soldiers, two more than a normal contingent of larger-framed U.S. paratroopers. Instructors demonstrated how each helicopter load, called a chalk, should be spaced along the PZ to allow the helicopters to land and load. While American soldiers did not view this as a complex operation, the South Vietnamese did. As the helicopters were landing, the ARVN soldiers became unglued and the integrity of the chalks dissolved. The U.S. advisor and his NCO began running around the PZ trying to restore some semblance of order. We were afraid that one of the ARVN soldiers might be decapitated running into a rotor blade. Because of the confusion, the helicopters aborted the landing. Harry Godwin called it a "monumental cluster fuck." Dave Hackworth pointed to the U.S. advisors trying to reorganize the mess and said, "It's no wonder everyone wants out of MACV. Look at those poor guys." That day we coined the expression, "Looking like a Vietnamese airmobile!" In the 327th, it replaced an earlier generation's "SNAFU" . . . Situation Normal, All Fucked Up.

On the day after New Year's, we started a program of improving the base defenses. The task was two-fold; the bunkers on the perimeter needed some work and we also wanted to get the troops out of the holiday stand-down mode. Dave Hackworth made it a point to inspect the work of each company. During one of his visits, a disgruntled paratrooper was cutting logs with an ax. He placed his foot on the wood and swung his ax. Hackworth watched for a moment and then said, "Son, be careful, you're going to cut your foot off." The soldier stopped, looked at the XO and with a sheepish grin said, "Sir, I wish the fuck I would."

During our stay at Phan Rang, I realized that I had found my calling and that the Army was going to be my career. Fort Campbell provided a great introduction but service in Vietnam convinced me the military would be my lifelong profession. I did not experience a single moment of clarity, rather an evolution that began in June of 1965 upon arrival in Southeast Asia. Dave Hackworth was the key player in my maturation. His counsel, insights, and encouragement persuaded me that my boyhood desire to be a soldier was not an empty daydream. From that time, I never questioned the path I was on or wondered if my career choice had been a mistake.

New replacements arrived. We needed them because the rifle company strengths were below 75 percent. Very few of our sick and wounded had returned. Most of the new troops, privates, were fresh out of airborne school. One of the incoming sergeants was my Ranger School instructor in the fall of 1964. The man had very little time to respond to the notification that he was going to Vietnam. The NCO barely had an opportunity to resettle his family before he was on a plane headed to the combat zone. His situation was an indicator of the replacement system trying to keep up with increased casualties and buildup of U.S. forces. The war was heating up, affecting the entire Army; everyone was going to serve in Vietnam.

As the ranks of the battalion were replenished, Dave Hackworth observed that some new officers wanted to be in an infantry battalion a minimal amount of time and move to a staff position in a large headquarters. He called these men "ticket punchers." The term would become institutionalized as the war continued. It was a shock that some officers were putting self before service. These careerists, as they were called, wanted to get their obligatory combat command tours checked off and then complete the remainder of their Vietnam time in comfortable, less risky jobs. The U.S. Army put great stock in an officer's performance as a platoon leader, company commander, or battalion commander. To get promoted, successful command time was a must. Hack said, "We need to be careful . . . amateurs and ticket punchers are going to get all of us killed!"

Selected officers were transferred to MACV and the 173rd Airborne Brigade. This was the beginning of what was known as the Infusion Program. The authorities were concerned that company grade officers, captains and lieutenants, would reach DEROS (Date Eligible to Return from Overseas) at the same time. Theoretically, after a year in country, a battalion would have an influx of brand new officers and there would be a loss of continuity. DEROS for most officers in 1-327th Infantry was July 8, 1966, one year after the *Eltinge* sailed from Oakland. In reality, it was a non-issue. Casualties, evacuation for sickness, and job rotation created vacancies that were immediately filled by individual replacements. When early July 1966 rolled around, very few remained who had been part of the original group from Fort Campbell.

⸺ ❧ ⸺

Commanders were trying to get their arms around how to fight an elusive enemy. All agreed that we needed to take advantage of mobility provided by helicopters. LTC "Hank" Emerson, CO of 2-502nd Infantry, took the lead and came up with several concepts to saturate an area and then if it came up a dry hole to quickly move the troops to another location. He wanted to repeat the process until contact was made; then helicopters brought in reinforcements. To help the troops understand his concepts he gave them names: *Checker Boarding*, saturating several grid squares with platoon-size elements; *Jitterbugging*, moving the troops around by helicopter if there was no enemy activity; and finally, *Piling On*, once contact was made, bringing every ounce of combat power into the fight. There was no such thing as too much force when fighting NVA units.

The battalion began an extensive training period. Our base camp time was drawing to a close. The area around Phan Rang was ideal to re-hone skills and to integrate new soldiers. It was a quiet AO so rookie mistakes were not deadly. The brigade would not sit idle for long, but no one knew where we were going. Major Hackworth gave us a heads up about an impending move to Phu Yen Province, between Nha Trang and Qui Nhon. Communist forces in II Corps obtained most of their rice in Phu Yen, the breadbasket of central Vietnam. They requisitioned so much the previous year the government had to import tons of rice to feed the population. One of General Westmoreland's 1966 objectives was to deny this food source to the enemy. The South Vietnamese were unable to provide the necessary security for the harvest so the 1st Brigade, 101st Airborne Division would have to do it.[2] Hackworth was excited about the battalion's mission. He pushed for the creation of a special reconnaissance unit, the Tiger Force, and believed it would give 1-327th Infantry another combat multiplier. Tuy Hoa would test everyone, particularly the Tigers.

CHAPTER 5

The Tiger Force

[U]nlike other recon units, the Tigers had additional responsibilities. Not only were they supposed to find the enemy but they were to engage the enemy, at times acting like a commando unit. They were not there just to search but to destroy.
—*TIGER FORCE: A TRUE STORY OF MEN AT WAR*[1]

DURING THE KOREAN WAR, THE COMMANDER OF THE 27TH Infantry Regiment directed Lieutenant Hackworth to form a "Raider" platoon. Manned by volunteers, its mission was to gain intelligence along the regimental front, including taking prisoners.[2] Dave Hackworth believed a similar organization would improve our battalion's intelligence-gathering capability, plus provide two additional fighting platoons. Hence, Hack became the driver behind the Tiger Force because he wanted to "out guerrilla the guerrilla."

First Battalion (Airborne), 327th Infantry in 1965-1966 was organized with a headquarters company and three rifle companies. Each rifle company had three platoons and a weapons platoon (with three 81mm mortars and two 106 recoilless rifles). Three combat platoons were assigned to the headquarters company: a 4.2" ("four-deuce") mortar platoon; a reconnaissance platoon; and an antitank (AT) platoon. The recon platoon's scout teams were equipped with M151 ¼-ton vehicles (jeeps) with pedestal-mounted M60 machine guns. In peacetime jeep-mounted scouts raced up and down roads looking for the opposing force. This tactic did not work in Vietnam since the VC did not use roads, and main thoroughfares exposed a mounted unit to ambushes. The AT platoon's primary weapon was the 106mm recoilless rifle (RR) mounted on an M38 jeep. It was organized to fight Soviet tanks on the plains of central Europe. Since there were no enemy tanks in 1965, the AT platoon's role was limited to convoy security and road-clearing operations.

The reconnaissance platoon was an obvious candidate to be part of a larger force. The recon platoon was stretched trying to determine where the enemy was. Hackworth envisioned a two-platoon recon unit. The AT platoon was underemployed so was added to the mix. To bolster the strength, a call went out for volunteers. There was no shortage of men who wanted to join.

Each platoon was organized into four teams of seven men with an experienced sergeant or staff sergeant designated as team leader. Seven Americans with combat gear comprised a load for the upgraded UH1. Each team communicated with an AN/PRC 25 radio. Machine guns and grenade launchers were pooled and distributed in accordance with mission requirements. A platoon leader, platoon sergeant, medic, and two RTOs rounded out the thirty-three-man unit.[3] The entire force, two platoons and a small command group, consisted of seventy volunteers.

A solid citizen, LT Jim Gardner, was assigned as the first commander. Jim entered West Point in 1961 but resigned during Plebe Year, subsequently attending Officer Candidate School. Gardner put the unit through its paces. Upon completion of an intensive training period, camouflage fatigues with a bold tiger stripe pattern were issued, setting the troops apart. Colonel Timothy approved the concept and officially christened the unit as the Tiger Force. Other battalions followed Hackworth's lead; 2-327th Infantry formed the Hawk Force and 2-502nd Infantry established the Recondos. The recon model was another local improvisation to meet the challenges of finding an enemy who usually did not want to be found.

In January 1966, our battalion moved north to Phu Yen Province. Tuy Hoa, the provincial capital, was a sprawling coastal city bisected by a large bay. The 1st Brigade established its command post at an airfield north of the bay. On January 28, Colonel Timothy relinquished command to BG Willard Pearson, previously the assistant division commander of the 101st at Fort Campbell. All of us were sorry to see Colonel "Tim" go, but the MACV rotation policy kept battalion and brigade commanders in their positions for six months. You could set your clock by the leadership changes. Conventional wisdom postulated there was too much stress associated with extended command time. In reality, many commanders were hitting the peak of their effectiveness when they were replaced by the next aspirant in the queue.

The rice harvest security mission was called Operation *Van Buren*. The area was southwest of Tuy Hoa City, a farming region consisting of miles of rice paddies, interspersed with small hamlets. The 95th NVA Regiment of *Street Without Joy* fame operated freely in the area.[4] Prepared to fight for its food source, the 95th immediately confronted the 101st. C Company, 2nd Battalion, 502nd Infantry, commanded by CPT Bob Murphy, got into a fierce fight 30 kilometers south of the province capital. On the morning of February 7, 1966, Major Hackworth was directed to form a task force and move to assist Murphy near a village shown on our map sheets as "My Canh (2)". Task Force (TF) Hackworth, made up of B Company, the Tiger Force, and a small command element, loaded aboard UH1s and headed into the fray.

The TF landed north of My Canh (2), not far from Captain Murphy's company, and moved toward the sound of the guns. No one was surprised that Dave Hackworth was on the ground with his troops, not orbiting overhead in a helicopter. He sent B Company to set up a blocking position south of the village. The Tigers would hit the northern edge of the NVA perimeter once B Company was ready. His plan intended to take the pressure off Murphy's unit and force the defenders out of the hamlet into the blocker's kill zone. Like all combat plans, things went awry almost immediately.

B Company was caught in the open as it maneuvered toward a suitable blocking position. The NVA had prepared the ground where they were going to fight. Fields of fire were unimpeded allowing the enemy to open up on U.S. troops as they moved south. The paratroopers of B Company had to seek cover behind rice paddy dykes. CPT Al Heiser, B Company commander, managed to break contact and pull the unit into a tight perimeter. However the damage was already done; nineteen men were killed and twenty were wounded.

Jim Gardner thought he could reach My Canh using elephant grass as concealment, but the grass stopped short of the hamlet. Open rice paddies covered by machine-gun fire separated the objective from the Americans. The lead Tiger element suffered casualties as it moved across open ground, forcing a withdrawal. In an effort to silence the weapons that were raking the area, Gardner grabbed all the grenades he could carry and dashed across the field. He destroyed three machine-gun emplacements before he was mortally wounded near the fourth. He was posthumously awarded the Medal of Honor It was his twenty-third birthday.[5]

Jim's valor diminished the enemy fire but did not eliminate it. Hackworth radioed 2LT Dennis Foley, who was now in charge of the Tigers, and told him to prepare to move. A massive artillery barrage was orchestrated to keep the enemy's heads down. When it commenced, the Tigers left their concealed positions and raced across the open area. Foley and his men joined Murphy's unit without losing anyone. Darkness was fast approaching, but there were not enough troops to seal off the area.

During the night, My Canh (2) was pounded with artillery fire. At first light tactical air support (tac air) was added to the mix. When the barrage lifted, the task force entered a deserted village. The enemy force, the 5th Battalion of the 95th NVA Regiment, slipped out of the partial encirclement, leaving behind sixty-three dead soldiers and many weapons. Task Force Hackworth lost twenty-six killed and twenty-eight wounded.[6] Dave was awarded the Distinguished

Service Cross for his actions at My Canh (2). Without his leadership and tactical acumen, there would have been more friendly casualties.

One of the dead in B Company was LT John Sanford, a platoon leader, who had been in Vietnam less than thirty days. He arrived in country on January 14, 1966 and joined the battalion at the end of the month. He was so new that it was difficult to find someone in the battalion rear to identify the body and verify the information on the Casualty Feeder Report. New replacements in World War II were often killed before anyone really knew them. History was being repeated.

Early on February 8, the remainder of the battalion arrived as the Tigers, B Company, and C/502nd Infantry cleared My Canh. Task Force Hackworth was dissolved and 1-327th Infantry began to search for the 95th Regiment's stragglers. A field TOC was established in the village and Hack reverted to his role as XO. He was in a buoyant mood because all the visitors, including Lieutenant General Heintges, deputy MACV commander, were effusive in their praise of his conduct of the battle.

Over the next few days, nighttime probes let us know that the NVA were still in the area. One was aimed at the TOC. After midnight an outpost (OP) was hit; calls to the OP were not answered. Dave Hackworth and Doc Benjamin ran to the position and not knowing what possessed me, I joined them. Two troopers from the 4.2" mortar platoon were seriously wounded. One soldier had his arm blown off at the shoulder. A lighted cigarette lay at the bottom of the foxhole, indicating one of the men had been smoking. While Dave and Doc dragged the soldiers back to the perimeter, I picked up an M79 and fired a dozen 40mm rounds at the enemy muzzle flashes. With Hack and Doc out of the line of fire, it seemed wise to get out of there. With the mortar platoon now dropping four-deuce rounds on suspected enemy locations, I ran the fastest 50-yard dash of my life back to the battalion perimeter. Later, Doc Benjamin told me that both wounded soldiers died in the aid station.

I moved to the Tiger Force after that action, but there was some "push-pull" about the assignment. Dave Hackworth wanted me to run the Tigers with Dennis Foley as my #2. Dennis wanted to be the Tiger commander, rightly believing he won his spurs at My Canh (2). Lieutenant Colonel Rogers insisted that my classmate, LT Norm Grunstad, the weapons platoon leader in C Company, command the Tiger Force with Foley and me serving under him as platoon leaders. Norm, a prior serviceman, had been a cadet regimental commander at West Point and that held great sway with Lieutenant Colonel Rogers. Hack solved the issue by concurring with the CO but establishing a rating scheme where he wrote the report cards for Grunstad, Foley, and me. His rationale was the platoons operated independently so often that it made sense for him to be the rater of all three lieutenants. In fact, this was a Hackworth ruse so that he could ensure Foley and I were taken care of when grading time came around.

My first mission as a Tiger platoon leader was a joint U.S.-Vietnamese patrol. The 1st Battalion, 327th Infantry was attempting to operate with host nation forces and develop some synergy by working together. It was an experiment that would be adopted throughout the brigade if successful. A Civilian Irregular Defense Group (CIDG) unit of thirty men joined my platoon for a three-day patrol. The CIDG soldiers were irregulars, armed and trained by the U.S. Special Forces (SF). They were Montagnard tribesmen from SF detachment A221 at Cung Son, west of Tuy Hoa. The men knew the terrain and the local villagers. Senior U.S. commanders believed that such operations using indigenous personnel would improve our ability to find an elusive enemy. Montagnards were considered good soldiers who would stand and fight the VC and NVA; they would also fight the South Vietnamese, whom they detested as much as the enemy. Montagnards had a history of being discriminated against by ethnic Vietnamese who called them "*moi*," meaning savage or barbarian.

The CIDG platoon was accompanied by a Special Forces sergeant. He expressed great confidence that his "Yards," his word, would perform well in the event of a firefight. On the first day the Montagnards lived up to the sergeant's prediction. They showed good discipline and moved quietly looking for signs of the enemy. When an NDP was established that afternoon, the CIDG soldiers dug in and occupied a sector of our perimeter. There was no need to question their combat capabilities.

The following morning the patrol moved farther westward. As the day continued, the CIDG soldiers were noticeably edgy, fingering the amulets they wore to ward off evil spirits. Late in the afternoon it was time to set up for the night. A small river separated us from an excellent spot. A scout team was sent to check the far side of the river and the high ground where the platoon would prepare its NDP. After receiving an "all clear," we waded across the river and moved to the new site. SSG Larry Smith, the platoon sergeant, and I put the troops in position, established fields of fire for the machine guns, and indicated where to emplace Claymore mines. The SF NCO came to me and said: "Sir, my little guys say that this side of the river is Number 10!" Loosely translated, the Montagnards meant we were in a dangerous area and they did not like it. The sergeant was afraid they might leave and he would have to go with them. No sooner had he said it the CIDG platoon began to file down the hill heading east back to Cung Son. I shook hands with the man and he hurried after his charges. That was the last we saw of them. I called the Battalion TOC and apprised them of the departure of our local warriors. Contrary to the tribesmen's intuition, no contact materialized for the remainder of the mission. At the end-of-mission debriefing, Dave Hackworth said, "So much for U.S.-Vietnamese cooperation. We aren't going to do that shit again!"

The brigade S2 believed the NVA and main force VC units were basing in the mountains and making forays into the lowland to disrupt the rice harvest. Our battalion was directed to send out two long-range patrols to supplement the brigade's reconnaissance operations. The mission was tailored for the Tiger Force and given to my platoon. I would take one seven-man element and Sergeant Smith would lead the other.

The concept involved inserting two teams at dusk on February 25 in a mountainous region where elements of the 95th Regiment had been spotted. The teams would be 5 kilometers apart, establish OPs on the high ground, and watch the trail networks that laced the area. In preparation, we made an aerial recon with the pilots who would fly the mission. A primary LZ and several alternate sites for false insertions were selected. The pucker factor was high because the area was outside artillery range and communications would be maintained with a twenty-four-hour airborne command post. Radio listening silence was a standard operation procedure except for designated reporting times or in the event of a tactical emergency (TE). USAF gunships were on strip alert to support us if we had a TE.

Each soldier's equipment was specified with no deviations allowed. One night vision device, called a Starlight Scope, was issued to each patrol. These bulky telescopes, about 5 inches in diameter and 20 inches long, were the first generation of a series of night vision devices that years later would give the U.S. Army a significant tactical edge. Rehearsals and inspections were part of our preparation. No one smoked, shaved, or washed twenty-four hours prior to H-Hour since the smell of tobacco and soap were readily identifiable in the jungle.

When we linked up with our aircraft at the Tuy Hoa airfield, the pilots stated they needed to launch the mission an hour earlier than originally planned. The flight leader was a captain who tried to steamroll me, giving no reason for the change of plans. I adamantly objected because too much daylight endangered both patrols. We would be needlessly exposed while we were most vulnerable, right after touchdown on the LZ. I told the pilots I would abort the operation before I would allow it to go earlier than planned and was prepared to tell the brigade commander why. They backed off and agreed to fly the mission as briefed. With that unpleasantness behind us, the patrols made final preparations and boarded the aircraft just as the sun was setting.

Our two Hueys lifted off and flew west toward the designated LZs with helicopter gunships providing high cover. When the UH1s split off, my patrol landed after two false insertions and Smith's went in after one. Darkness came just as we hit the LZs. My team immediately moved up a ridgeline so we could put distance between the LZ and us. If enemy soldiers were nearby, they would key off the sound of the chopper and head to intercept us. We found a concealed site and hid. I reported via code that we were in position and Smith did the same. It was an uneventful night.

Before first light, my patrol moved to a concealed rocky outcropping overlooking several well-used trails. At midday of the 26th, Staff Sergeant Smith broke radio silence and said he had men missing. Two scouts were sent forward on a quick recon and did not return. Smith was going to continue the mission while attempting to find the men. All efforts to locate them were unsuccessful. The missing soldiers were Sgt. Donald S. Newton, an experienced scout, and PFC Francis D. Wills. Looking back, I should have insisted on termination of Smith's mission then and there. The operation was compromised and the patrol was in even greater danger. An immediate extraction would have allowed the battalion to initiate a ground search . . . we might have found Newton and Wills before the enemy did. Five decades later I continue to question my decision not to press for that solution.

Both teams were extracted several days later. If the 95th Regiment had detachments in the area, they remained well concealed. An aerial search was immediately launched in the area Smith's team operated. The exact location the two were last seen was identified, but there was no trace of the missing scouts. Each member of the Tiger Force carried a signal mirror and smoke grenades. We hoped the distinctive sound of the helicopters would alert Newton or Wills and prompt them to signal us. The chopper carrying Smith and me was escorted by two gunships, so we were prepared to rescue them if they were sighted. After two futile days I was ordered to terminate the search.

The battalion S2 later received an agent report that one American POW was paraded through a local village. The hamlet was in the general vicinity of Smith's patrol. The information was so sketchy that neither the battalion nor the brigade acted on it and I was not apprised of it. The author, Shelby Stanton, published a detailed account of the incident based on a Department of the Army letter.

"On 11 March 1966 the mystery was apparently resolved after South Vietnamese Lt. Tran Hua Tien, the intelligence officer for Tuy Hoa District, contacted an informer in Phu Sen village. The villager related that ten days earlier two Americans, one white and the other black, had dug an overnight foxhole near the village and were unaware of partisans watching them. On the following morning an observation aircraft flew overhead and the Americans tried to signal it with three red smoke grenades. The partisans realized that both men were trouble and attacked. The black soldier was slain after killing three partisans, and the white soldier was captured after he was wounded in the arm and ran out of ammunition. The partisans stripped the black soldier's body and tossed it into the river, and used the white captive in a propaganda march through Thanh Hoi village. . . . The captive was also paraded through Phung Ha village and seen by the widow of a VC-murdered hamlet chief. She reported the communists redressed the prisoner in a plain khaki uniform and moved him across the river into Heiu Xuong district."[7]

Newton and Wills were the men cited in the report. They were officially listed as Missing in Action (MIA), the first 101st paratroopers not accounted for. Wills, an African American, was declared dead a year later; Newton was carried on the rolls as MIA until August 20, 1974 when he was also declared dead. Neither soldier's remains have been recovered.

⁓

There was no pause for mourning. Tiger Force was immediately tasked to conduct a reconnaissance in force in an area north of the village called My Phu, another nondescript hamlet that meant little to us except as a reference point on a map. On the morning of March 3, the Tigers initiated a two-platoon sweep where enemy elements were reported. Before the mission I talked to my friend, Harry Godwin, about it. Looking at the map, both of us reckoned that the area was "bad shit." Harry remarked, "That's Indian Country!! Watch your ass." It was the last time I saw him alive.

Our route resembled a cloverleaf, moving to the south almost to My Phu and then swinging north back to the battalion fire support base. The terrain was wide open, dotted with harvested rice paddies and small houses. What few villagers we met were sullen and non-communicative. All of us sensed that the place was full of "dinks," the GI term to dehumanize the NVA. Instincts were verified when we surprised a not-so-attentive outpost; our point man, James N. Wilson, killed two enemy soldiers. They were dressed in fresh khaki uniforms and armed with new AK-47s. The presence of "Regular, By God" dinks affirmed Harry's speculation that the area was bad shit.

As soon as we started the return leg of our patrol route, two NVA soldiers were spotted running south toward My Phu. They were well beyond small-arms range. Norm Grunstad ordered my platoon to chase them, but I balked and questioned why two soldiers, who were well hidden, would needlessly expose themselves unless they were trying to lure us in that direction. I was emphatic that we not follow into what would certainly be an ambush. He took my advice. When a SITREP was rendered, the battalion XO directed us to return to the FSB. During the debriefing, we carefully described the incident. When our report was combined with other indicators, it was determined that a battalion of the 95th NVA Regiment was operating not far from where the Tiger patrol had been. My Phu was obviously a center of enemy activity. The 1st Battalion, 327th Infantry (A and B Company) planned to conduct an air assault south of the village the next morning, March 4, and sweep north to secure it.

March 4 turned out to be a very bad day. ABU Company took casualties as it approached the hamlet. One of the wounded was SSG

Milton McQueeny, an iconic, longtime ABU soldier, who was hit multiple times by machine-gun fire. 1SG Robert Press, now A Company's top NCO, found McQueeny leaning against a paddy dike with a cocked .45 pistol in his hand. He refused to accept medical aid until other wounded paratroopers were cared for. The company also had an act of overt cowardice. A soldier feigned being hit and, when discovered, refused to rejoin the unit. It was a bad omen that increased the sense of foreboding.

My Phu was an entrenched redoubt. ABU was caught in the open in a fusillade of automatic weapons fire, wounding several paratroopers. Harry Godwin ran forward and pulled two wounded men back behind a rice paddy dike. Then, just like Jim Gardner had done a month earlier, Harry raced across the paddy and, using his M16, wiped out a machine-gun bunker, killing five enemy soldiers. His bravery stopped some of the fire and allowed the 2nd Platoon to seek cover. While attempting to silence an adjacent automatic weapons emplacement, he was mortally wounded.

Second Platoon soldiers revered their leader, Harry Godwin. He had been with them the entire tour, more than a lifetime for a combat infantry lieutenant. "Harry the Horse," as he was known, was a legend for his fearlessness and his concern for his men. SP4 Reuben Garnett, aka Sweet Daddy Grace, was killed trying to get to Harry's body. Reuben, a boisterous African-American paratrooper, was from Steelton, Pennsylvania, just outside of Harrisburg. He had been raised in a tough area near a Bethlehem Steel mill. He said when he got back to Steelton he was never going to use his fists again . . . now he knew about guns and grenades. Reuben was a product of the inner city, and Harry was a white man from the rural South, El Dorado, Arkansas. However there was a bond between them that overcame any of the racial discord that was germinating in the Army.

As the day progressed, casualties increased. Both company commanders, Hal Eaton and Al Heiser, were hit. Had it not been for Doc Benjamin being on the scene, the number of KIAs would have been higher. He rendered first aid and stabilized several men who would have died without his medical expertise. Doc pulled seriously wounded soldiers out of the line of fire and was awarded the Silver Star for his gallantry.

Tigers were standing by at the battalion firebase listening to radio reports of the fighting. We heard Major Hackworth's call that The Horse was down; everyone knew who that was. Reinforcements were needed so a warning order was issued to be ready to go. No one required prodding because our buddies were in trouble and we wanted to help. As the day dragged on, the Tigers continued to stand by. After dark, Hack called me and said get "saddled up" because five helicopters were going to bring in my platoon as reinforcements. If the first lift was successful, the choppers would return for Dennis Foley's guys. A night landing into a hot LZ was a high-risk mission. Night vision goggles were far off in the future, so we were operating with what we could see with the naked eye. At 9:00 P.M., the choppers arrived and we lifted off looking for an LZ near the 327th tactical CP. Keying on the flames from My Phu and tracers, we found a spot about 500 meters south of the hamlet. The descent was slow because all of us were looking for trees and other obstacles that might wreck our helicopters. The Hueys made great targets but none were hit. As the platoon moved toward My Phu, I found Dave Hackworth who told me to reinforce A Company. Hack later claimed our five-ship mission was the first nighttime combat assault in the history of the 1st Brigade, 101st Airborne Division.[8]

1LT Bob Anderson, ABU XO and a Fort Campbell hand, took command of the company when Hal Eaton went down. Bob said he needed help on his left flank because the company simply did not have enough men to cut off the western escape route out of the village. He asked me to tie in with his left-most platoon and block that potential exit. We tied in with both ABU and the North Vietnamese who were trying to flee My Phu. It was an all-night gun battle with hand grenades, NVA shoulder-fired rocket-propelled grenades (RPG), and automatic weapons fire. The RPG was designed to be an antitank weapon, but the North Vietnamese used it against infantry troops. The RPG was not accurate, but it had great shock value. When the 80mm round exploded, the sound was deafening and shards of metal were sent out in all directions.

At first light, we found a dozen dead NVA soldiers in our sector. No one had the inclination to verify if they were killed earlier in the day or in our fight that night. Body count was higher headquarters' measure of effectiveness, not ours. I was glad we did our job without any friendly casualties. Several of us had cuts from shrapnel and were patched up with iodine and bandages. Our unwritten rule in the Tiger Force was that a Purple Heart required medical evacuation; RPG splinters and grenade fragments "didn't count."

The morning of May 5 was spent cleaning out the village. In his book, *About Face*, Dave Hackworth described ABU company as "dazed and defeated, hunkered down behind rice-paddy walls."[9] I did not see rock-bottom morale. To this day, Bob Press takes great exception to the description and denies that was the case. Some paratroopers from A Company refused medical evacuation so they could remain with the company. At a recent 101st reunion, Bob and I recalled Dave never let facts encumber a good story and thus was prone to take literary liberties.[10] When his book came out in 1989, I cautioned friends that it was interesting, some of it was controversial, and some of it was even true.

Notwithstanding the disagreement about the state of morale, it had been a tough fight. B Company had eight killed and eleven wounded. ABU suffered fifty-one casualties, thirteen KIA and thirty-eight WIA.[11] The unit that moved out of My Phu was not the one I was in three months earlier. Few of the ABU originals remained. My old platoon, the 3rd, was left with only a handful of paratroopers from the original contingent that had arrived on the *Eltinge* and two of them would be gone soon. PFC Clarence Griffin would die a few days later and SP4 Galen Mitchell, a grenadier, would be seriously wounded on April 7.

Officially, one hundred North Vietnamese bodies were in the rubble.[12] We were far more concerned with the twenty-one paratroopers who were killed. Shortly after dawn, I found Harry Godwin's body, which was covered with a poncho. Helicopters evacuated the dead after we got all the wounded out and fresh supplies in. More than one soldier said that there would have been fewer ABU casualties had CPT Hal Eaton used his machine guns to provide covering fire and employed M79 grenade launchers and mortars for suppression. Instead he chose to frontally assault a fortified position and his troops paid the price. Bob Press decried Eaton's failure to use supporting fire.[13] It was a case of aggressiveness overcoming good tactical sense. Not many men were left who remembered his November speech when he took over the company.

1LT Harry Marlin Godwin, age twenty-six, was posthumously awarded the Distinguished Service Cross. Those who saw the incident said Harry deserved the Medal of Honor, but timing and military award quotas prevented it. First Battalion, 327th Infantry had just submitted a recommendation for the Medal of Honor for Jim Gardner, so the awards people were reluctant to forward another submission so soon. The paperwork never got past the 1st Brigade commander. Medal of Honor politics ruled the day.

After the My Phu battle, the battalion moved into the western reaches of Phu Yen Province. The bulk of the rice was harvested, so the brigade commander pursued NVA units in the mountains. Tigers established a patrol base at Dong Tre, in an isolated Special Forces camp where Detachment A-222 operated. The SF commander let us use several of the camp's old buildings. I assigned a new NCO, Staff Sergeant Vest, the job of making the new place livable. He had an aviation maintenance background but had volunteered to be in an infantry unit. Since he was airborne-qualified, some fluke in the personnel system put him in the 1st Brigade, 101st. The trickle-down effect landed him in the Tiger Force. Vest did not have the field experience to be a platoon sergeant or a scout team leader but was quite happy in the job I created, assistant platoon sergeant. Sergeant Vest, an inveterate chain smoker, doubled as an armorer and general handyman who could fix anything. One night I saw him with a cigarette dangling from his lips and exploded about violating light discipline. The glow of a cigarette at night made a great sniper target. Vest said, "Aw Sir, it ain't lit. I just like to feel it in my mouth!"

We did not have to look very hard to find a fight around Dong Tre. Until the 101st came, the NVA ruled the area beyond the camp's wire. Multiple recon teams were inserted into the AO, and often as not, we had to extract them under fire. Prisoner reports indicated that the 95th NVA Regiment had dispersed into small units and was moving out of the region. One Tiger said, "The little fucks ain't hidin' here." In early April, our battalion killed twenty-eight NVA. This fight brought the total enemy killed during operations in the mountains west of Tuy Hoa to 134, compared to eight KIA from the 1st Brigade.[14]

In mid-April, Brigadier General Pearson left 2-327th Infantry in Tuy Hoa and moved the remainder of the brigade south to Phan Thiet. Those who thought we might return to our base camp in Phan Rang for a short break were mistaken. We passed over it as we flew south. Phan Thiet was a coastal town known as the *nuoc mam* capital of Vietnam. The amber-colored liquid extracted from fermenting fish and salt was a staple of the Vietnamese diet and the GI-equivalent of Tabasco Sauce. You could smell the pungent condiment even in the countryside.

Several soldiers who had been hospitalized returned to the battalion while we were there. One was SP4 Charlie Lostaunau, an ABU paratrooper, who was wounded at An Khe and evacuated to Japan. Charlie rejoined the company in an assembly area. He asked one soldier where the 3rd Platoon was and got the response, "This is the 3rd Platoon." Later, Charlie only recognized one man, Tom Joyce, a machine-gunner. Joyce, unscathed in a year of combat, would be the only man of our original forty-two to serve his entire twelve-month tour in 3rd Platoon, ABU, 1-327th Infantry. The authorities did not have to worry about a mass departure of our original soldiers when the July 1966 DEROS date arrived. Most were already gone.

We set up our base and started sending recon teams out to look for the NVA. The dry season was at its height so the heat was particularly harsh. Compared to where we had just come from, contact was minimal. General Westmoreland never left the brigade in one place very long if there was not a fight. Soon we had orders to move to the jungles around Nhon Co, astride the boundary between II Corps and III Corps, a known infiltration route along the Cambodian border. I was sick when we arrived in our new AO. Terrible chills were punctuated by periods of profuse sweating and zero energy level. I kept pushing until I collapsed. Doc Benjamin worked on me in the aid station and put me on a med evac chopper.

I woke up in the 8th Field Hospital in Nha Trang with an acute case of falciparum malaria. I recall very little of that time but I did not need to be a physician to know that I was a sick man. One night my temperature went into an uncontrolled spike. To bring it down, I was placed in a bathtub with buckets of ice floating in the water. It was a question of whether I would die from hypothermia or from my fever being over 106. The ice water bath won and my temperature dropped. My doctor told me malaria fever is a killer that, if it cannot be controlled, fries your brain.

Not long afterwards, Doc Benjamin and Dave Hackworth visited me at the hospital. They somehow managed to spring me on a short pass. It was a huge mistake. We had a great lobster dinner at a little restaurant on the Nha Trang beach. The rich food sent me into a major relapse and they rushed me back to the hospital. My doctor had two alternatives: court-martial me or ship me back to the U.S.A. He saved my fledgling career and chose the latter.

In early June, I was placed on a stretcher, loaded on a C-130, and flown to Clark AFB in the Philippines. I eventually moved to Walter Reed Army Medical Center in Washington, DC. By the time I got to Walter Reed, my June DEROS had come and gone. The 1st Brigade, 101st Airborne Division was locked in a tough fight at Dak To in the Central Highlands. The battle made news headlines because a great Army football player, West Point's "lonesome end," CPT Bill Carpenter, called in an airstrike on his position to keep the North Vietnamese from overrunning his company. I felt guilty sleeping in a clean hospital bed while friends were toe-to-toe with North Vietnamese regulars.

———

LTC Walter E. Meinzen replaced Lieutenant Colonel Rogers prior to the battle of My Phu. I only saw him during patrol debriefings. However, as the battalion commander, Meinzen was the top man in my rating chain. The laudatory comments he wrote in my report card, the Officer Efficiency Report (OER), were offset by the last sentence: "... he needs to discipline himself socially to acquire additional polish."[15]

In 1966, there was no requirement to show the rated officer his OER, so I did not see the report until several years later. A single comment like that might be a career stopper in today's military. Fortunately, social discipline and polish were not high on the Army's list of attributes for combat infantrymen in the Vietnam era.

CHAPTER 6

Second Korean Conflict

[T]he Second Korean Conflict has drifted into obscurity, a curious episode, a footnote to the Vietnam era.
—"Scenes from an Unfinished War:
Low Intensity Combat in Korea, 1966–1969"[1]

MY SUMMER OF '66 WAS SPENT IN A MALARIA WARD AT WALTER Reed Army Medical Center. So much blood was drawn that my bruised arms and veins looked like they belonged to a certified heroin mainliner. When the doctors deemed I was cured and released me in late August, Judy Lasley and I got married and headed to Fort Ord, California's U.S. Army Training Center (USATC). Training troops was a common assignment for Vietnam returnees. Fort Ord was an anomaly because it was located in a beautiful area, unusual for military installations. Our married life started in an Army house perched on a manzanita-covered hill overlooking the Monterey Bay, a home with a million dollar view.

The USATC was a wartime operation churning out new soldiers and support troops, cooks, mechanics, and bakers. I took command of a basic combat training (BCT) company and was responsible for turning civilians into soldiers. After eight weeks a company of 240–250 new soldiers graduated on Friday morning and a fresh batch of recruits arrived that weekend to begin another cycle. Prior to each graduation, we were required to submit names of soldiers to attend Officer Candidate School. The guidance was to pick the best that you have even though some might not be very good. ROTC and West Point could not keep up with the demand for lieutenants, so OCS had to fill the void. In less than a year, the Army expanded the OCS program from two schools, one at Fort Benning, Georgia, and the other at Fort Sill, Oklahoma, to eight courses training new officers for the infantry, artillery, armor, engineers, signal corps, transportation corps, ordnance corps, and quartermaster corps. At the height of the war, Infantry OCS at Fort Benning graduated 7,000 new second lieutenants a year. However, some marginally qualified officers joined the ranks because of wartime exigencies, and liberal draft exemptions allowed many able men to avoid military service. Lieutenant Calley of My Lai infamy was a product of rapid expansion of the officer corps.

The USMA Class of 1964 was promoted to captain on January 3, 1967, thirty-one months after we were commissioned. The Army needed captains and the way to grow them was to speed up promotions. The personnel system was transitioning to a period when second lieutenants became first lieutenants in twelve months and promotion to captain occurred after two years of service. Shortening promotion time was another wartime measure. Similar policies were implemented during World War II and the Korean War.

Melinda Louise, we called her Mindy, was born at Fort Ord Army Hospital. Although not classified as premature, she weighed less than 5 pounds and was put in the "suspect nursery" to measure her progress during the first few days of life. Typical of the 1960s, I was not allowed in the delivery room. As new parents, Judy and I were always afraid the child had some fatal malady and was not long for the world. We learned parenting on our own and we were better off for it.

Life in the Monterey area changed when a call came from my classmate, Bud Henry, a fellow Fort Ord company commander. His first words were, "Hold on to your hat! We have orders for Korea." I was speechless because in October 1967 I fully expected to go back to Vietnam. Bud said that we had a November departure date and I should contact my assignment officer to acknowledge the orders. His sources revealed that we were part of a levy sending combat-experienced captains to Korea. Bud Henry always knew things before anyone else.

I placed a call to Infantry Assignments Branch in Washington. MAJ Leon Bieri, a 1st Cav veteran, came on the line. I told him that I had just received orders for Korea but wanted to go back to Vietnam. His response is forever etched in my mind: "Hey, Howard, if the Army wanted you to go to Vietnam, you'd be sent there! The Army needs you in Korea. Any questions?" His abruptness meant that there was only one response: "No, sir." "Follow your orders," he said and hung up. Ours was not a kinder, gentler personnel system.

Dave Hackworth was now a lieutenant colonel working in the Pentagon. I called him hoping he could get my orders changed. There had to be an infantry captain with Vietnam experience who would prefer a tour in Korea to returning to Southeast Asia. Korea was a backwater, a low-priority operation, not unlike the China-Burma-India Theater of World War II. I gave Dave a rundown on my short conversation with Major Bieri and asked him to pull some strings to get me headed back to Vietnam. Dave said he was on it and was sure that a change would be forthcoming.

Hack called the next day. His opening words were, "Johnny, you're fucked!" He explained there was no chance of getting the orders changed because the U.S. commander in Korea, GEN Charles H. Bonesteel III, appealed to the chief of staff of the Army for assignment of forty to fifty infantry captains with combat experience. The 2nd Infantry Division and the 7th Infantry Division, the U.S. divisions in Korea, were in a leadership crisis. Captains leaving the theater were not being replaced, so infantry battalions were run by second lieutenants and a lieutenant colonel. Vietnam was top priority and it was all the Army could do to keep up the officer strength there. Dave said that Bonesteel's request was the result of things being in a mess in U.S. Forces Korea (USFK) and intelligence indicators predicting increased North Korean aggressiveness. The Army chief of staff, GEN Harold K. Johnson, supported the theater commander and told the personnel people to get the captains to Korea ASAP. Upon hearing that, I resigned myself to a tour in the "Land of the Morning Calm."

A week later I was summoned to the office of Fort Ord's commanding general, MG Thomas Kennan. His friend, MG William Enemark, was taking over the 7th Infantry Division and needed an aide, and the same major I talked to earlier nominated me for the job. The CG wanted to know if I was interested and gave me a day or so to think about it. Another call went to Dave Hackworth. Dave said he would run a background check on Enemark, including contacting COL Hank Emerson, the former CO of 2nd Battalion, 502nd Infantry. Return calls came from both Dave and Colonel Emerson. Gunfighter, Colonel Emerson's call sign in Vietnam, left little to the imagination: "Johnny, don't do it! Enemark is a scorpion." His advice was to go to Korea and command a company on the DMZ. Colonel Emerson said that Korea would be a tough assignment because, "The place is on its ass." How right he was!

I immediately told Major General Kennan that I appreciated General Enemark's offer but I wanted to be a rifle company commander, a response that seemed to sit well. General Kennan did not need to know that his colleague had a terrible reputation as a "people-eater." It turned out to be one of the best decisions I ever made.

The family resettled in our hometown, Salisbury, Maryland. We had about three weeks to travel across country, find a place to live, and set up housekeeping before I departed the day after Thanksgiving. Orders instructed me to proceed to Fort Lewis, Washington, and report to the replacement depot. Korea-bound soldiers flew out of

McChord AFB, which was adjacent to Fort Lewis. Bud Henry and I met at the airport and reported for duty. Unlike daily flights to Vietnam, Korea-bound aircraft were limited to one or two per week. Our sole duty was checking each morning for departure instructions. The Fort Lewis Officers' Club provided a diversion and a chance to talk to others heading to the same destination. By the time our flight was ready, the news from Vietnam had us on edge. The 173rd Airborne Brigade had been in a bad fight on a mountain, Hill 875, in the Central Highlands. Two members of the Class of '64, Hal Kaufman and Mike Kiley, were killed there. Mike was my Beast Barracks roommate in the summer of 1960.

—

"The Miracle on the Han River," the Republic of Korea's amazing economic recovery, was only a strategic planner's vision in 1967. The country was still suffering from the devastating effects of the Korean War and the ensuing poverty that followed. Long-range recovery programs were in place, but time was needed to revitalize the nation. Aid from Japan and the United States, partially for Korea's contributions to the war effort in Vietnam, was instrumental in the country's modernization efforts. Roads outside of Seoul were in poor condition and rural electrification was sparse. People in the countryside had a hard life in an unforgiving climate.

USFK was responsible for 18 miles of the DMZ, paralleling the Imjin River (see Map 6-1). Five infantry battalions were deployed there occupying a series of cantonment areas that followed the southern trace of the demilitarized zone. Camp Greaves and the 3rd Battalion, 23rd Infantry, where I was assigned, anchored the left flank of the U.S. line. The camp was a cluster of Quonset huts built at the end of the Korean War. Access to Greaves was via Freedom Bridge, a single-span across the Imjin River where U.S. POWs were repatriated in 1953. Demolition charges were in place to blow it in the event of an attack.

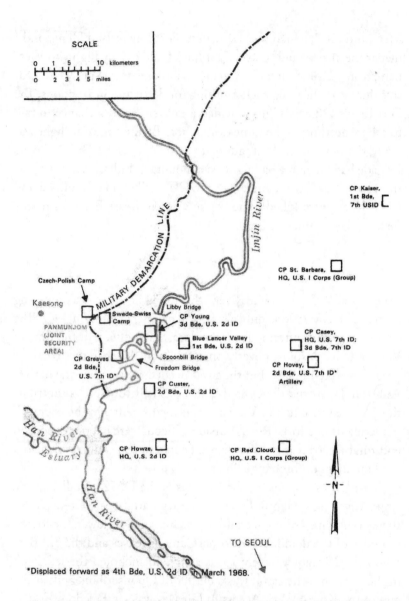

SCALE

0 1 5 10 kilometers
0 2 3 4 5 miles

CP Kaiser,
1st Bde,
7th USID

Imjin River

MILITARY DEMARCATION LINE

Czech-Polish Camp

CP St. Barbara,
HQ, U.S. I Corps (Group)

Kaesong

PANMUNJOM
(JOINT
SECURITY
AREA)

Swede-Swiss
Camp

Libby Bridge

CP Young
3d Bde, U.S. 2d ID

Blue Lancer Valley
1st Bde, U.S. 2d ID

CP Casey,
HQ, U.S. 7th ID;
3d Bde, 7th ID

Spoonbill Bridge

CP Greaves,
2d Bde,
U.S. 7th ID*

Freedom Bridge

CP Hovey,
2d Bde, U.S. 7th ID*
Artillery

CP Custer,
2d Bde, U.S. 2d ID

Han River

Estuary

CP Howze,
HQ, U.S. 2d ID

CP Red Cloud,
HQ, U.S. I Corps (Group)

Han River

-N-

TO SEOUL

*Displaced forward as 4th Bde, U.S. 2d ID in March 1968.

(From Daniel P. Bolger, "Scenes from an Unfinished War: Low Intensity Conflict in Korea, 1966–1969," p. 19.)

Map 6-1

There were no civilians "North of the River," a GI-term for the DMZ area. All had been resettled farther south following the 1953 armistice, the agreement that terminated fighting on the Korean peninsula. South Koreans working for the U.S. military arrived by bus early in the morning and departed in the evening. Having an area with only authorized Korean workers, mostly mess hall personnel and mechanics, was a blessing. For U.S. Army units south of the Imjin River, theft was a major problem. Korean "Slicky Boys" were notorious for stealing from Americans. No unattended equipment was safe when the Slicky Boys were around. Cyclone fences and 24/7 guards were required to protect installations. The difference in the standard of living in the Korean villages and the adjacent U.S. compounds was the source of the predicament.

LTC Charles "Chuck" Garwood, the battalion commander, was genuinely glad to see me and said I would command B Company. He gave two pieces of guidance: Anything you do will be better than what B Company is doing now, and if you fire a man, have someone at least as good to replace him. Garwood also said that the first sergeant and several NCOs intimidated the young lieutenants, so their initiative was stifled. The problem was more serious in B Company than the rest of the battalion.

Chuck Garwood needed help. His executive officer was an older Field Artillery major . . . a nice man but with minimal talent. The rest of the officers were lieutenants on their first assignments. These young men simply did not have the experience to cope with all the challenges. The battalion sergeant major and the first sergeants were second stringers, delighted to be in Korea rather than Vietnam. B Company's first sergeant, Jack Sharp, was a World War II and Korean War veteran; he already had two awards of the Combat Infantryman Badge with no desire for a third one from Vietnam. Marking time until retirement, his primary focus was a teenage Korean girlfriend in Munsan, the first large town south of the Imjim. Sharp was full-blown middle-age crazy and the prime contributor to the company's woes.

Most of the NCOs were young buck sergeants (E-5s) who had attended Fort Benning's NCO Candidate Course (NCOCC). NCOCC, modeled after OCS, was established to meet the need for enlisted wartime leadership, turning privates into sergeants in twenty-one weeks. The operational issues faced by these young soldiers were tough, but they were particularly ill equipped to cope with drug and racial problems festering in USFK. They tried hard, but because there was no help from the first sergeant, they were in over their heads. The troops referred to these men as "Shake and Bakes" and in some cases treated them with not so subtle disrespect.

B Company had more than its share of Project 100,000 soldiers, readily identified by unique serial numbers. In 1966, Secretary of Defense McNamara called for induction of men from the lowest mental categories. Heretofore, these individuals had been barred from entering the Army but the war caused admission standards to be lowered. Again, deferments for financial hardships, marriage, and college attendance allowed better qualified individuals to be exempt from military duties, forcing the authorities to take those who should have never served. At Fort Ord, Project 100,000 recruits were grouped into separate units and given extra training just to get them through BCT. Most came from low-income families and were high school dropouts. Their low intelligence levels and short attention spans made the simplest tasks very difficult. In B Company, these easily swayed men were already a source of trouble. By and large, they were uneducated, unhappy, and unruly.

Almost 20 percent of the company strength was KATUSA, Korean Augmentation to the US Army. Their presence masked serious shortfalls in the US enlisted ranks. The KATUSA program was initiated during the Korean War when ROK soldiers fleshed out understrength U.S. units. Now this shell game was vastly expanded so more U.S. soldiers could be diverted to Vietnam. Most of the Korean soldiers had no understanding of English and were weak in basic soldier skills. Each company had a KATUSA NCO with a modest mastery of English to serve as the KATUSA first sergeant.

He was always with First Sergeant Sharp, not an ideal mentor. I had two Jack Sharps on my hands . . . one Korean and one American. The personnel situation was a mess, and as long as the war in Southeast Asia was raging it would not change. We would remain understrength and undermanned. Slothful senior NCOs, inexperienced junior NCOs, Project 100,000 soldiers, and a disproportionate number of KATUSAs presented a challenge of the first magnitude. I thought of Dave Hackworth's warning: "You can't make chicken salad out of chicken shit!"

The mission was surveillance along the demilitarized zone to prevent infiltration. The armistice established a 2-kilometer demilitarized swath on each side of the 160-mile Military Demarcation Line (MDL); no crew-served weapons, armored vehicles, artillery, or fortifications were allowed there. The North Korean Peoples' Army (KPA) regularly flouted the armistice provisions but the United Nations Command (UNC), the headquarters with operational control over all allied forces, was reluctant to do the same. Deadly incidents along the DMZ began in 1966 when the KPA infiltrations increased; most were now aimed at the U.S. sector.

General Bonesteel devised an anti-infiltration strategy to detect and delay KPA incursions. Affordability was a problem because most of the Defense dollars were spent on the Vietnam War. To overcome USFK budgetary constraints, the general persuaded U.S. Army Combat Developments Command (CDC) to fund an anti-infiltration test, which allowed research and development money to be used. Bonesteel, a Rhodes Scholar and brilliant officer, knew how to work the military and political bureaucracy.

The heart of the system was a 10-foot-high chain link fence, known as the Barrier, running along the entire south tape of the DMZ. Permanent fighting positions were emplaced to observe the fence and towers were constructed overlooking likely avenues of approach. Within the demilitarized zone itself, engineers built a fortified guard post in each company sector. The system could only impede KPA infiltration, not stop it.[2] Rifle companies were required to man a guard post, patrol the DMZ, and occupy positions on the Barrier. People issues and the lack of competent leaders made this a formidable task.

There was no formal change of command ceremony. Lieutenant Colonel Garwood walked with me to the Quonset hut that served as B Company's orderly room and introduced me as the new commander. I signed the assumption of command order and we got to work. LT Jim Hurley was happy to have the weight of running the company off his shoulders. The first order of business was to determine how to accomplish the mission with the people available. In the haste to address all tasks, unit integrity had been lost. The Barrier contingent, manning the positions along the fence, was formed from a "hey you" duty roster maintained by the first sergeant. It became the first item on a growing list of things that needed to be fixed; unit integrity had to be restored. A platoon was given responsibility for the guard post and patrolling in the DMZ. The remaining platoons manned the fighting positions and the towers. A skeletal force, two squads, occupied it in daylight while the evening contingent required most of the men in the company. The weapons platoon stored its 81mm mortars and recoilless rifles and became a rifle platoon. The first sergeant and the platoon sergeant protested, but we could not afford to have underemployed men. UNC regulations prohibited indirect fire in the DMZ so the weapons platoon was incorporated into the surveillance plan.

CDC was evaluating cutting-edge sensor technology and B Company's sector was the test site, making it of great interest to the senior leadership. Questions about the sensors, infrared devices, acoustical warnings, and pressure-activated systems were met with comments such as, "The damned things don't work" or "They always are giving false alarms." CDC constructed a large concrete bunker to be the monitoring station that also doubled as the company CP. Sensor consoles were manned by the sick, lame, and lazy, including two Project 100,000 soldiers who could hardly read and write let alone render coherent reports. The sensor bunker needed to be upgraded and staffed by new people. Several "craftsmen" were tasked to spruce the place up. Among draftees you could always find an artist, a carpenter, and a handyman. These young men took great pride in their work and were happy to use their civilian talents. A schematic of the company's sector was painted on a 4' × 8' sheet of plywood, providing a visual representation of the sensor locations, our guard post, towers, and fighting positions. Tech manuals were pulled out of the file cabinet, and new men were trained as system monitors. Civilian contractors came to the DMZ to ensure the devices were still operational. They brought a xenon searchlight so we could illuminate the sector when a sensor activated.

Lo and behold the devices worked and things were coming together! The bunker was cleaned up and became a regular stop for VIP visits. It also served as my nighttime place of duty. One of our carpenters built scale models of each type of sensor for visitor "show and tells." None of this was rocket science, but because my predecessor was inexperienced and bullied by a lethargic first sergeant, it seemed like it.

Fatigue, monotony, and the harsh winter were enemies as well as the North Koreans. Days were short so platoons were trucked out to the Barrier at 4:00 p.m.. In December and January, darkness lasted fifteen or sixteen hours. The North Koreans kept up a steady barrage of propaganda broadcasts over giant loudspeakers. Some were in English, decrying the U.S. mission in Korea and branding us as "imperialist bandits." Other times the KPA aimed their message at the KATUSAs, exhorting them to turn on U.S. soldiers and defect to the North. Both the English and Korean broadcasts were so stilted with awkward Marxist phrases that no one took them seriously or wanted any part of President-for-Life Kim Il Sung's communist utopia. One night when I was checking the line, I stopped at a fighting position manned by a U.S. draftee and a KATUSA. The North Korean broadcaster was cranked up, ranting and raving in English about U.S. crimes in Vietnam. I asked the GI what he thought of the harangue. His response was, "Sir, nobody believes that fuckin' bullshit!"

Nighttime temperatures hovered around 0 as the wind ripped across the DMZ. Cold weather injuries were major threats, so warming tents were placed behind the fighting positions. The tents were heated with diesel-burning potbellied stoves. Throughout the night, platoon leaders and platoon sergeants had to ensure the troops rotated into the warming tents and then went back on the line. Because of the fierce weather, all soldiers wore bulky boots made of layers of rubber, felt, and wool that protected feet to minus 25 degrees. Officially called vapor barrier boots but known as "Mickey Mouse Boots," they prevented frostbitten feet after a long night at the Barrier.

Facilities suffered because of the Eighth U.S. Army budget crunch. The 2nd Infantry Division and the 7th Infantry Division occupied more than 100 small camps; the sheer number of installations stretched the facility engineers to the breaking point. The old Quonset huts were literally falling down around us. Because the toilets were constantly clogged, I had outdoor latrines constructed to prevent a major sanitation problem. The assistant division commander (ADC), BG John Guthrie, questioned me about it during one of his visits. He energized the engineers, but there were not enough crews to handle all the problems. The situation was fixed for a short period and then reverted back.

Vehicle maintenance suffered from the lack of spare parts. Any item—alternators, distributors, batteries, and filters—could be obtained in the "ville," the GIs word for Munsan. Korean shop owners had stocks of parts pilfered from U.S. depots by Slicky Boys or sold on the black market by rear area GIs. The Korean version of Napa Auto Parts kept our trucks and jeeps operational. Expended brass collected at our small test fire range as well as cans of GI coffee were taken to Munsan as barter for spare parts. It was another example of the strain and far-reaching effect of the Vietnam War.

One cold afternoon, I was returning from the Barrier and saw the first sergeant at the bus stop. He told me he was taking a pass to visit a friend. I was shocked that the senior NCO in the company would be taking a break when no one else was getting one. The first sergeant was not sharing the hardships that everyone else endured, so the next day a policy was initiated where I approved all passes. None were issued. When the battalion sergeant major counseled that I was getting into sergeants' business, I told him that I had to because the NCOs were not taking care of business. I added that I would fire Jack Sharp if there was a repeat incident of taking a pass when all the troops were working eighteen hours a day, seven days a week.

In January 1968, Lieutenant Colonel Garwood said we were hanging on by our fingernails and any incident could send us down failure's slippery slope. To bring a little civility to our day, the battalion commander directed that the officers who were not on the Barrier would eat supper together. Occupying a hillside with a picture window overlooking the Imjin River, the officers' club was a structure from a more placid time. The rule of the mess was that we did not talk business over our meal. Following supper, company commanders excused themselves and headed to the Barrier while Lieutenant Colonel Garwood spent his nights in the TOC. We were trying to prevent a fatal slide.

Fixes were made, but the root problems were beyond our control. Our mission was secondary in the larger scheme of things. We would have to operate on a shoestring while a bigger war was being prosecuted. Accordingly, maintenance issues, shortages of qualified people, and tight money would dog us. Nor was time on our side; all intelligence pointed to tough days ahead in the form of increased KPA incidents. During 1967, USFK suffered sixteen Americans KIA and fifty-one wounded, compared to six killed in 1966.[3]

The biggest threat to South Korea occurred on the night of January 17, 1968. The North Korean dictator, Kim Il Sung, was going for broke. A thirty-one-man team from the KPA's elite 124th Army Unit, a highly trained commando organization, successfully infiltrated the DMZ. The team's mission was the assassination of the ROK president, Park Chung Hee. They planned to follow isolated mountain trails all the way to Seoul. Their operation went well until the afternoon of January 19 when they encountered four South Korean woodcutters. The infiltrators used the opportunity to extol the virtues of North Korean communism and then released the woodcutters. Fortunately, the South Koreans disregarded the admonition to go home and immediately went to the police. By the next morning, the entire theater was on alert. The KPA soldiers, wearing ROK Army uniforms, were discovered on the streets of Seoul near the Blue House, the president's official residence. An alert policeman questioned the disguised platoon leader and when he stumbled with some of his answers, firing broke out. In the chaos, the team scattered, attempting to get back across the DMZ.

Our battalion assumed a maximum surveillance posture. Having to orient north and south called for extreme measures. Mess halls and motor pools closed; cooks, clerks, and mechanics formed a provisional platoon to augment observation along the DMZ. All duties except those directly related to Barrier operations were suspended. We gambled that surviving Unidentified Infiltrators (UI—the official term for KPA infiltrators) would attempt to cross the DMZ after dark. Our reinforcements supplemented our night positions and patrols, but no Blue House raiders came through 3rd Battalion, 23rd Infantry. One UI was captured, one or two escaped to North Korea, and the rest were killed. Three American soldiers were killed and three were wounded. South Koreans suffered much heavier casualties: sixty-eight were killed (including nearly two dozen civilians) and sixty-six were wounded.

The incident created a crisis in confidence between South Koreans and Americans. The North Korean prisoner, Lt. Kim Shin Jo, told his interrogators that the 124th came through a portion of the line manned by 2nd Battalion, 38th Infantry, the western-most unit in the U.S. sector. The terrain there offered excellent cover and concealment. Kim Shin Jo was brought up to the DMZ and pointed to the exact spot where the thirty-one-man team penetrated the Barrier. The UIs cut holes in the fence and moved undetected past a position manned by sleeping soldiers. To make matters worse and causing further embarrassment for the U.S. command, men of the 2nd Battalion, 38th Infantry repaired the holes and did not report the fence had been cut.

On January 23, 1968, a U.S. intelligence ship, USS *Pueblo*, was seized in international waters off the coast of North Korea. U.S. sailors were taken as hostages and one was killed. The *Pueblo* incident added to the trauma of the abortive Blue House raid. Some ROK generals made inflammatory statements that the ROK army should attack the KPA since the lack of a U.S. response was perceived as appeasement. There were indications that President Park was considering pulling South Korean troops out of Vietnam and bringing them home to defend the country. American troops were scorned as being substandard and calls for their replacement along the DMZ were sounded. When a high-level Washington delegation arrived to bring some calm to the situation, Park Chung Hee initially refused to see President Johnson's emissary, Cyrus Vance. Kim Il Sung had no idea how close he came to fracturing the ROK-U.S. alliance.[4]

The word of the apparent cover-up in 2-38th Infantry's sector spread throughout the 2nd Division. We were firmly convinced many in the chain of command would be relieved and those directly involved with the cover-up would be court-martialed. Even at our level it was obvious that the incident was big trouble, but the depths of the ROK-U.S. problems were way above our pay grades.

Amazingly, no action was taken and the expected relief never materialized. The battalion commander and the company commander remained on the job. The battalion commander was even selected for promotion and later pinned on the rank of colonel! Second Infantry Division was held together by a slim thread, and senior officials decided a massive relief might snap it. General Bonesteel let DEROS dates take care of the problem. Soon a new commander arrived as part of normal rotation.

Events elsewhere overshadowed the Korean crisis. The communists initiated a massive, country-wide offensive in Vietnam just after midnight on January 30, 1968, the outset of the Chinese New Year, Tet. Intense combat dragged on for weeks culminating in the ARVN and U.S. Marines fighting house-to-house to clear the Hue Citadel. Tet was a watershed for the Vietnam War because the military victory did not offset the political fallout. Former supporters of the effort in Vietnam now believed that the war was unwinnable. In a television speech on March 31, President Johnson announced he would not seek a second term as president. "That bitch of a war," as Johnson called it, hounded him out of office. His address to the nation was followed four days later by the assassination of Dr. Martin Luther King Jr. With rioting in major U.S. cities, it appeared our country was coming apart. Most of this news came belatedly as we maintained our DMZ alert posture. We were lucky to get days old copies of the *Stars & Stripes* newspaper and no one had time to listen to Armed Forces Network Korea. Colonel Garwood was as miffed as the rest of us and asked, "What in the hell is happening in our country?"

The Blue House raid and the *Pueblo* incident prompted several policy changes that helped flagging morale. Effective April 1, 1968, all personnel on the DMZ were awarded sixty-five dollars a month combat pay. Later, the Armed Forces Expeditionary Medal was authorized for those who had served there. Soldiers who were involved in firefights were eligible for the Combat Infantryman Badge or Combat Medical Badge. Recognition of service "North of the River" was a small gesture but it showed we were not forgotten. We would have to hold things together with what we had. Our shooting war along the DMZ was insignificant when U.S. casualties in Vietnam averaged 1,190 KIA per month.[5]

Part of the fallout from the Blue House raid was my reassignment to be S3 of 2nd Battalion, 38th Infantry. The unit was getting a new team and I was part of it. BG Ray Lynch, the new ADC, paid a visit and apprised Lieutenant Colonel Garwood and me of my new assignment. General Lynch spent thirty minutes giving his take on what needed to be done and told me to be at my new job the following morning. LTC Charles Dougherty, the new commander, was contending with the stigma of the January fiasco. His primary mission was to ensure the UIs did not succeed again and he set about it with a zeal and tactical expertise that the previous commander lacked. Together we conducted a detailed terrain analysis and carefully assessed the likely routes of infiltration, walking the ground to gain a better appreciation. Friendly positions along the barrier were moved so the soldiers had better surveillance along the avenues of approach, and more checks were made to ensure the men were alert. Dougherty had a tactical command post dug in just behind the Barrier, in the center of the 2-38th Infantry sector. Roads were improved so the Quick Reaction Force (QRF), equipped with M113 armored personnel carriers, had better access throughout the AO. Dougherty and I were in the Tac CP at night, co-located with the QRF.

On September 19, 1968, the changes paid off. An alert U.S. soldier reported seeing five infiltrators cutting the fence. Rather than fire on them and getting killed, he called in the incident as the UIs crawled past his position. The QRF intercepted them. Following their training and indoctrination, the UIs fought to the last man. By midday, it was over; four North Koreans were killed and one seriously wounded commando was captured. Two friendly soldiers were killed and four were wounded. When we were clearing the area, five Soviet PPS 43 submachine guns were found along with an assortment of grenades. The PPS 43, produced by the USSR during World War II, was obsolete in the Red Army. We were surprised an elite North Korean commando team would be armed with an older weapon, not the superior 7.62mm Kalashnikov assault rifle, the AK-47. Colonel Dougherty mused that perhaps North Korea was at the end of the Soviet/People's Republic of China (PRC) supply line and the good stuff went to the North Vietnamese.

A month later, a 2-38th Infantry daytime patrol in the DMZ observed an enemy squad just as it crossed the MDL. During the firefight, one U.S. soldier was killed and five were wounded. One intruder was KIA. The incident was among dozens that occurred in the U.S. sector after the Blue House raid. Every North Korean raid across the DMZ was turned back and the UIs suffered casualties. Momentum had finally shifted. Since attempts across the DMZ met with failure, Kim Il Sung tried another tactic. One hundred twenty men from the KPA 124th Army Unit landed on the ROK east coast, many miles south of the MDL. Their mission was to start an insurrection, but local villagers were in no mood to begin a revolution; they notified the national police immediately. South Korean troops swarmed into the area and over a two-week period killed most of the intruders.

By the end of 1968 the Second Korean Conflict was over.[6] Victory was not readily apparent, but the ROK-U.S. alliance had been severely tested and remained intact. Every North Korean initiative aimed at destabilizing the South had failed. Because of continuing resource problems and the demands of constant vigilance, we waited for the next provocation, knowing we were only one step away from disaster. No one realized that the Republic of Korea and the United States had won . . . except Kim Il Sung.

Unlike Vietnam, Korea was a thirteen-month tour. Officially my DEROS was December 29, 1968, so I was due to spend a second Christmas in ROK. The personnel people came to my aid with a Christmas "drop." Soldiers who spent Christmas of 1967 in Korea had their tours curtailed so they would be home for the 1968 holidays. My next assignment was the Infantry Officers Advanced Course (IOAC) at Fort Benning. The course was originally designed to prepare officers to command companies. In peacetime that usually occurred between six and eight years of service. Now most attendees, including me, had already commanded two companies. Even though the school system was out of whack because of the war, IOAC was a requirement for anyone staying in the Army. After two overseas tours, nine months at Fort Benning would be a welcomed break.

Frustrations over the past thirteen months did not dampen my sense of accomplishment in a tough environment. That satisfaction level increased markedly in late October 1968 when the Department of the Army released the names of captains to be promoted to major. I was selected for promotion with just over four years time-in-service, a wartime expedient. So much had changed since May 1961 when West Point officials were unsure I possessed the aptitude to be an Army officer. Perhaps surviving that USMA challenge was one of my subconscious motivators. Two years had passed since LTC Walt Meinzen rated my performance with the Tiger Force. Apparently, I had acquired sufficient social discipline and additional polish to move to the Army's next level.

Ranger School rubber boat training, December 1964. Three members of the class of 1964 in this photo were killed in Vietnam: Alex Hottell (front row, second from left with pipe), H.P. Kindleberger (fourth from left kneeling on the boat), and Bill Black (standing on the far right). Author is behind Alex Hottell to the right and the author's Ranger buddy, Dan Deter, is seated on the far left. DEPARTMENT OF THE ARMY PHOTO

3rd Platoon and Weapons Platoon, Company A (ABU), 1st Battalion (Airborne), 327th Infantry, 101st Airborne Division, May 1965. Author is fourth from the left in the first row; from his left—CPT Donald C. Hilbert, 1SG Duane E. Finley, SFC John Humphries, and SSG Travis Martin. DEPARTMENT OF THE ARMY PHOTO

ABU Company's four platoon leaders after our arrival in Vietnam, August 1965. Left to right: Harry Godwin (2nd Platoon), Chuck Littnan (Weapons), George Reynolds (1st Platoon) and author, 3rd Platoon Leader. AUTHOR'S COLLECTION

3rd Platoon sergeant John Humphries
and author in Qui Nhon, October 1965.
COURTESY OF SGT ADRIEN BELANGER

CPT (Doctor) Raphiel "Doc" Benjamin,
MC. Doc was decorated four times for
bravery. COURTESY OF R.J. BENJAMIN, MD

Doc Benjamin examines a fragment
in MAJ Dave Hackworth's arm
while CPT Ben Wills (foreground)
opens a can of Pabst Blue Ribbon
beer. COURTESY OF R.J. BENJAMIN, MD

Infantry sweep on March 4, 1966 near the village of My Phu. The 1-327th Infantry hit elements of the 95th NVA Regiment later that day. DEPARTMENT OF THE ARMY PHOTO

Left to right: MAJ Dave Hackworth, author, and CPT Don Chapman. Photo taken at My Canh (2) on February 8, 1966, the day after Hackworth won the Distinguished Service Cross. COURTESY OF R.J. BENJAMIN, MD

The author applying camouflage prior to a long-range patrol, February 25, 1966. DEPARTMENT OF THE ARMY PHOTO

"Rucking up"—getting ready to board helicopters for a long-range patrol mission on February 25, 1966. DEPARTMENT OF THE ARMY PHOTO

SGT Donald S. Newton of the Tiger Force. Newton was MIA on February 26, 1966 on a long-range patrol mission near Tuy Hoa. He was declared dead in 1977. His remains have not been recovered. AUTHOR'S COLLECTION

MAJ Donald C. Hilbert, S3, 1st Battalion (Airborne), 327th Infantry. AUTHOR'S COLLECTION

NCOs of 3rd Platoon ABU Company in Qui Nhon in 1965: SSG Travis Martin, SSG Billy Robbins, SSG Bill Bowlin, and SFC John Humphries. AUTHOR'S COLLECTION

The Barrier: part of the U.S. sector of the DMZ—the fence along the south tape of the DMZ, fighting positions, and a tower. AUTHOR'S COLLECTION

Aerial view of the center of An Loc taken in May 1972. COURTESY OF LT BILL CARRUTHERS, FAC AT AN LOC

Russian T54 tank knocked out in the center of An Loc. A crater from a U.S. bomb is to the left of the tank. AUTHOR'S COLLECTION

B-52 airstrike at An Loc. COURTESY OF LT BILL CARRUTHERS, FAC AT AN LOC

FAC's view of An Loc: The road, running from left to upper right, is QL 13, heading south toward Lai Khe. COURTESY OF LT BILL CARRUTHERS, FAC AT AN LOC

The devastation along QL 1 following the retreat from Quang Tri Province in May 1972. Huge amounts of U.S. equipment delivered as part of the Vietnamization program were lost. Not shown in the photo were the bodies that were left in the vehicles and along the road. DEPARTMENT OF DEFENSE PHOTO

Outside An Loc, June 18, 1972: An MK 82 500-pound bomb explodes several hundred meters from the 6th Airborne Battalion. The strike was part of a flight of USAF F4 Phantoms employed to destroy NVA positions. The An/PRC 77 in the foreground was the advisors' link to US airpower.
AUTHOR'S COLLECTION

SP4 Joe Javor awarded the Silver Star in An Loc, June 1972. Behind Javor: the author, CPT Jerry Metcalfe, and Captain McCoy of the An Loc District Advisory Team.
AUTHOR'S COLLECTION

CPT Woody Furrow, June 1972, Quang Tri. The Soviet T54 tank in the background was knocked out during the engagement the previous day. Furrow was hit in the arm. COURTESY OF THE FAMILY OF CPT GAIL W. FURROW

Quang Tri Citadel prior to its destruction in 1972. DEPARTMENT OF THE AIR FORCE PHOTO

MAJ Le Van Me, commander of the 11th Airborne Battalion, Vietnamese Airborne Division, September 1972. He is shown wearing the French paratrooper "lizard hat." Me was a soldier's soldier. AUTHOR'S COLLECTION

Last formation of Airborne Division Assistance Team, February 6, 1973. DEPARTMENT OF THE ARMY PHOTO

CHAPTER 7

Vietnam Redux: May 1972

*Vietnam is a graveyard of lost hopes, destroyed vanity, glib prom-
ises and good intentions.*

—CHARLIE MOHR, *TIME* 1963

NO STATESIDE ARMY INSTALLATION SHOWED THE IMPACT OF THE
Vietnam conflict more than Fort Benning, Georgia. "Home of the
Infantry," Benning was going full-bore training combat soldiers.
Paratroopers, Rangers, Infantry second lieutenants, "instant" NCOs,
and combat-tested captains were school products. The war had an
insatiable need for infantrymen and leaders. In 1968, nearly 17,000
U.S. military personnel, mostly grunts, were killed in Vietnam. To
keep up with the vacancies, OCS turned out 100–150 second lieutenants every week and NCOCC graduated 6,000 brand new sergeants a year.

Twelve hundred captains and majors were attending the Infantry Officers' Advanced Course when I arrived in January 1969.
Every advanced course student had been to Vietnam, some twice.
The faculty knew that IOAC was simply a pause in anticipation of
returning to Southeast Asia, so no one took our periodic inatten-
tion too seriously. Much of the curriculum focused on conventional
warfare, fighting the Soviets, with an occasional class on Vietnam.
The school's emphasis on combined arms operations would be put

to good use in a few years. A gentleman's course, the instruction did not generate any academic competition so we maintained a sense of humor and an irreverent attitude. During a chemical warfare class, the instructor showed us how easily an HVAC system could be contaminated. While he was lecturing, harmless phosphorous powder was placed in the ventilation ducts. At the end of the hour, he turned on a black light to show we were "glowing." When the lights came up, a member of the class looked at his seatmate who was undergoing reconstructive facial surgery as a result of being seriously wounded and exclaimed, "Jesus Christ, Norm, look at what that shit did to your face!"

President Nixon announced the start of Vietnamization during our IOAC. As part of the president's initiative, the first Army troop withdrawals began in August 1969. By the end of 1970, U.S. troop strength was projected to be at 344,000, down by one-third from an authorized peak of 549,500. Part of this drawdown included the 1st Infantry Division, 199th Infantry Brigade, 25th Infantry Division, and the 4th Infantry Division. These reductions affected many assignments. I fully expected a second Vietnam tour but was told that I would be going to graduate school in Operations Research/Systems Analysis (OR/SA). When Robert McNamara became the secretary of defense in 1961, his "Whiz Kids" overwhelmed the Pentagon staff with quantitative analysis and OR/SA techniques. The Defense establishment was playing catch-up, trying to educate selected officers in the discipline. Naval Postgraduate School (NPS) in Monterey, California, designed a two-year OR/SA master's program with allocations for each service. Since the West Point curriculum was predominantly focused on mathematics, USMA graduates were prime candidates to attend. When apprised of my selection, I was told this was where the Army needed me and this was where I would go. Like my previous assignment to Korea, what I wanted to do was not factored into the equation.

Another PCS took us from Georgia to California's Monterey Peninsula, a few miles from Fort Ord where Judy and I started married life and Mindy was born. It was our fourth move in the same number of years. The NPS campus was located on the former Del Monte estate, a beautiful property the Navy had taken over in World War II. The idyllic surroundings masked what was in store for us. Our classes began in March 1970 with graduation slated for two years later. Those of us who had been away from academia were sent to a short refresher course, which provided a taste of the rigorous classwork that was to follow. A math professor breezed through my two years of West Point calculus in the same number of weeks. The dean added more stress by announcing that each of us would be evaluated at the end of the first year and those who did not measure up to course standards would be given a BS degree and sent "back to the Fleet." The dean's admonition was not an idle threat because a Marine Corps friend received his baccalaureate "pink slip" and was banished to Okinawa. The Army sent me to NPS to get a master's degree, so anything short of that was not meeting expectations.

Courses with names like Stochastic Processes I & II, Linear/Dynamic Programming, and Non-parametric Statistics kept me fully occupied, but I made the first year cut and continued in the graduate program. In addition to normal coursework, there was also a thesis requirement and semester spent training with industry, in our case the Department of Defense. All my time was not spent studying, because my daughter Mary was born in June 1971. We found that raising child #2 was far easier than the first. Late night studying put me on the schedule for the last feeding and a diaper-change. The parenting experience was not nearly as traumatic as when Mindy was born in 1967.

Our institution was a hotbed of tranquility compared to other places of higher learning. Outside the confines of NPS, colleges were in turmoil. Allied attacks into Cambodia in the spring of 1970 set off a firestorm of protests. Campuses were literally ablaze. On May 4, 1970, Ohio National Guard troops were sent in to protect facilities at Kent State University. In the confusion they fired on demonstrators, killing four and wounding nine others. Hundreds of colleges and high schools closed because four million students went on strikes. The unrest prompted Congress to pass legislation that prohibited U.S. ground troops from being sent outside South Vietnam, the Cooper-Church Amendment.

Less than a year later South Vietnam launched an operation into Laos to disrupt an NVA offensive buildup. U.S. aircraft supported the incursion, code named *Lam Son 719.* The mission did not spark the domestic unrest generated by the previous year's strike into Cambodia. Lam Son 719 was not a success and resulted in a high loss of life and equipment, particularly U.S. aircraft. Notwithstanding a poor ARVN showing, Vietnamization continued to reduce U.S. ground combat capability as the fighting tempo ebbed. In the fall of 1971, I received orders to return to Vietnam and was apprised that OR/SA skills were critical to the withdrawal effort. In all likelihood I would be working on the MACV staff at Tan Son Nhut Air Base. The NVA Easter Offensive would change lots of plans, including how the Army was going to use my new advanced degree.

After graduation on March 24, 1972, we moved to Salisbury, Maryland. The family was going to stay in our hometown like they did when I went to Korea. With both sets of parents there, they had a strong support group. While we were getting settled, Vietnam suddenly became the top news story. The largest communist offensive of the war, an "all-in" blow involving the DRV's entire combat capability, started on March 30. Unlike Tet in 1968, Viet Cong insurgents had only a minor role in the attack because there was no realistic expectation of a popular uprising in the South. Instead, Hanoi's leaders directed a three-prong conventional attack, making no attempt to mask the North Vietnamese participation. Heretofore the guise of the National Liberation Front waging a revolutionary struggle against the "American imperialists and their puppets" provided a smoke screen for NVA forces. This mythology was completely discarded.

Vo Nguyen Giap, the defense minister and victor at Dien Bien Phu, was the reluctant architect of the offensive. He believed a full-scale attack in the spring of 1972 was premature but other Politburo members, led by Party Secretary Le Duan, insisted that now was the time to act. The triumph in Laos validated the North's conventional warfighting capability. Declining U.S. combat strength would diminish the firepower that had decimated their ranks during previous fighting. Warming relations between the United States and the DRV's communist benefactors, the Soviet Union and the People's Republic of China, added to the sense of urgency. A stunning defeat of ARVN might limit fallout caused by U.S.-USSR détente and America's rapprochement with the PRC. North Vietnam's leaders correctly gauged the mood in the United States that there was no political will to reintroduce ground combat units after so many troop withdrawals. Operation *Nguyen Hue* was meant to be Hanoi's masterstroke.

The offensive caused confusion among the ARVN leaders and U.S. officers. Three NVA divisions rolled across the DMZ on the 30th, the strike at Loc Ninh in III Corps commenced on April 5, and the attack in the Central Highlands began on April 14. The situation was muddled because intelligence analysts were unable to determine the main attack. Hanoi's planners believed President Thieu would commit his reserves to protect the northern-most provinces and the old imperial capital of Hue, leaving Saigon exposed when the North Vietnamese struck Loc Ninh and An Loc. If An Loc fell, few ARVN troops would be positioned to defend the capital, 60 miles away. Binh Long Province, which encompassed Loc Ninh and An Loc, was also expected to be the new home of the Provisional Revolutionary Government (PRG), the shadow administration created by the southern revolutionaries. In the third or Central Highlands phase, two divisions attacked Kontum Province. If the ARVN lost Kontum City, a provincial capital, the NVA would easily capture Pleiku further south, then turn eastward to link up with the forces fighting in the coastal region of Binh Dinh. This would split South Vietnam in two, a VC and NVA objective dating back to the 1960s.

The three main assaults involved 120,000 soldiers organized into fourteen divisions and twenty-six independent regiments supported by 500 tanks and heavy artillery.[1] The Politburo surmised

Vietnamization was a failure and U.S. public opinion would prevent a strong reaction from President Nixon. The importance of the U.S. presidential elections in November 1972 was an additional consideration. A similar situation existed in 1968, and although the NVA and VC suffered a staggering military defeat during Tet, they won an incalculable political victory. America turned against the war and President Johnson did not seek a second term. Now, given the maximum use of conventional military power, the perceived weakness of the ARVN and the political climate in the United States, the probability of North Vietnam's success seemed high.

Communist successes in April reinforced the optimism of the Politburo hardliners and marginalized the members who had counseled caution. South Vietnam was in a precarious position with total collapse a very real possibility. Along the DMZ Quang Tri was lost; An Loc was under siege, fighting for its life; the Highlands city of Kontum was threatened and barely holding on. From Hanoi's perspective, the campaign was progressing well. However, the DRV leadership made a strategic miscalculation by grossly misreading Richard M. Nixon. Disregarding advice from senior civilian officials to let the Easter Offensive be a test of Vietnamization, Nixon responded strongly. He directed the mining of North Vietnam's seaports, reinforced the South with additional airpower, and resumed bombing North Vietnam under the code name *Linebacker I*. To the enemy's alarm, not only did a majority of Americans support the president's decision, but the U.S.-USSR Summit in Moscow scheduled for later in May proceeded as planned. Leonid Brezhnev, general secretary of the Soviet Communist Party, viewed improved relations with the United States as being as important as solidarity with the North Vietnamese. President Nixon's actions were announced on May 8 during a primetime TV address. Navy and Marine A6 fighter-bombers were sowing electronic mines outside Haiphong as he spoke to the nation. One hundred more B-52 bombers were on the way to Guam and Thailand. Eventually 206 B-52s and over 800 tactical aircraft, USAF fighters, and carrier-based jets were available for airstrikes in both

North and South Vietnam.[2] Since these initiatives did not immediately affect the battle, the early May situation in South Vietnam remained grim.

———

I said goodbye to the family and headed back to the war zone before the presidential address. In 1972, soldiers traveling on military orders wore the Army green uniform, even though you might be the subject of hostility from fellow citizens. At the Baltimore airport, I was asked where I was headed. When I told the ticket agent I was going back to Vietnam, he only shook his head. Not only had the American public grown war-weary, but it appeared that the whole thing was going down the drain. The flight from Baltimore to San Francisco was punctuated by one moment of levity. Sitting on the aisle across from me was a young African-American private who had just finished Army basic training. He too was traveling in uniform and was clutching a brown envelope containing orders to his next duty station. His drill sergeant had warned him not to let the packet out of his hands so he had it in a death grip. As we were taxiing out to the runway, the plane's brakes were squeaking and at one point, the pilot made an abrupt stop. The young private looked at me and in all seriousness said, "Sir, do you think this motherfucker knows what he's doin'?"

I took a bus from San Francisco to Travis Air Force Base in Fairfield, California, and reported for duty. There was a late night flight so all passengers loitered in the terminal until assembly time. I struck up a conversation with an Army doctor who had recently escorted a patient back to the U.S.A. The doctor explained the wounded NCO later died of a staph infection. The soldier, later identified as SFC Alberto Ortiz, an advisor with the Vietnamese Airborne Division, was hit in the butt and one of the shell fragments cut his rectum. The medical personnel were unable to control the infection. The discussion was a grim way to start one's return to Vietnam.

Our aircraft was filled with senior NCOs, captains, majors, and lieutenant colonels. The lack of junior enlisted soldiers and lieutenants indicated the days of U.S. ground combat units were over. Even though the Easter Offensive was raging, the troop withdrawals continued and more Americans were departing than arriving. In the first week of May 1972, U.S. troop strength in Vietnam dipped below 68,000. Only two U.S. combat brigades, the last residual of what had once totaled seven Army divisions, two Marine divisions, and three separate brigades, remained; they were committed to guarding air bases and would not counter the NVA. US advisors and airmen were the only American combatants.[3]

We arrived in South Vietnam's airspace after dark, making a spiral approach into Tan Son Nhut to minimize exposure to ground fire. As we taxied to the terminal, I was impressed by all the activity. U.S. aircraft were taking off and landing every minute. Portable lights were set up in the concrete revetments allowing maintenance crews to work on the jet fighters, preparing them for first-light missions. When we finally stopped near the terminal, the aircraft doors were opened and hot, humid air rushed in. I was taken back to 1965 because you never forgot the smell of Vietnam and its heat. MACV personnel were told to expect specific assignments within twenty-four to forty-eight hours. In the meantime, we were billeted at the replacement detachment called Camp Alpha, not far from the sprawling MACV headquarters complex. Checking the assignment roster was my sole duty. Several days later, on May 9, my name appeared on the bulletin board with the notation, "Airborne Division Assistance Team, MACV Team 162." The Army was now in a hurry because someone scrawled in red pen, "BEGIN PROCESSING ASAP."

MAJ Julian Turner, the man in charge of MACV officer assignments, was in the administrative center. Julian and I had served together at Fort Ord in 1966 and 1967. We talked for a few minutes before he looked at my assignment sheet and said, "Oh, Jesus Christ, you shouldn't go there! Let me change those orders." I was surprised by what he said but realized he was just trying to do me a favor and keep me from getting shot. I begged off because my philosophy, go where the Army sends you, had worked in the past, so there was no need to change now. During the ensuing months, I questioned my judgment for not taking Julian up on his offer. Processing was expedited and Team 162 was informed I needed transportation to the detachment headquarters, co-located with the Vietnamese Airborne Division across Tan Son Nhut Air Base.

<hr />

When there was a large U.S. military presence in Vietnam from 1965 to 1970, advisory duty was never deemed as career-enhancing as service with an American unit. Command of a platoon, company, or battalion in combat was viewed as the premier assignment. There was the belief that officers who served with U.S. units were promoted ahead of those who were battalion and regimental advisors. Stories also abounded about advisors being left by the Vietnamese when bullets started whizzing around. Those perceptions were some of the unintended consequences of the Americanization of the war. As many officers gravitated to U.S. combat units, the advisory effort often got the short end of the quality stick, slowing the improvement of the ARVN.

From the outset of the buildup, U.S. units were less than enthusiastic about working with the Vietnamese. Some Americans were demeaning of their fighting ability and held them in thinly veiled contempt. One said, "You can kill one hundred dinks in an AO that's been cleared by Marvin!" "Marvin the ARVN" was a term of scorn that applied to any South Vietnamese in uniform, regular Army soldiers, the militia, or the national police. U.S. soldiers did not know or care enough about our ally to sort out all the players. The political maneuverings of senior military leaders did little to enhance the Vietnamese Army's stature. President Thieu personally selected all general officers, so loyalty outweighed competence and professionalism. Corruption was assumed, and it was noteworthy if a senior officer was not "on the take."

The Airborne Division was different. It was held in high regard by Vietnamese civilians and U.S. military personnel. The ARVN paratrooper had a terrific fighting reputation and his leaders were competent. Being an airborne advisor was considered a great assignment, on par with serving in a U.S. unit. The Airborne Division Assistance Team (ADAT) was the largest division combat assistance team (DCAT) in MACV. Over 1,200 officers and NCOs ultimately served with ADAT and more than thirty were subsequently promoted to general. GEN Norman Schwarzkopf, the 1991 coalition commander during *Desert Storm*, and GEN Barry McCaffrey were the team's most noted alumni. Barry, a classmate and longtime friend, was in some of the Airborne Division's hardest fighting. He won the first of two Distinguished Service Crosses as a lieutenant deputy advisor with the 2nd Airborne Battalion. When the battalion senior advisor, CPT Gary Brux, was killed, McCaffrey's gallantry rallied the paratroopers and kept the unit from being overrun. He was seriously wounded in that October 1966 fight. Between 1962 and 1973, twenty-six men from Team 162 died, the largest number of casualties of any DCAT. Five were killed during the Easter Offensive.

The Vietnamese Airborne Division was close to the center of power. From Tan Son Nhut Air Base, a task force could be at the Presidential Palace in ten minutes. President Thieu kept an element of the Airborne Division near the capital to prevent a possible coup. The division commander, LTG Du Quoc Dong, was a strong ally and ensured reliable paratroopers were available in the event another general tried to seize power. When a unit was assigned as palace guard, its US advisors kept out of sight because MACV did not want the perception that U.S. military personnel were involved in Vietnamese politics. Guarding the president meant R&R for U.S. advisors. Old-timers in the detachment fondly remembered those days. The advisors occupied their own BOQ, called the "Manor," complete with a chef and jovial bartender. Inconveniences such as the periodic loss of electricity and the influx of newly arrived Americans inflating prices at their favorite bars were the sources of complaints. That period was referred to by some as the "Cake Walk Days." One wag paraphrased Margaret Mitchell saying those times were "gone with the wind." In the spring of 1972, the entire division was committed to stopping the communist attacks. It would be in the thick of the fighting for the remainder of the war, never returning to Saigon.

~~~

Vietnamese paratroopers traced their lineage to the Indochina War, 1945–1954. In August 1951, the 1st Vietnamese Paratroop Battalion was organized to augment the overextended French Expeditionary Corps. Five airborne battalions were eventually activated. As the Indochina War dragged on, the French finally began to train Vietnamese officers and NCOs. Many of those young paratroop officers rose to high positions in the RVN military. Lieutenant General Dong was French-trained as was the head of Joint General Staff, GEN Cao Van Vien. They were among a group of Vietnamese officers who fought the Viet Minh, forerunners to the Viet Cong, during the latter stages of the Indochina War.

After partition, the South's new president, Ngo Dinh Diem, quickly consolidated his power. He used paratroopers to eliminate the gangsters who operated in the Chinese quarter of Saigon. Eradication of the Cholon Mafia, known as the *Binh Xuyen*, caused the U.S. MAAG chief to take a special interest in the airborne troops. Initial assistance addressed organizational and logistical issues, equipment upgrades, and supply accountability. The U.S. Army's growing influence prompted the Vietnamese to redesignate the unit as the Airborne Brigade. As fighting increased U.S. help evolved from technical to operational. By 1961, battalion advisory teams were accompanying the ARVN on combat operations. The first airborne advisor fatality was CPT Don York, killed in action on July 14, 1962.[4]

By 1965, additional infantry battalions were added and the formation was designated the Airborne Division, *Su-Doan Nhay Du*. It ultimately mirrored the 82nd and 101st Airborne Division, with three infantry brigades and nine infantry battalions, numbered 1 through 11. In keeping with Vietnamese superstitions, there was no 4th or 10th battalion since both numbers conjured bad luck. Team 162 grew to more than seventy-five Army and Air Force personnel. Battalion combat assistance teams (BCAT) were headed by a U.S. captain supported by a lieutenant and a senior noncommissioned officer. When the Vietnamese Airborne Division upgraded the battalion commanders' positions to majors and lieutenant colonels, the BCATs went through a similar transition; battalion senior advisors became majors and their deputies were captains.

Vietnamese airborne battalions consisted of a headquarters company and four rifle companies. On operations, the battalion often split into two elements. The battalion commander, accompanied by his senior advisor, maneuvered the headquarters and two companies with the NCO light weapons advisor accompanying the lead company. The battalion executive officer, assisted by the deputy advisor, was in charge of the other two rifle companies. Advisors acted as liaison officers to nearby American units and coordinated a vast array of U.S. assets, helicopter support, tactical airstrikes, artillery fire from U.S. batteries, resupply, and medical evacuation.

At MACV headquarters, the Airborne Division enjoyed a special status giving it top priority for equipment and support. General Westmoreland, himself a former commander of the 187th Airborne RCT and the 101st Airborne Division, watched it closely. Americans at all levels bent over backwards to support the paratroopers. The Airborne Division had the best equipment, the best housing, the best medical care and, with jump pay, was the best compensated. Vietnamese paratroopers were also in the hardest fighting. In 1967 and 1968, eight airborne battalions and task forces were awarded the prestigious US Presidential Unit Citation.[5] The selection of airborne advisors reflected its "favorite son" stature. The division senior advisor could pick and choose the U.S. officers and NCOs assigned to Team 162. Volunteers lined up to join so there was no need for draftees nor were there any "weak sisters."

As part of General Abrams's 1969 program to improve ARVN, the Airborne Division teamed with the 1st Cavalry Division screening along the Cambodian border. Called Operation *Dong Tien* (*Progress Together*), airborne brigades and battalions worked closely with Cav units and became very proficient in airmobile operations. They also enjoyed Cav logistical support. If Vietnamese supply channels did not work as rapidly as expected, the 1st Cavalry Division provided whatever was requested. Lieutenant General Dong had the opportunity to co-locate the Airborne Division command post with the Cav's tactical CP. He turned down multiple offers, saying that he and his officers were too busy. The division commander and his staff missed a golden opportunity to operate in a field headquarters environment.

A wake-up call came when the Airborne Division led the attack into Laos, Lam Son 719. The Cooper-Church Amendment prevented advisors from accompanying their counterparts. Cooper-Church stated that no U.S. ground forces could be employed outside of South Vietnam; advisors were considered ground forces. The prohibition did not apply to tactical aircraft, B-52s, or helicopters. The attack into Laos was the first time the division headquarters operated as a tactical entity, creating problems from the outset. Orders to subordinate units were often delayed, lacked clarity, and were not properly coordinated. At the same time, difficulty communicating with U.S. aircraft and a lack of procedural knowledge slowed much-needed support. Operational troubles plagued all brigades and battalions. Tactics that worked prior to 1971, firebases and small unit sweeps, courted disaster when the NVA arrayed its forces in regimental strength augmented with tanks and heavy artillery.

The commander of the Airborne Division, had his nose out of joint from the outset. He outranked LTG Hoang Xuan Lam, the CG of I Corps and the overall commander of the operation. His displeasure was evident when he publicly pointed out shortfalls in Lam's plan. Most of the time, he did not attend key briefings or interact with the corps commander. His uncooperative attitude was a major concern for senior U.S. officials. Dong was quick to complain about many things, including "lack of US support."[6] His criticisms were freely shared with his subordinates, who parroted his comments. In the midst of Lam Son 719, the Airborne Division senior advisor, COL Arthur W. Pence, was relieved. LTG James W. Sutherland, the commanding general of XXIV Corps and the senior American officer in the AO, believed Pence had lost his objectivity and had been thoroughly co-opted by his counterpart. COL James B. Vaught was selected to be his replacement and was rushed to Khe Sanh Combat Base, the division CP. The CG performed an about face, dampened his inflammatory words, and became more cooperative. A better politician than a soldier, he was politically astute enough to realize he could not continue to act in such a petulant manner. General Dong accepted Colonel Vaught's recommendations and told his staff that Vaught spoke for him.

Despite glowing reports of victory following Lam Son 719, the Airborne Division was a major player in what was an overall disaster. It suffered 455 killed, nearly 2,000 wounded, and an unknown number of missing, including the 3rd Brigade commander. After the operation, MACV directives reduced the size of ADAT. The sting of changes caused by Vietnamization, coupled with lingering resentment over the absence of advisors during Lam Son 719, created tensions. Colonel Vaught explained that the ADAT cuts were not as severe as they were in other ARVN units. The Airborne Division retained its battalion advisors when similar positions were eliminated throughout MACV. BCATs temporarily augmented with extra trainers to assist in post-Laos reconstitution. When I arrived, a U.S. major, captain, and sergeant were still authorized in each BCAT and every effort was made to keep the positions filled. Casualties were immediately replaced by another advisor.

Captain Gorley, head of the rear detachment, picked me up at Camp Alpha and drove me to the detachment. Entering the Airborne

Division area was like stepping back in time. The hustle and bustle of the American side of the air base was left behind. Gate guards wearing white gloves snapped to attention and rendered smart salutes. We were in a peaceful enclave where soldiers walked on tree-lined sidewalks, some accompanied by lithe young women in white *ao dais*, the double-slit, full-length dress and pantaloons that were traditional attire for Vietnamese ladies. Team 162's headquarters building, like the rest in the division complex, was a comfortable reminder of French colonialism. Thick stucco walls, red tile roofs, and window shutters made the buildings resemble villas, more appropriate for the Riviera than Saigon. Air conditioners, a staple in the temporary American facilities, were not needed; slow-moving fans circulated the air while high ceilings and large windows provided sufficient ventilation. It was hard to imagine a war raging not far from this tranquil spot.

I reported to COL Robert A. Hyatt, the division senior advisor. He was a 1951 West Point graduate and a former battalion commander in the 25th Infantry Division. His first question was: "Are you a volunteer?" There was no "hello" or "welcome," not even a handshake. Perhaps Hyatt had been sent other replacements who were less than enthusiastic about being there. I assured him I was a volunteer, not telling him that I rejected an offer for a staff job in MACV headquarters that very morning.

Hyatt gave me a quick rundown of the situation in each of the brigades, all of which were in the field, spread from Quang Tri to An Loc. I was to be assigned as the senior advisor to the 6th Airborne Battalion. The job was going to be a challenge because the 6th Battalion was nearly destroyed outside An Loc. Several NVA regiments overwhelmed the unit on the morning of April 20, 1972. Split by the ferocity of the assault, two companies withdrew into the town but the commander and what was left of the other two were forced to escape annihilation by retreating to the south. 1LT Ross S. Kelly, the acting senior advisor, employed air support to cover the retreat. When the battalion commander, LTC Nguyen Van Dinh, refused to exert any battlefield leadership, the movement had the makings of a rout. Dinh's security squad dug a hole and the battalion commander went "to ground." U.S. troops had an expression for losing it under fire called "blowing your shit." Kelly's tenacity and professionalism held the formation together. He employed multiple airstrikes and a timely B-52 mission to keep the survivors from being overrun. The young American's exertions pulled Dinh out of his funk. A day later, Vietnamese Air Force (VNAF) helicopters managed to extract the remaining soldiers of the 6th Airborne Battalion. VNAF pilots, never known for stout-heartedness, were overly concerned for their own safety. They hovered the aircraft instead of putting the ships on the ground to allow proper loading. As the paratroopers were struggling to get the wounded on board, the helicopters abruptly took off and some soldiers were left behind.[7]

Kelly, with less than two years of service, was recommended for a Distinguished Service Cross. Colonel Dinh lost face because his performance was lackluster and an American first lieutenant's actions saved the day. The incident made the man virulently and openly anti-American. The division senior advisor was aware of the Dinh-Kelly dustup but chose not to make an issue of it. "Don't rock the boat" was the order of the day, so the counterpart relationship was mine to mend. My mission was to perform an attitude adjustment and assist in the battalion's reorganization in Chon Thanh District, not far from Lai Khe, a now major ARVN base northwest of Saigon. Colonel Hyatt said it was just a matter of time before the unit would be back in the fight.

Following the interview, Captain Gorley took me to get my gear. The Vietnamese Airborne Division paratroopers wore a light green camouflage uniform while other ARVN units and U.S. personnel wore olive green jungle fatigues. Team 162 advisers wore the same airborne camouflage, plus U.S. and Vietnamese rank as well as the red Airborne Division patch. "Cheap Charlie," the Vietnamese tailor just off the base, sewed the insignia on the camouflage fatigues and fitted me with a field cap and red airborne beret. Within a short time, I had all my uniforms plus equipment drawn from the team supply room, including a CAR 15, a compact version of the M16 rifle, pistol, rucksack, and a survival radio. The last piece of gear was a "flak vest." On my previous tour, we did not wear protective vests since they were heavy and hot. However, with shrapnel flying around from NVA artillery, it was good to have one. We stowed everything in a jeep and drove to the BOQ.

Missouri BOQ was one of dozens of converted hotels in Saigon that housed U.S. personnel. ADAT majors and company-grade officers occupied the third floor of the Missouri, a five-floor structure. Each two-man room had a bathroom and a window air conditioner. Compared to U.S. base camps, it was luxurious. Located on Pham Van Hai Street, the BOQ was near the Airborne Detachment and the 3rd Field Hospital. Our accommodations were more spartan than other local American facilities in Saigon, but it didn't matter because neither our standards nor expectations were very high.

Another recent arrival, CPT Jerry Metcalfe, was my roommate. Jerry was slated to be the senior advisor to the 8th Airborne Battalion, but the unit was in An Loc so getting there was a problem. We talked about our reception in the Airborne Division including his office call with Colonel Hyatt, which was similar to mine. Both of us were dismayed by first impressions. Jerry was a 101st Airborne Division veteran who had seen hard fighting in Quang Tri Province during 1968. He opined that the Missouri BOQ was a hell of a lot better than anything he saw at Camp Evans, a former 101st Airborne Division base in I Corps. Both of us commented on the number of NCOs in Team 162 who extended their tours with the Airborne Division. Jerry could not recall a single 101st Airborne Division NCO serving in an infantry company who requested an extension. Being a platoon sergeant in a rifle company was hard soldiering with a high mortality rate. If a unit got a break, it was for a few days at a rustic base camp like Evans, well away from civilization.

I knew one other officer in Team 162. LTC Arthur E. Taylor was the senior advisor to the 1st Airborne Brigade, fighting in An Loc. Taylor had been the S3 of the 1st Battalion, 327th Infantry when I reported to Fort Campbell in January 1965. He deployed to Vietnam with us and later became the S3 of the 2nd Battalion, 502nd Infantry, working for LTC Hank "Gunfighter" Emerson. Anyone who thrived under the Gunfighter was a good soldier. Knowing one senior officer was reassuring, because I had the feeling that I would need support working with my new counterpart, LTC Nguyen Van Dinh. I was not comfortable it would come from the division senior advisor.

For the Airborne Division advisors, the Missouri BOQ was an overnight rest stop and a place to store extra gear. The third floor rooms differed from others in the BOQ because each contained additional cabinets filled with weapons and ammo, M16s, AK-47s, sawed-off shotguns, .45-caliber pistols, stacks of loaded magazines, grenades, pen flares, and tear gas. Several advisors from Team 162 were stuck in the Missouri when the Tet Offensive began. Fighting was raging outside the BOQ, giving the advisors some dicey moments because they were only armed with .45-caliber pistols. They vowed it would never happen again. Now the third floor was an arsenal containing enough weapons and ammunition to hold off a large NVA force. With three North Vietnamese divisions not far from Saigon, one never knew when the arms might be needed.

CHAPTER 8

An Loc I: April–May 1972

On the question of the B-52s and tac air, it's very clear to me that
. . . this government would now have fallen, and this country
would now be gone, and we wouldn't be meeting here today, if it
hadn't been for the B-52s and the tac air.
—GEN Creighton Abrams, Commander MACV[1]

On May 10, my first full day in Team 162, I tried to fly to Chon Thanh to join the 6th Airborne Battalion, but all U.S. helicopters were committed on operational missions. Captain Gorley assured me something would be available in a day or two. In the meantime I needed a better picture of the situation because my knowledge was limited to articles from the *Stars and Stripes* and Colonel Hyatt's short briefing. MACV headquarters was nearby so it was the logical place to get the latest information. MSG Fred Brandner, the detachment first sergeant and a former member of the 1st Battalion, 327th Infantry, knew people in the J3 operations section and lined up an afternoon appointment for me.

⌐✦⌐

Binh Long Province, translated as *"Peaceful Dragon,"* was divided into three districts: Loc Ninh, adjacent to the Cambodian border;

An Loc, home to the provincial capital of 15,000; and Chon Thanh, little more than a district town defined by a small cluster of houses and shops at the intersection of QL 13 and an east-west secondary road (see Map 8-1). The province, the former AO of the U.S. 1st Infantry Division and the 11th Armored Cavalry Regiment, had been the scene of heavy fighting since 1965. Acres of rubber trees once provided the main employment for the local folks, but the war crippled the industry.

The second phase of Operation Nguyen Hue started in early April when the NVA struck Loc Ninh. The district town held out for two days but fell on April 7 after enduring human-wave assaults, heavy artillery fire, and repeated tank attacks. Two U.S. advisors were killed and four became prisoners of war. One man, MAJ Tom Davidson, the Loc Ninh District advisor, evaded the NVA and escaped on foot to An Loc.

By April 9, An Loc was receiving strong probes from the advancing enemy. Three divisions were identified: the 5th VC Division, the 7th NVA Division, and the 9th VC Division. The 5th and the 9th were VC in name only because they were manned by North Vietnamese soldiers and equipped by their communist allies, the USSR and PRC. The main attack kicked off four days later. NVA struck from the north and west, spearheaded by Russian T54 and PT 76 tanks. The communists were stopped by massive U.S. airpower, including Air Force and Navy fighters, B-52 bombers, and Army Cobra gunships firing TOW (Tube Launched, Optically Tracked, Wire Guided) antitank missiles. The TOW, brand new in the U.S. Army inventory, proved extremely effective against Soviet armor.

Large-scale attacks continued over several days but were pounded from above. TOW missiles, airstrikes and timely Operation *Arc Light* missions, three B-52 aircraft each carrying 108 500-pound bombs, took a toll on the NVA. Still, when the fighting abated, the enemy was holding positions in the northern half of the town.

On April 14, the 1st Airborne Brigade conducted a series of airmobile assaults into LZs southeast of An Loc. American helicopters

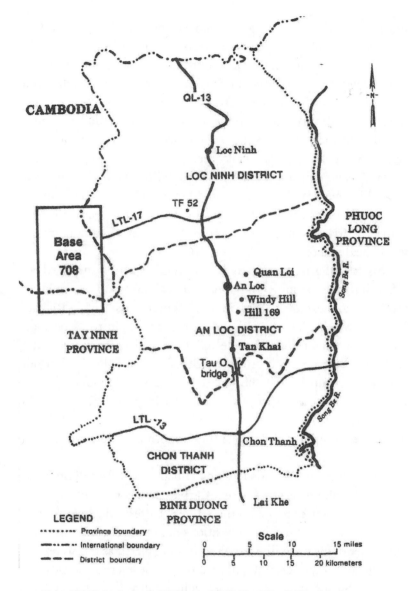

(From LTC [Ret.] James H. Willbanks, "Thiet Giap! The Battle of An Loc, April 1972," p. 6.)

Map 8-1

provided the airlift ensuring the soldiers landed at the specified LZs at the appointed time. The paratroopers were given two tasks: establish a firebase on the high ground outside An Loc and reinforce the town's defenders. One battalion, the 6th, would secure two hills while the other units—5th Airborne Battalion, 8th Airborne Battalion, and the attached 81st Airborne Ranger Group, a commando battalion—would fight their way into the town. Once the infantry secured the area, U.S. CH-47 Chinook helicopters would sling-load six 105mm howitzers and emplace them on "Windy Hill," the highest piece of ground in the area. A firebase would provide much-needed support for the defenders since all the guns in An Loc had been destroyed. If the 1st Brigade could hold the base, NVA lines of communication would be disrupted.

Sixth Airborne Battalion's insertion on April 14 surprised the NVA, but not for long. The paratroopers were soon under heavy artillery and mortar fire. The battalion's senior advisor, MAJ Richard Morgan, was hit by shrapnel and evacuated late in the afternoon. USAF gunships provided some relief when darkness came. Fifth Airborne Battalion, 8th Airborne Battalion, and the 1st Brigade command group landed the next day; the 81st Airborne Ranger Group followed on April 16. A tactical brigade CP, secured by the brigade reconnaissance company, was established on Hill 169, just south of Windy Hill, while the 5th, 8th, and 81st moved into An Loc.

Sixth Battalion defended Windy Hill and the village of Srok Ton Cui, several kilometers to the east. The battalion commander ordered his executive officer to secure the artillery battery with two companies; he established defensive positions around the hamlet with the remainder of his force. The battalion was organized as if it were conducting search and destroy operations against guerrilla squads and platoons. Such dispersion increased vulnerability. With the two task forces no longer mutually supporting, they became prime targets to be picked off one by one. Military textbooks called it "setting the stage for defeat in detail."

The NVA was determined to wipe out the artillery battery and the 6th Battalion. Both hills and Srok Ton Cui hamlet were pounded by indirect fire; all six howitzers were destroyed by NVA artillery fire. MAJ John Peyton, Morgan's replacement, was wounded by an incoming round and med evac'd on the 19th. LT Ross Kelly, the deputy advisor, was the sole American on the scene; he moved from Windy Hill and joined Colonel Dinh in Srok Ton Cui.

On April 20, NVA infantry struck the 6th Battalion's positions, first the hills and then the hamlet. Two companies of the 6th Battalion and brigade personnel were overwhelmed and withdrew into An Loc. Troops in Srok Ton Cui were beaten so badly that the only option was retreat to the southeast. Approximately eighty paratroopers, including the battalion commander and his U.S. lieutenant advisor, were pursued by the enemy throughout the afternoon and night. Ross Kelly orchestrated U.S. firepower that kept the enemy from overrunning the small force. Had he not been there directing timely airstrikes and providing sorely needed leadership, all would have been killed or captured.[2] The incident ignited LTC Nguyen Van Dinh's anti-U.S. sentiments.

Airborne reinforcements, the 5th, 8th and 81st, strengthened An Loc's wavering defenses. Because advisors were with the battalions, airstrikes were visually adjusted, often very close to friendly positions. SFC Jesse Yearta accompanied the 81st Airborne Ranger Group on a night counterattack to restore part of the perimeter. Yearta, the light weapons advisor, directed a rolling barrage from a C-130 gunship using pen flares to mark the front lines. NVA forces were beaten back and the defensive line restored.

Paratroopers also provided much-needed discipline within the garrison. Troops from the 7th and 8th Regiments, part of the 5th ARVN Division, looted civilian homes and hoarded food airdropped into the town. Leadership in the 5th ARVN had completely broken down because battalion and regimental commanders rarely left their bunkers. With the arrival of the 1st Airborne Brigade, civilians received rations and limited medical assistance. The bond between the town and the 81st Airborne Ranger Group was especially strong. After the siege, the people maintained a small cemetery where the remains of sixty-seven Airborne Rangers were interred.

Throughout the remainder of April and into early May, An Loc was barely holding on. Shortages of ammunition, food, and medical supplies hindered their ability to withstand another coordinated attack. Since the 7th NVA Division blocked QL 13 between Chon Thanh and An Loc, the defenders were totally dependent on aerial resupply. USAF tried a variety of airdrop methods but more parachutes were falling outside the lines than were recovered. Supplies that landed within the perimeter were not effectively distributed. Gunfights between competing groups erupted as 5th ARVN Division soldiers fought to get to the bundles. In desperation, BG Le Van Hung, the 5th ARVN Division commander and the senior commander on the ground, assigned COL Le Quang Luong, 1st Airborne Brigade commander, responsibility for securing all airdrops. This brought order to the drop zone and ensured limited supplies were equitably shared. Still, serious shortages existed. After much trial and error, USAF perfected the high-altitude Ground Radar Aerial Delivery System (GRADS), improving drop accuracy. From May 4 through 10, 492 bundles were dropped with a 94 percent recovery rate. The new technique reduced the threat of ground fire that previously downed three low flying C-130s. Now An Loc received the minimum sustenance needed to continue the fight.[3]

The volume of artillery fire was increasing and the defensive perimeter was being probed. All intelligence reports indicated another major attack soon, probably on May 11. MG James A. Hollingsworth, CG of Third Regional Assistance Command (TRAC), and his deputy, BG John R. McGiffert, were on top of the situation. They appealed to General Abrams to ensure An Loc received top priority for tactical air and B-52 strikes. General Hollingsworth, a Texas A&M graduate who had been a Patton protégé in World War II, was extremely competent, flamboyant, and one of the great combat leaders of the Vietnam War. He made superhuman efforts to rescue the advisors at Loc Ninh during the early stages of the campaign. His timely use of airpower in April was responsible for stopping the NVA. Danger 79'er, the general's radio call sign during a previous tour in Vietnam, was in his element . . . he knew how to fight this kind of war. The J2 and J3 officers told me Hollingsworth planned thirty B-52 strikes (a strike consisted of three aircraft each carrying 54,000 pounds of bombs) for May 11. The Strategic Air Command's Advanced Element at Tan Son Nhut allowed targets to be changed when the bombers were en route to An Loc. This flexibility was new in the air war. Each target was plotted on map sheets as a 1 kilometer by 3 kilometer rectangle. MACV and TRAC were able take advantage of up-to-the-minute intelligence reports and shift the "boxes." When I left MACV HQ on the afternoon of the 10th, I had a clear picture of the situation. One of the officers recommended that I check in with TRAC Forward, a small cell of U.S. officers at Lai Khe, on the way to Chon Thanh.

Hollingsworth's prediction was accurate. At 0530 hours on May 11, the NVA attacked An Loc from the north and west. An extensive artillery preparation put more than 8,000 rounds on the city's defenses. After several hours of fighting, it was obvious that the North Vietnamese were attempting to cut the town in half. When the armor spearheads hit the ARVN defenders, tanks and infantry became separated. Most of the tanks traveled very slowly and some ran out of fuel because they attacked without external fuel drums. Although the enemy commander failed to take advantage of his armor's speed and shock value, he still succeeded in establishing two significant penetrations.

On May 11 alone, 297 sorties of tac air and thirty B-52 strikes were used. When the ARVN was toe-to-toe with the attackers at night, AC-130 gunships with 40mm and 105mm cannons destroyed many tanks and disrupted any attempt to coordinate operations.

USAF gunships were particularly effective in "danger close" situations. Airpower gave the defenders time to rally. The 5th Airborne Battalion moved into the gap between the penetrations. CPT Mike McDermott, advisor to the 5th Battalion, distinguished himself in the action, probably setting a record for the number of airstrikes directed.

Stopping the NVA was not without a price. Russian-made SA 7 missiles and clusters of antiaircraft artillery (AAA) batteries downed five U.S. aircraft between May 11 and May 14. One forward air controller (FAC), 1LT Henry A. "Pep" McPhillips, was shot down on Mother's Day, the 14th. As his parachute drifted to the ground, there was a footrace between the NVA and ARVN paratroopers to get to him. Fortunately, the 5th Battalion won. After a brief stay with Mike McDermott, McPhillips was hustled to the 1st Airborne Brigade CP. His limp was later diagnosed as a broken ankle.

By the 15th, NVA could no longer sustain its assault. Continuous B-52 strikes and close air support aircraft decimated their ranks. Forty tanks, mostly T54s, were destroyed over four days of fighting. These armored vehicles had been part of two NVA tank regiments, the 202nd and the 203rd, which rolled down QL 13 after Loc Ninh fell. Infantry units suffered the same fate. More than one NVA regiment was decimated when caught in a B-52 box just as the soldiers were commencing their attack. Still, the Communist B2 Front commander, LTG Tran Van Tra, had plenty of artillery and enough ground troops to maintain a state of siege. Tra could not occupy the province capital, but he could stop ARVN attempts to re-open the road into An Loc.

There was little humor in An Loc, so when a funny incident occurred it was repeated over and over. The saga of Jimmy Takata became a legend. SP7 James Takata was Team 162's sensor operator, a position that had survived the most recent MACV cuts. Technicians in the Army of the 1960s and 1970s held the rank of Specialist and the grades went from Specialist 4 (E4) to Specialist 9 (E9). In the mid-1960s, Specialist 8 and 9 ranks were discontinued but "Spec 7" (E7) was retained as an enlisted rating until after the war.

Jimmy Takata, a Japanese American, had been in Vietnam a long time, having extended his ADAT tour several times. When the U.S. effort was scaled down in 1971, the sensor tech position remained although there were few devices to employ. As a result, Specialist 7 Takata did not have much of a job and was often hard to find. Because of his ability to disappear in Saigon for days on end, he received the nickname, "Jimmy the Ghost."

When the 1st Airborne Brigade was committed to the battle of An Loc, Takata went with them. He was there from the middle of April until the end of May. It was the first time in years that the team leadership knew where Jimmy was. No more extensions were allowed, so Takata had to accept his summer DEROS date. During the big May battle, he was hit by shrapnel; it was not life-threatening so Takata was listed among the "walking wounded." When there was a lull in the action, Lieutenant Colonel Taylor arranged for a helicopter to evacuate Jimmy the Ghost.

U.S. helicopters landed in An Loc only in direct support of U.S. advisors. VNAF refused to fly into the maelstrom. Because of ground fire, U.S. insertion and extraction missions were planned in great detail with only a few Americans apprised of the impending sortie. In April several U.S. helicopters had been mobbed by ARVN soldiers trying to get out of An Loc. Some were called "Olympic wounded" because, although they had been injured, they could still run fast and jump high. The press published photos of ARVN soldiers clamoring to get on U.S. aircraft. One receiving wide circulation showed two South Vietnamese soldiers hanging from the skids of a U.S. Huey as it took off. To prevent U.S. aircraft from being overwhelmed by undisciplined ARVN troops, helicopter door gunners carried Mace to keep unwanted passengers away.

When the coded call came that the helicopter was inbound, Jimmy went to one of the foxholes that ringed the PZ. Helicopters always drew fire so the aircraft spent just a few seconds on the ground. Incoming personnel jumped off on the right side, bringing a bag of mail and sundry items, and the outgoing soldiers hopped on from the left, a carefully choreographed operation.

As the helicopter touched down, Takata ran toward it but the door gunner assumed Jimmy was Vietnamese and sprayed him with Mace. Takata screamed in pain and yelled, "I'm an American, you motherfucker! I'm an American!" The door gunner grabbed his arm and pulled him on board just as the helicopter was lifting off. Jimmy made it out of An Loc, but not by much. As the Duke of Wellington said after Waterloo, "It was a damned close run thing."

— ⋅ —

When the NVA did not renew the assault, SFC James Clanton and I drove a jeep from Saigon to Lai Khe. Colonel Hyatt had instructed us to remain at the detachment when the big attack commenced on the 11th. We were standing by in the event one of our fellow Americans was wounded or killed. We were "on deck" replacements. When the attack appeared to have run its course, the senior advisor authorized our departure to Chon Thanh.

Fifth ARVN Division support units, the 21st ARVN Division Headquarters, and the TRAC Forward Command Post were set up in Lai Khe. MAJ Pete Bentson was the TRAC G3 operations officer at the CP. Pete had been a year ahead of me at West Point, and more recently we had been together in the OR/SA program at the Naval Postgraduate School. He graduated in the fall of 1971 and had started his second tour in Vietnam in November. Pete gave us an update on the fighting and verified the 6th Airborne Battalion's location. Since it was getting late in the day, he suggested that Clanton and I remain at Lai Khe for the night and drive to Chon Thanh in the morning. The stretch of QL 13 to the north had been the scene of heavy fighting in April. It was thought to be clear now, but there was no sense in taking chances in the dark.

We arrived at the battalion command post the following morning. The first order of business was to introduce myself to LTC Nguyen Van Dinh and get Ross Kelly back to Saigon. Given the tensions that had developed on the retreat from An Loc, nothing could be gained by his presence. Ross and I went over all the equipment, especially the two AN/PRC 77 backpack radios, and the codes and the cipher set, KY38, which allowed us to talk in the secure mode. After Clanton left with Kelly, I tried to spend a little quality time with my new counterpart. He was proper but not forthcoming about the battalion's state of training or future plans. Aloof best described his demeanor. Like any relationship, I figured we needed a little time.

Over an evening meal, I learned that Colonel Dinh had attended the Infantry Officers Advanced Course at Fort Benning, Georgia. If U.S. Army Infantry School was a useful or positive experience, he did not mention it. Two things did impress him, and he cited them more than once. The first was the partnership established with the U.S. 1st Cavalry Division in 1969 and 1970. Airborne battalions were supported by Cav helicopters and an airmobile logistical system. ARVN paratroopers had everything they needed and then some. He also mentioned how bad the Laos incursion was. I already knew about the casualties suffered in Laos, including the capture of a brigade commander. The division had the reputation for never leaving a fallen comrade. I gathered from our short conversations that the 6th Airborne Battalion left dead and wounded in Laos. Dinh did not bring up the recent retreat out of An Loc or those who were left behind there, but the subject seemed to be the 500-pound gorilla stomping around the camp.

Replacements arrived but they were not an impressive lot. The 6th Airborne Battalion had to rebuild the unit around the men who escaped the An Loc fight. The infusion of 400 new soldiers was a huge task. ARVN authorities were scouring the streets of cities, the jails, and universities to find men to fill the ranks. Six weeks of heavy fighting created a country-wide manpower shortage. Military planners were hard-pressed to replace all the casualties. Even so, I did not see any extraordinary efforts to ensure the new men were integrated into their respective companies.

A small rifle range was set up near the battalion perimeter. Sergeant Clanton and I checked it out and walked down range when the first group of firers went forward to look at their targets. Results were not good. Clanton and I had been involved with basic rifle marksmanship in our training center days, so we watched closely when the next order moved to the firing line. The second group had the same results. Later, Clanton pointed out that the Vietnamese NCOs and lieutenants were using slipshod teaching techniques. They were going through the motions but no one's heart seemed in it. The trainers needed adult supervision from the company commanders and battalion commander, but that was not forthcoming.

Some of the troops had vision problems. Optical exams were not part of the ARVN induction process, nor were glasses issued by the military. Clanton asked me, "Sir, how many of these guys are wearing glasses? A lot less than there should be." Only one wore spectacles. Glasses were considered unmanly and the troops made fun of any soldiers who wore them. They were branded as university boys, not a complimentary term. I wore glasses so they probably poked fun at me behind my back. We were seeing another case where cultural issues eroded military effectiveness.

When the battalion co-located with 31st Regiment, 21st ARVN Division, I met LTC Charles L. Butler, regimental senior advisor. Butler was a member of the Class of 1950 from West Point and was one of the lieutenants sent directly to Korea following the North's attack on June 25, 1950. He was seriously wounded not long after his arrival. Charlie Butler had an excellent perspective on advisory duty having served with an ARVN battalion during a previous Vietnam tour. He was not a cynic, but he did not subscribe to the Team 162 philosophy that everything in advisor land was universally wonderful. Butler stressed that we did not help the Vietnamese by acquiring equipment for them. For too long the ARVN supply system did not have demands placed on it because the American advisor could get it whatever was needed quicker through U.S. channels. Now with most U.S. forces out of Vietnam, the period of abundance was over. The ARVN logisticians had to learn to cope with constrained resources and make their system work.

The 6th Battalion was dug in when I returned from my visit to the 31st Regiment. All the positions had overhead cover to protect the occupants from indirect fire. The noticeable exception was the advisor bunker adjacent to the TOC. It was just a hole in the ground. I was told there were not enough sandbags, so I accepted Lieutenant Colonel Butler's offer to stay with him. Clanton and I grabbed our rucksacks and headed to the 31st Regiment. At dusk, an airborne lieutenant came to us and stated that our bunker now had overhead cover. Dinh seemed to be probing the limits of my tolerance, but I was still optimistic that his attitude would change.

The training pace was leisurely. No one seemed concerned that the unit would soon be back in combat. The lack of any sense of urgency was distressing. Even though the troops needed more training, the battalion commander was not particularly focused on what was going on. His preferred place of duty was his hammock. Company commanders followed Dinh's lead. Sergeant Clanton said that, unlike the U.S. Army, Vietnamese subordinates did not make recommendations to senior officers, nor did leaders solicit input. The battalion commander issued orders and that was it; company commanders executed the orders. When the captain passed on instructions to his lieutenants, the same phenomenon occurred. It was ingrained in the Vietnamese military operating procedures.

Colonel Dinh was not interested in discussing future operations. Even attempts at small talk were rebuffed. I had time on my hands, so I started a daily journal and maintained it throughout my tour. Dinh's refusal to interact gave me more opportunity to talk with Charlie Butler, who made several points that were eye-openers. Butler said the U.S. military leadership never really criticized our ally or held the ARVN's feet to the fire. Instead of denying resources to commanders like Dinh, the United States tolerated unacceptable behavior and thus perpetuated it. The U.S. Army always insisted on setting standards and ensuring adherence to them. We seemed to discard that approach when working with the Vietnamese. Reluctance to use tough love did not benefit the ARVN. His other observation concerned overall U.S. military policy in Vietnam. At no time during our extensive involvement did anyone seriously address the idea of a unified command structure. In the midst of the Korean War a supreme commander for all forces was designated. It helped mold the ROK Army into a credible fighting force. Two ROK divisions and an ROK marine brigade served in Vietnam. At the height of the conflict, the Korean commitment was the equivalent of twenty-two maneuver battalions. In contrast, the Australians received far more publicity but furnished just two.[4]

I was struck by a continuing sense of isolation. Communicating by mail with the folks at home had not changed from my first tour. At best, sending a letter to the East Coast took ten to twelve days; the reverse process was similarly lengthy. Getting the mail to the right place in the field was an additional challenge. Delivery of the *Stars & Stripes* was sporadic because most copies did not make it past Lai Khe. Neither Sergeant Clanton nor I had a transistor radio so AFVN was not a news option. We did not learn Governor George Wallace, a Democratic candidate for President, had been seriously wounded in an assassination attempt until a week after it happened.

Other issues highlighted future difficulties for the Dinh-Howard relationship. A written statement attesting to Ross Kelly's heroics was sent to me requesting Colonel Dinh's signature as a witness. There was nothing derogatory about the battalion commander in the statement, but he refused to sign it saying, "Kelly very bad officer. . . ." It should have come as no surprise Dinh responded as he did, for it resurrected an unpleasant situation. He was offended that he was asked to confirm Kelly's bravery and blamed me for bringing the statement to him. A little more sensitivity to the Vietnamese concept of face could have prevented rubbing salt in Dinh's psychological wounds.

The second incident was a request to send Sergeant Clanton on a company night ambush. Other than some ineffective 122mm rocket fire, there was no enemy activity. Because of personnel shortages, advisors no longer went with company formations. We could not operate like battalion advisory teams did in earlier years. This was explained to the battalion commander, but he was already aware of it. I asked why he made the request since I was not apprised of any threat. Dinh glared at me and walked away. It was another test to see how far he could press the envelope. Still, he sent a message to the division commander saying his advisor was not supporting him. Within a day or two, I had to respond to a nasty note from Colonel Hyatt questioning my actions. His wording shocked me. In my response, I repeated the guidance he gave me weeks earlier: "Team 162 no longer sends advisors on company operations." I assumed the division commander had been informed of this. Hyatt fell another notch in my estimation.

These events rattled my confidence. I was acutely aware that I had no experience working with the ARVN and scant knowledge of their customs and traditions. My interaction with the South Vietnamese during my first tour was limited to a single patrol where the indigenous troops left in the middle of the operation. Critics accused former secretary of defense Robert McNamara of trying to put a Ford engine in a Vietnamese oxcart. At my low level, great pains were taken not to replicate similar arrogance or to appear to be overbearing. Since my arrival, I had tread carefully and only spoke when I believed there was something that needed saying. I tried to apply the Golden Rule, "Treat others as you want to be treated," but it was not working. Dinh viewed me as one of his flunkies, so my frustration level rose.

My situation was not materially different from what CPT Mike McDermott, advisor to the 5th Airborne Battalion, experienced. A seasoned combat veteran with three tours with the 101st Airborne Division, Mike performed heroically in An Loc. He was all over the battlefield, adjusting U.S. airstrikes that prevented the battalion from being overrun. He was exposed to enemy fire so often it was a miracle that he was still alive. LTC Art Taylor, senior advisor with the 1st Airborne Brigade, called McDermott the bravest of the brave. Yet his counterpart, LTC Nguyen Chi Hieu, hardly acknowledged his assistance and never considered him anything other than a useful functionary. He was ignored unless U.S. firepower was needed. Hieu's visible indifference toward his advisor was an indication of fraying advisory ties that would become more evident as time progressed. When Mike departed An Loc, the battalion commander turned his back on him, refusing to say goodbye or shake hands.[5] But U.S. officials lauded his service, recognized his valor in An Loc, and awarded him the Distinguished Service Cross and the Silver Star.

The pace in the 6th Battalion did not change although Clanton and I speculated that there was a major operation in the offing. When I queried Dinh, he professed to have no knowledge of any plans. Within a few days, a message instructed me to attend a briefing at TRAC Forward and to meet the new light weapons advisor. Sergeant Clanton was being transferred and the 6th Battalion was getting another light weapons advisor, SSG William Phelps. He would be at Lai Khe when I came to the briefing. Phelps had been in Vietnam for several years, serving with an ARVN Ranger battalion. The man had volunteered for the Airborne Division, an action that attested to his mettle.

My friend, Pete Bentson, thought to include me in the TRAC meeting. The meeting was chaired by Major General Hollingsworth and Brigadier General McGiffert and restricted to U.S. personnel. We were told that the enemy was strengthening defenses along QL 13 and was intent on keeping it closed. General Hollingsworth was pressing the III Corps commander, LTG Nguyen Van Minh, to clear the highway but little progress had been made. Something had to be done to break the stalemate. A foothold was established at Tan Khai north of Chon Thanh but COL J. Ross Franklin, the senior advisor to the 21st Division, was not confident that the ARVN would move north from there. He was miffed by their lethargy and over reliance on B-52s to eliminate the enemy. He described in great detail the failure of the 21st Division to employ all its assets. I knew J. Ross Franklin by reputation. Like Charlie Butler, he was a 1950 USMA graduate and had served multiple tours in Vietnam. Colonel Franklin was a warrior-scholar with a PhD from American University, a hero in the Korean War, and was fluent in several languages.

Part of the new allied initiative was to insert a battalion behind the NVA main defenses and have that unit fight its way north to link up with the An Loc defenders. The mission would go to the 6th Airborne Battalion. The enemy situation, availability of air support, and Army/USAF communications were discussed at length. The free-flowing dialogue was a godsend. General Hollingsworth used his colorful speech to amplify what needed to be accomplished. In closing, the TRAC CG reminded us of the need for confidentiality. It was not to be shared with anyone because the ARVN command structure was riddled with informants. When we were leaving, Danger 79'er put his arm around my shoulder and told me to "kick my counterpart's ass if I had to but make sure that battalion made it to An Loc."

Staff Sergeant Phelps was standing by when the meeting concluded. I gave a quick rundown on what had transpired. He had not been idle while waiting for me. Bill Phelps knew something important was going to happen and figured we might need a few things. The back of the vehicle was crammed with supplies he "found." He obtained extra batteries, a signal beacon to assist with airstrikes, rations, and a half-dozen cartons of cigarettes. Phelps said we would fight and smoke our way into An Loc. The man was going to be a great asset. He had a sense of humor, initiative, and awareness. His knowledge of the language and the culture would be invaluable.

Phelps recommended that we not mention his ability to speak Vietnamese. He could learn more just by listening and then discussing it with me in private. I told him about Dinh's attitudes. He thought for a moment and then said, "Sir, don't worry. We'll show the man we know what the fuck we're doin'!" I had learned long ago that good NCOs are able to grasp the essence of any issue in short order. With Phelps's sage observation, we got in the jeep and drove up the road. For the first time since arrival in the 6th Battalion, I was not operating in an information void.

CHAPTER 9

An Loc II: June 1972

The only way to approach the battle of An Loc is to remember that the ARVN are there and the North Vietnamese aren't.
—U.S. ADVISOR IN AN LOC, JUNE 1972[1]

THE LAST DAY OF MAY STARTED WITH A GREAT FLURRY OF ACTIVITY. Soldiers were packing equipment as 2½-ton trucks rolled into the base camp. Obviously the battalion was moving out, but no reason was offered. Bill Phelps and I knew a warning order had been issued instructing the 6th Battalion to move to Lai Khe. The link-up mission was obviously a "go." We would get further details and changes from Pete Bentson at TRAC Forward. As the convoy moved south, Phelps and I discussed Dinh's attitude and his reluctance to let us be part of the team. Bill asked the question I couldn't answer: "Why do we have to put up with shit like this?"

The combat assault was set for June 4. VNAF helicopters would take the battalion from Lai Khe to an LZ near the 21st ARVN Division's forward-most firebase at Than Khai. The specified missions were to break through the encirclement at An Loc and bring replacements to the 15th ARVN Regiment that was cut off just south of the town. Phelps and I were left out of the preparation until the last day, June 3. Colonel Dinh did not seem to fathom or care that we normally would have needed time for planning too. He was willing to sacrifice combat effectiveness to make the point that two advisors were second-class citizens. Thanks to the earlier briefing, we had already coordinated with the Air Force and the Army personnel at TRAC Forward and had everything we needed. ARVN officials believed we would land behind the 7th NVA Division defensive positions and quickly link up with the An Loc defenders. Phelps and I were not so sure. The enemy had more than eight weeks to establish primary and alternate positions all along the highway. The battalion commander wanted to use QL 13 as his axis of advance, the obvious avenue of approach where the NVA was the strongest. My recommendation to move farther east along a covered route well away from the main highway was received with a sneer.

Lieutenant General Dong and Colonel Hyatt flew to Lai Khe to see us off. It was the first time I met General Dong. He barely acknowledged me, perhaps due to my counterpart's earlier message that I was not supporting him. My only recollection from the encounter was the general's designer sunglasses. The few times I saw him later, Dong was wearing oversized shades. General officer uniform affectations have been with armies for a long time. Even by Vietnamese standards, Dong was over the top. While the helicopters were cranking, Colonel Hyatt drew me aside and emphasized the importance of the mission. I assured him that Phelps and I would do everything in our power to get the 6th Airborne Battalion to An Loc. Mission accomplishment would mean our counterpart's redemption from the ignominious retreat in April.

The straight-line distance from Lai Khe to Tan Khai was 40 kilometers. It was the scariest helicopter flight of my eight-year Army career. Our VNAF pilot employed violent evasive maneuvers that appeared to over-torque the aircraft. After one sharp jerk red lights on the instrument panel were flashing . . . never a good sign. I said a quick prayer requesting divine intervention to prevent enemy fire or pilot error from knocking us out of the sky. Regardless of how many NVA were waiting for us on the ground, chances of survival were better there than in a VNAF Huey.

The landing was unopposed but not for long. As the battalion consolidated, the NVA struck with RPGs, automatic weapons fire, and mortar rounds. They heard the choppers and were rushing to eliminate the threat to their rear. Phelps and I put in multiple airstrikes, the sole means of fire support. Terrain was open so we could see where the bombs were hitting and were able to adjust quickly. Sergeant Phelps worked with Major Tung, the XO, identifying targets for the next set of inbound aircraft while the FAC and I adjusted the ongoing strike. It was the first time I had directed airstrikes for the 6th Airborne Battalion but the Howard-Phelps-Tung combination seemed to work fine. While the three of us hunkered behind a termite mound, Colonel Dinh's security squad, his bodyguards, were frantically digging a bunker. When it was completed, he used the freshly dug hole as his personal CP.

That night AC-130 gunships kept the NVA from mounting a coordinated assault against our perimeter. Called "Spectre," the aircraft was the Cadillac of gunships. The model supporting the 6th Airborne Battalion, the AC-130E, was equipped with state-of-the-art electronics, including a TV camera and infrared sensors. It mounted a 105mm howitzer, two 20mm guns, and a 40mm cannon. When the AC-130 acquired its target, it was an accurate killing machine. In the morning, we counted thirty enemy dead near our position; one ARVN paratrooper died in the action. Spectre's 105mm cannon did terrible damage to the enemy. Body parts, pieces of weapons, and tattered equipment were scattered throughout the area. Unlike encounters on my first tour, North Vietnamese soldiers made no attempt to recover the remains of their soldiers.

Dinh's personality changed; he became more talkative and informed us of the day's plans. His attitude bordered on being professional. U.S. airpower was the decisive factor in his success and we controlled it. I remarked to Staff Sergeant Phelps about the battalion commander's new demeanor. In his taciturn manner, Phelps said, "Dinh may be an asshole, but he ain't a fool. He knows we can bring down the wrath of God with these fuckin' radios."

The FACs, who used "Rash" and "Sundog" as radio call signs, were absolutely superb. They were from the 21st Tactical Air Support Squadron (TASS), stationed at Tan Son Nhut. FACs flew the Cessna 0-2 Skymaster, known as the "Suck and Blow." One engine was mounted on the nose of the airplane, and the other was a pusher at the rear of the fuselage. They provided us 24/7 coverage and flew in the same time slot day after day, night after night. We knew them only by their call signs. The buzz of the O-2's engine was very reassuring and became our security blanket.

The 6th Airborne Battalion did not move quickly; caution trumped aggressiveness. Once north of our initial LZ, we were in stands of rubber trees. Geometrically arranged rows made excellent fields of fire for enemy machine guns. On June 5, there was sporadic contact but no major fights. An aerial bombardment had carved a path for us. Many rubber trees were destroyed in the process; the damage was the least of our concerns. The dripping latex from broken trees looked like pools of Elmer's Glue, both on the ground and on NVA corpses.

Our secondary mission was to bring replacements to the 15th ARVN Regiment, part of a task force that tried to link up earlier with the garrison. The regiment occupied an old French rubber processing plant, Thanh Binh, south of An Loc. The regiment was chewed up so badly that it lacked the strength to move. Only one hundred able-bodied soldiers manned a tight perimeter. The NVA was content to let the 15th Regiment stay in Thanh Binh since it was not a threat to their operations.

Colonel Dinh made a provisional company out of the replacements but kept them out of the fighting. At 0900, June 6, we hit a determined NVA force near the 15th Regiment's positions. Due to the proximity of the regiment and the 6th Battalion, employing tac air was a delicate operation. We made sure that Dinh was cognizant of the "danger close" situation, but he insisted the strikes go in. Before each one, the FAC asked me to authenticate, meaning I was accepting responsibility for any friendly casualties. Fifteen paratroopers were killed and scores were wounded before the 6th Battalion fought its way to the 15th Regiment. Dinh was emphatic that enemy fire accounted for the casualties, not our airstrikes. Phelps and I found some of the friendly KIAs who were obviously killed by bombs. Hand grenades, RPGs, and gunfire did not dismember human bodies in such a manner.

I realized the battalion commander was willing to accept friendly casualties from our airstrikes, even when the situation was not dire. I was stunned by his cavalier attitude and wondered if it were another example of our cultural abyss. He was an addict . . . hooked on airstrikes. From my experience in the 101st Airborne Division, taking casualties from friendly fire was a last resort measure and was only sanctioned to prevent a unit from being overrun. I chose not to make an issue of it. No verbal or written report was rendered, but U.S. authorities needed to know that an ARVN commander was using airstrikes without regard for the safety of his own troops. It was an error on my part.

The 7th NVA Division was determined to maintain pressure on An Loc and stop any attempts to relieve the garrison. The approaches near the town's perimeter were blocked by a formidable system of trenches and bunkers, sited so the enemy could fire in multiple directions. All afternoon on June 7, the 6th Airborne Battalion tried to breach the obstacles, the last hurdle to link up. Airstrikes were ineffective because vegetation obscured the positions, making it difficult for the FACs and fighter pilots to acquire targets. Adjusting the strikes was equally troublesome. After dark, a Spectre gunship was sent to assist us. The AC-130 aircraft's awesome firepower was enhanced by cutting-edge sensor technology that identified both enemy and friendly locations. This data was fed into the fire control computer and the 105mm howitzer or the 40mm guns locked on to the target without fear of hitting the good guys.

I needed to be forward of the battalion lines so I could adjust the strikes. We were within 500 meters of the target, but I could not get a good fix on the obstacles. I was reminded of my September 10, 1965 experience of engaging a target without seeing it and vowed that would never happen again. Sergeant Phelps stayed in the TOC with one AN/PRC 77 while I moved out with the other radio. Colonel Dinh provided a security squad to accompany me, but in the darkness we became separated. Once we cleared the battalion perimeter, they disappeared. I suspected it was intentional, since the squad leader did not seem very enthusiastic about leaving the relative security of friendly lines. Duc, our faithful Vietnamese radio operator, and I were on our own. I could talk directly to the Spectre because the plane was equipped with FM radios. To ensure the crew had a fix on our location, my hand-held transponder, the one Phelps "liberated" in Lai Khe, was activated. The device provided verification via a radio signal of my location so Spectre would not inadvertently hit Duc and me. In 1972, this was hi-tech stuff.

The pilot of the AC-130 said his sensors picked up a mass of "hot spots" at the coordinates I provided. Technology confirmed what we already knew, but now the aircraft had the exact location. NVA was there in full force determined to prevent the 6th Airborne Battalion from getting to An Loc. Spectre let loose with a barrage from the 105mm cannon. The explosions were readily visible. The situation became high adventure when I received another radio call saying some "hot spots" were moving in our direction. Whether they were trying to escape Spectre's fire or guessed Duc and I were nearby made little difference; a dozen or so NVA were coming our way. We could stay and fight or high-tail it back to friendly lines. Neither option was good. Six to one were not very good odds and the second course of action offered a high probability of being shot by South Vietnamese paratroopers. The decision was taken out of my hands when the aircraft attacked the moving target with two 20mm weapons. The pilot tersely said, "Get down," and commenced firing. A dozen bursts either killed or wounded the soldiers moving toward us. The aircraft commander assured me he "got 'em," but it was close. He said they were less than 50 meters from us, but I didn't see or hear them because my head was in the dirt. With that unpleasantness out of the way, the Air Force went back to hosing the main enemy position. When the AC-130 needed to refuel and rearm, another replaced it. I was lavish in my praise and thanks. At dawn, the last Spectre returned to its home base. We probably "overkilled" the trench line and bunkers, but in that situation there was no such thing as too much firepower.

Duc and I needed to get back within the battalion perimeter. I asked Staff Sergeant Phelps to ensure everyone knew we were returning. I was not confident Dinh would get the word out, and we would end up being fired upon by our own people. I radioed Lieutenant Colonel Taylor, senior advisor with the 1st Airborne Brigade in An Loc, and requested his counterpart, the brigade commander, notify Dinh we were coming back. It was the first time I talked to him. In our brief conversation, he called me "ABU" so I knew that he remembered me from our Fort Campbell days. It brought a rare smile to my face.

As the morning of June 8 progressed, the battalion moved through the destroyed entrenchments. Friendly losses from the previous afternoon and evening were eleven KIA and thirty-one wounded. Phelps and I counted over one hundred dead NVA soldiers and a large quantity of AK-47s, RPGs, mortars, and machine guns. We couldn't resist grabbing two Type 51 Chinese pistols, copies of the Soviet Tokarev, for souvenirs. At 1745 hours, the 6th Airborne Battalion officially linked up with the 8th Airborne Battalion.

Our unit was incorporated into the defensive perimeter in the rubber stand south of the city. Senior officials from the chairman of the Joint General Staff to the division commander were effusive in their praise of the 6th Airborne Battalion. The Saigon press gave laudatory coverage to the event. Nguyen Van Dinh had redeemed himself, and our relationship was at a high point. I suspected things would only go downhill later. Once we left An Loc and he was no longer at risk, Dinh reverted to his old ways.

The town still remained isolated and depended on aerial resupply. USAF C-130s maintained the logistical lifeline as drop accuracy improved daily. I used the battalion position for drops rather than the central drop zone in town because recovery and distribution was much easier. Paratroopers stockpiled boxes of Uncle Ben's Instant Rice and the C-ration staples, Boned Chicken and Turkey Loaf. When we got the call that Wagon Train, the call sign for the C-130s, was about to make a drop, the battalion commander was immediately informed. Bill Phelps moved through the area to tell the young soldiers to look skyward. You had to stay alert because ammunition and food pallets hit hard and could crush a man. From May 26 to June 30, USAF C-130s flew ninety-eight sorties and dropped 1,568 tons of supplies, 1,440 tons of which were recovered.[2]

The North Vietnamese units were destroyed by U.S. airpower. B-52 missions had been particularly decisive. Whole regiments were rendered combat ineffective by timely B-52 strikes. Their offensive capability was eliminated, but they had plenty of artillery weapons and air defense systems. The shelling was a constant reminder that the NVA was still a force to be reckoned with. Clearing operations reduced some of the threat and allowed some VNAF medical evacuations to be flown.

Everyone developed a sense where an artillery round was headed by hearing the initial firing in the distance. It was an acquired skill. If you reckoned the round was going to land in another location, no one flinched. Otherwise, if it was headed your way, you had several seconds to hit the ground or find a hole after the initial report. It was said the Lord will look out for you but you had to help Him by not walking around in artillery fire. We were worried about Lieutenant Colonel Taylor because his hearing was poor. He would not seek cover when rounds were on the way. The Vietnamese were impressed; they said, "*Trung Ta* (Lieutenant Colonel) Taylor very brave!" No American broke their bubble by saying Art Taylor was a little deaf.

On June 12, Major General Hollingsworth flew into An Loc. It was a morale booster for everyone. More than any man, Danger 79 saved An Loc. During his visit, he talked to SP4 Joe Javor, Taylor's RTO. Javor had spent the duration of the siege in An Loc so Hollingsworth awarded him the Silver Star. A day later, there was a brief ceremony when Taylor pinned the medal on Joe. Jerry Metcalfe and I attended. Making the trip from our positions south of town was exciting. On several occasions we had to dodge the NVA salvos sent our way.

Follow-up paperwork for Javor's award was required so the appropriate order and citation could be issued. Jerry Metcalfe relayed how it transpired. CPT Ed Donaldson, Taylor's deputy, was tasked to complete the paper work. He interviewed Javor and the conversation went like this: "Javor, how many airstrikes did you put in?" Javor's response was, "None, sir." "Javor, how many resupply air drops did you direct?" "None, sir." "Javor, which counterattacks were you in?" "None, sir." "Javor, what in the fuck did you do??" "Sir, I made cocoa for Colonel Taylor." Javor's comments were probably embellished to make a better story, but they were a source of laughter when that commodity was in short supply.

<hr />

We were apprised, "The situation has stabilized." That same night a 122mm rocket nearly vaporized Duc, who had just left the bunker to take a leak. While he was outside, a rocket came screaming in and hit 6 feet from him. Phelps and I hit the ground anticipating a huge explosion but the round was a dud. Our man, Duc, was traumatized by the incident and did not move. We were able to pull him back into the bunker. Phelps opined, "I didn't think the NVA was supposed to do that now that the fuckin' situation has stabilized!"

For several days, we monitored the status of the advisor with the 15th Regiment. The unit was still in the same position where we brought the replacements. The lone American with the 15th, call sign *Superman,* AKA LTC John Johnson, was deathly sick. Johnson finally reported that if the ARVN moved, he would be left behind. True to form, COL J. Ross Franklin mounted a relief operation. No other U.S. officer was available so Franklin decided he would replace *Superman.* During the mission the lead U.S. Huey carrying Colonel Franklin was shot down, but the pilots managed to make a controlled crash landing. A chase helicopter picked up Franklin and the crew and returned to Lai Khe. He immediately got on another helicopter and tried again. This time he was successful and Johnson was evacuated. Colonel Franklin was *Superman!* Airborne advisors said Ross Franklin was "a bad motherfucker," a term of great endearment. He was a genuine war hero.

The evenings were punctuated by small talk with the FACs. If there was no enemy contact, we put one of the radios on an alternate frequency and the FACs read articles from the *Stars & Stripes* to us. In our isolation we knew nothing about the outside world. We heard about Senator McGovern's presidential campaign pledge to go anywhere in the world to negotiate an end to the war. Being surrounded by North Vietnamese, we did not think the senator's comments were very helpful. We were incredulous that an intelligent man, a World War II bomber pilot to boot, would make a statement encouraging our enemy, especially when U.S. soldiers were still fighting. Some politicians did not seem to be concerned about increasing the risk for Americans in harm's way. Jerry Metcalfe said, "Maybe McGovern can come to An Loc and negotiate with those shitheads firing all the artillery at us." News of the acquittal of the Communist Party activist, Angela Davis, also drew many responses. The most common was, "Fuck her and fuck communism."

The strength of the An Loc garrison increased to 7,600. Elements of the 18th ARVN Division were airlifted in to replace the battered troops of the 5th Division. On June 16, Lieutenant Colonel Taylor told us that the 1st Airborne Brigade was ordered to break out of An Loc, move south to a pickup zone, and be airlifted to Lai Khe. From there we would move to Saigon and prepare for a new mission in I Corps. I was not surprised the information came through advisory channels rather than from my counterpart. Art Taylor provided the route, order of movement, radio frequencies, and passage of lines instructions. The mission of stopping the NVA at An Loc was accomplished and the ARVN paratroopers were needed to support a counter-offensive.

The 1st Airborne Brigade and its three infantry battalions left the An Loc perimeter before dawn on June 18 using QL 13 as our axis. Moving parallel to the highway showed an amazing lack of innovation. The 6th Airborne Battalion was in the lead, but enemy resistance soon stopped us. A Sundog FAC had a good fix on the line of bunkers, so I asked him to juggle both the Cobra gunships and the fast movers. I called the Cobra leader and told him to contact Sundog on VHF (Very High Frequency), a radio that I did not have. The FAC would sequence strikes on the target while I adjusted. One gunship pilot was reluctant to be handed off to an Air Force FAC. I had a sharp exchange with the pilot: "Hey, we aren't fucking around down here so if you can't work with us, RTB (Return to Base) and cool off." The conversation was recorded and in his book, *Vietnam's Last Battle*, Dale Andrade attributed the quote to someone else.[3]

Elimination of the strongpoint took longer than expected, causing me to find another vantage point. I moved to a small berm and was immediately hit by a sickening stench. Two NVA bodies, bloated and blackened, were sprawled several yards away. They were killed earlier, perhaps when we were fighting our way into An Loc. An explosion or concussion caused the bodies to split open and unremitting heat hastened the rotting. Man's inhumanity to man was captured right there. The smell of decomposing flesh stayed with me, permeating my senses more than my clothing.

On the 20th, a U.S. AH1G Cobra, flying near our position, was shot down by an SA 7 missile fired from a concealed position. The gunship never had a chance. The missile streaked upward and knocked the tail boom off the helicopter; the Cobra went into an uncontrolled spin and exploded when it hit the ground. No one survived. The pilots, Chief Warrant Officer (CWO) Burdette Townsend and 1LT Louis Breuer, were from F Troop, 9th Cav, a 1st Cavalry Division unit that had been in the An Loc fight since early April. We secured the wreckage until a U.S. team flew in and recovered the remains of the two pilots.

The Vietnamese were reluctant to move fast or bypass NVA fortifications. The efficacy of U.S. airpower was etched in their psyche, so they relied on it to beat down the NVA. In three days we only moved 10 kilometers. On June 21, our task force linked up with the 31st ARVN Regiment. LTC Charlie Butler, who had befriended me at Chon Thanh, was still the regimental advisor so I went to the 31st CP to see him. We spent thirty minutes cross-leveling information, telling stories, and smoking cigarettes. The visit terminated when a call came that U.S. helicopters were inbound to pick up the airborne soldiers. I said farewell to Butler and rejoined the 6th Battalion.

1st Cav pilots were amazed to see two U.S. soldiers with a Vietnamese battalion. Bill Phelps and I were filthy, but there was no doubt that we were Americans because we towered over the Vietnamese soldiers. They welcomed us on board with big smiles and handshakes. We were flown to the airstrip at Lai Khe, where the operation started three weeks earlier. It was a far better helicopter flight than the one we had experienced on June 4. As Colonel Dinh made preparations to move the troops to Tan Son Nhut, I sought out Colonel Franklin. A replacement advisor had joined the 15th ARVN Regiment, so Franklin had resumed his duties with the 21st ARVN Division. His first words were, "Charlie Butler was killed by incoming fire a few minutes ago." His bunker took a direct hit. The news devastated me. Colonel Franklin said I must have been the last

American to see him alive. Charlie Butler's perspective and suggestions were very helpful during my initial days in the 6th Battalion. I meant to tell him so when we were together but missed the chance, and now I would never have that opportunity. Colonel Butler was the second regimental advisor from the 21st ARVN Division to die that week. The other officer, LTC Burr Wiley, was killed on June 19 as the 32nd ARVN Regiment was making another futile attack to clear QL 13.

From April to June 1972, twenty-six U.S. advisors from ADAT participated in the An Loc fighting. The number included *co vans* (Vietnamese word for "advisor") who served with the 81st Airborne Ranger Group who were part of Team 162. Eleven were wounded in the fighting. One, SFC Alberto Ortiz Jr., died of wounds after he was medically evacuated to the United States.

ARVN defenders in An Loc sustained 5,400 casualties, including 2,300 killed or missing. Those numbers paled when compared to NVA losses. The North Vietnamese frittered away three fine divisions and tons of sophisticated equipment. U.S. airpower accounted for the bulk of the 25,000 NVA casualties, 10,000 of which were killed. Enemy forces operating in Binh Long Province were on the receiving end of 262 B-52 missions and 9,200 airstrikes. In and around An Loc over eighty burned-out NVA tanks littered the landscape. Few buildings were untouched.[4] The town was a large demolition project rather than a place of human habitation.

The fighting slowed but not the dying. BG Richard Tallman, the new deputy TRAC commander, and some staff officers flew to An Loc on July 9. As they were moving off the LZ, an NVA artillery round landed in the midst of the group. COL Stanley J. Kuick, chief of staff of TRAC, MAJ Peter M. Bentson, G3 operations officer, 1LT John A. Todd Jr., aide to the deputy commander, and Sergeant Son, a Vietnamese interpreter, were killed instantly. General Tallman was seriously wounded but died on the operating table in the 3rd Field Hospital. Pete Bentson was having a "day out of the office" after working so hard at TRAC Forward ensuring the survival of An Loc.

Capt. Jim Willbanks, who wrote the book, *Battle of An Loc*, and MAJ Joe Hallum were wounded as they met the general's party.[5] Jim later became a noted Vietnam War author, lecturer, and scholar.

The last U.S. casualty prior to the implementation of the January 1973 ceasefire accords occurred in An Loc. LTC William B. Nolde, Binh Long Province senior advisor, was killed by incoming artillery fire on January 27. Nolde died eleven hours before the ceasefire took effect. An Loc was claiming U.S. lives right to the end of our involvement in Vietnam.[6]

———

It was dark by the time the 6th Airborne Battalion was completely assembled in Lai Khe. I hoped we would head to Saigon in the morning, but Colonel Dinh was determined to travel down Thunder Road at night and Phelps and I had to go with him. I did not want to have survived An Loc only to get zapped in an ambush somewhere along QL 13. Luckily, the ride was uneventful except for the reckless speed we drove.

Upon arriving at the Airborne Detachment at Tan Son Nhut, Lieutenant Colonel Taylor said we had to accomplish two tasks: All advisors were ordered to call our families; following those phone calls, we would go to the 21st TASS to meet the FACs who had supported us throughout the siege.

Major General Hollingsworth, ever the considerate commander, arranged for us to make calls to the U.S.A. Given the press coverage of the battle, Hollingsworth believed it was imperative that our loved ones know we were safe. In 1972, the only telephone connections with the States were for priority military use. That call was the only one I made during my two years in Vietnam.

We had established strong ties with the Rash and Sundog FACs. We only knew one by name; the rest of them were known by their call signs. LT Pep McPhillips, who was shot down on May 14, was the face of the FACs. We wanted to show them our appreciation for all they had done for us. We found their private bar on the air base. The sign read "Crew Training Facility" to skirt the USAF prohibition against unit clubs. All the FACs were assembled and it had the makings of a hard drinking night. The advisors were not a handsome group. Our bodies reeked and the red dirt from An Loc was caked on our uniforms.

Most of the FACs were first lieutenants. Their professionalism and dedication in the skies over An Loc belied their rank and experience. The young pilots wanted to have a serious party, but we had a low tolerance for alcohol. The evening did not last very long. We just wanted to get back to the Missouri BOQ, take a shower, and sleep in a real bed.

Arrangements were made for a formal dinner at the Tan Son Nhut officers' club the following evening. Unlike the Crew Training Facility, it was a traditional club with a dining room and linen on the tables. The clientele were primarily senior officers from MACV headquarters and the air base. We were cleaned up, had enjoyed a good night's sleep, and were able to drink more than the previous night. A steak dinner with shrimp cocktail was on the bill of fare. The festivities started well. Appropriate toasts were made and conversations contained minimal profanity. Even the presence of the wing commander, TASS squadron commander, and Art Taylor, always the consummate gentleman, did not keep the evening from rapidly degenerating. Bar games were punctuated by a medley of offensive songs, sung with great gusto. These antics did not sit well with the rest of the club patrons, and when the main course was completed, we were asked to leave.

A ceremony was held on the division parade field the next afternoon. Colonel Luong awarded each American advisor the Vietnamese Cross of Gallantry.[7] The decoration evolved from the French *Croix de Guerre* and was generously bestowed on many Americans. Still, the award was a fine gesture and we appreciated it. Lieutenant Colonel Taylor was awarded the Cross with Palm; the rest of the officers received the Cross of Gallantry with Gold Star. The U.S. NCOs were awarded the Cross with Silver Star. The Vietnamese adopted the French tradition where awards for valor followed precedence in accordance with the recipient's rank. A palm affixed to the Cross of Gallantry was a higher award than the Cross with Gold Star. A gold star was higher than a silver device.

The following day, I traveled by jeep to the resort town of Vung Tau to join the 6th Airborne Battalion. Called *Cap Saint Jacques* by the French, the town was located on the tip of a peninsula overlooking the South China Sea. The 6th was the only battalion in the Airborne Division that was stationed outside the greater Saigon–Bien Hoa area. According to airborne lore, it was ostracized to the coastal city in 1960 when it had been involved in an unsuccessful coup to oust President Diem. Because Colonel Dinh did not engage in small talk, I never found out why the battalion was there. During my entire tour in Vietnam, I spent only that one night in Vung Tau. On June 25, 1972, we loaded C-130s and flew to Phu Bai, the nearest airfield servicing Hue. The arrival of the 1st Brigade brought the Airborne Division to full strength. The campaign to retake Quang Tri, Lam Son 72, was about to begin.

All of us were in a state of post–An Loc euphoria. In the afterglow of victory, we rushed to write laudatory after-action reports and purposely downplayed the role of U.S. airpower. We were encouraged to recommend our counterparts for U.S. awards, so I complied. In an interview with a *Stars & Stripes* correspondent, I was able to laud the individual soldier. The young paratroopers did everything asked of them and more.[8]

I was guilty of wanting to improve my relationship with my counterpart and used the awards system to that end. In the report and award recommendation I prepared, I overlooked that Dinh rarely left his bunker. Other ADAT officers were equally disingenuous with their words and praise. Our "can do" spirit won out over reasoned analysis. All of us were aware of Colonel Hyatt's aversion to criticism of our ally, so none was offered. Opportunity for objectivity and a factual assessment was lost. Inadvertently, we continued to validate the Vietnamization policy and put a good face on America's ongoing disengagement. Those actions were later added to my list of wartime regrets.

CHAPTER 10

Quang Tri: July–September 1972

We are goin' to get our asses kicked if some changes aren't made around here.

—BOB RIDDELL, QUANG TRI CITY, JULY 1972

QUANG TRI WAS VIETNAM'S MOST SPARSELY POPULATED PROVINCE and, since it abutted the DMZ, was the most fought over (see Map 10-1). Places like Khe Sanh, Con Tien, and Camp Carroll had been in the news since U.S. Marines began fighting there in 1965. Prior to the Easter Offensive, local people lived in Quang Tri City, the provincial seat, Dong Ha, or small hamlets along QL 1. Even by Vietnamese standards Quang Tri City was a small town, a dusty enclave on the Thach Han River. Prior to the Easter Offensive, its population numbered 12,000. Quang Tri's Citadel, built in 1824 by the Emperor Minh Manh, was in the center of the town; it was a smaller version of Hue's imperial stronghold. With thick stonewalls, four ramparts, and a wide moat, the Citadel resembled a medieval fortress.

Abandoned on May 1, 1972 in the face of the NVA onslaught, Quang Tri City assumed a psychological significance far beyond any military value. The North Vietnamese recognized this and turned it into a massive fortification, knowing President Thieu would accept high casualties to take it back. Lam Son 72 was launched on the night of June 27-28. The attack across the My Chanh River and a

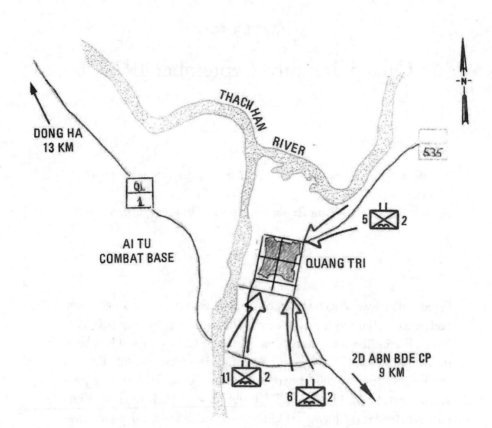

Map 10-1: 2nd Airborne Brigade Attack on Quang Tri Citadel, July 1972

large airmobile assault precipitated a large-scale NVA retreat. Within two days, ARVN forces advanced to the outskirts of Quang Tri City. Momentum was lost when Lieutenant General Truong, I Corps commander, halted his forces. The corps commander later stated that the delay was imperative because he was forced by presidential decree to change direction of the attack. He maintained that his original plan did not include the capture of the provincial capital. Truong claimed he wanted to bypass the city and not get bogged down in an urban battle. Since the president personally approved the detailed concept of the operation, Truong's assertion is unlikely.[1] A pause in the fighting gave the North Vietnamese time to resupply, reconstitute, and improve their positions. The Citadel was the hub of their defensive system, supported by a series of strongpoints scattered throughout the town. House-to-house fighting would be required to get near the fortress walls.

———

The Airborne Division established its command post at a former 1st Cavalry firebase, LZ Sally, just north of Hue. Located on the west side of QL 1, Sally was a sprawling camp but like others turned over to the Vietnamese, it was stripped of anything that could be sold. Sergeant Phelps said it had been Vietnamized. The division was operating as a field headquarters for the first time since the incursion into Laos. Little effort had been spent modifying tactics found lacking during Lam Son 719. The firebase concept, an insurgency era tactic, was still fully ingrained in the planning mentality. The division staff seemed reluctant to accept the reality of conventional warfare where the enemy operated in strength backed by heavy firepower.

First Brigade and its three battalions, the An Loc veterans, closed into assembly areas near LZ Sally on June 25 and were given a few days for rest. On July 1 the 6th Airborne Battalion was directed to reinforce the counter-offensive. In typical fashion, Staff Sergeant Phelps and I were not given any notice of the new mission. Someone would say, "We go now," and you needed to be ready to move. We were used to it, so when the soldiers started packing up, we did the same. I wondered what would happen if I had said, "You didn't tell me you were moving out. I'll join you later." Colonel Dinh would have waited because USAF fighters and Navy air "moved" with Phelps and me. However, Colonel Hyatt would have had apoplexy because his *modus operandi* was to bend over backwards to accommodate our counterparts. Dinh and others like him were given free rein to jerk us around. Denial of resources to change behavior was never considered. Since Dinh screamed for airstrikes whenever contact was made, this approach may have altered his attitude and caused him to be more professional.

Our earlier recon with 11th Battalion made up for the lack of information from the commander. Phelps and I knew we were headed for Quang Tri. Consequently, when the ARVN soldiers started scurrying around, we got our gear ready. The battalion's new mission was to be 2nd Airborne Brigade's reserve and occupy positions just south of the main line of fighting. Late in the afternoon, the unit moved by truck convoy up QL 1 and dismounted just short of our defensive site. Artillery fire increased as the battalion closed into the area. It did not take a tactical genius to realize we were observed and the NVA was responding. No attempt was made to disguise our arrival or use the night to cover our movement. The lack of common-sense security procedures would continue to dog us as the operation proceeded.

The following day, a new officer, CPT Robert C. Riddell II, joined the battalion as the deputy senior advisor, bringing the BCAT strength to its authorization of three for the first time. Bob went to Berlin, Germany when he graduated from West Point in 1969. He volunteered for Vietnam after serving only two years of a normal three-year European tour. At 6'3" and 225 pounds, he was an imposing man possessing a tactical sense and vigor that would be welcomed attributes as we attacked Quang Tri City.

Nasty weather accompanied Riddell's arrival. Over several days, MAJ Mike Flynn, G2 advisor, was sending out warnings that the fringe of a bad storm was projected to sweep along the coast dumping lots of rain on us. We were used to being wet but typhoons meant no air support. With a major storm brewing, the aircraft carriers would move further offshore out of its path and planes based in Vietnam would be grounded. Bad weather and heavy overcast skies allowed the NVA to move freely because there was no risk of overhead detection. Periods of limited visibility created opportunities for the enemy to launch an attack. Bill Phelps said the ARVN paratroopers were like any soldiers, who would be more concerned with staying dry than being observant. Since checking the troops was not a strong attribute of the leaders, we decided the three of us would alternate checking the line when the predicted storm hit.

On the night of July 2, my thirtieth birthday, we were in the midst of a low-grade typhoon. The ground was quickly saturated and the foxholes filled with water. Our bunker collapsed and several layers of wet sandbags filled the hole. We managed to salvage the radios out of the mess. Ever resourceful Bill Phelps had the foresight to put a carton of cigarettes in a plastic bag. There was no need to worry about the troops sleeping. Everyone was awake, wet, and miserable. Bob Riddell's personal transistor radio survived too. As it started to get light, he tuned into AFVN in Da Nang for a weather update. John Fogerty was belting out Creedence Clearwater Revival's 1971 hit, "Have You Ever Seen the Rain?" Riddell's question was, "Is this a coincidence or what?"

Another week passed before the 2nd Brigade kicked off its attack. The delays gave the NVA more time to improve their positions and bring up additional artillery. Enemy forward observers were able to put effective fire on us with mortars, rockets, 122mm howitzers, and 130mm field guns. All we could do was hunker down, keep our flak vests on, and wait it out. The Russian-made M46 130mm, superior to any allied artillery piece, had a range of 27,000 meters, well beyond that of our 155mm or 8-inch howitzers. The only ARVN weapon that ranged the M46 was the 175mm gun, but they were few in number. Four were lost on April 2 when the 56th ARVN Regiment surrendered at Camp Carroll. With little fear of counter-battery attacks, the 130mm guns fired on us at will. USAF FACs attempted to find the M46 firing positions, but they were well camouflaged and protected by antiaircraft weapons, including the SA 7. They proved very difficult to spot and even tougher to knock out. Consequently, indirect fire accounted for most of our casualties.

The attack on the Citadel was set for July 10. The plan violated multiple tenets of conventional doctrine. The most glaring violations were:

1. Ensure the assaulting force has a 3:1 numerical advantage at the point of attack.
2. Weight the main attack. Augment the main attacking force with additional troops and give it priority of fires.
3. In an urban environment, isolate the objective area to prevent the enemy from resupplying and reinforcing the defenders.

NVA held the Citadel and strong points outside the fortress walls with two reinforced regiments. Both were from 320B Division, an organization with a long combat record. They outnumbered the 2nd Airborne Brigade nearly two to one. Fifth Airborne Battalion was instructed to conduct the main attack, but additional troops were not provided to reinforce. In fact the battalion was still understrength from the fighting in An Loc. At the last minute, a short artillery preparation was employed when the attack commenced. Two other battalions, the 6th and the 11th, were to conduct supporting attacks from the south. No attempt was made to cut Quang Tri City off from communist logistical bases farther north. The North Vietnamese could cross the Thach Han River during the night to bring provisions and replacements.

The attack was a disaster waiting to happen. I never found out whether the division senior advisor or the G3 advisor expressed reservations about the plan. Most likely, General Dong chose not to share the details with them. When the operations order filtered down to the 6th Battalion, even Colonel Dinh, who never shared his observations with me, voiced some anxiety. By the time I passed my concerns to the 2nd Brigade senior advisor, it was too late. Day D, July 10, was the next day. None of us knew whether this ill-conceived plan was due to political exigencies, a lack of appreciation of sound doctrine, or faulty intelligence on enemy strength, but the battalion advisors, CPT Earl Isabell with the 5th Battalion, Woody Furrow, and I believed it had the makings of a monumental "fuck up."[2]

One of many ironies of the Vietnam War was that the attack on Quang Tri's Citadel was very similar to the one executed by the Viet Cong at the outset of the Tet Offensive. On the night of January 31, 1968, one VC battalion followed the axis of advance now being used by the 5th Airborne Battalion while another swept around the Citadel and entered the city from the south. Both immediately got bogged down. The enemy did not seize the Citadel in 1968 . . . nor did we four years later.[3]

The 6th Airborne Battalion managed to gain a foothold in the southern part of the town. Progress was slow because the NVA fought from house to house, withdrawing to successive positions after inflicting casualties on the attackers. The battalion CP was established in a masonry structure on Le Huan Street where a prosperous citizen once lived. Colonel Dinh had a shelter dug underneath the staircase. The rest of us, including the battalion aid station, were camped out in the former owner's living room. Riddell and I reckoned the enemy would use the two-story structure as an artillery registration point.

The Fifth Battalion made its first coordinated assault on the night of July 11. Paratroopers planned to breach the wall of the Citadel and take the northeast ramparts. The U.S. Air Force flew eighteen sorties to soften up the objective area and four batteries of 105mm and 155mm howitzers fired a short preparation as the attack commenced. The airstrikes and artillery had little effect on the NVA. They were well dug in and stopped the 5th Battalion short of the Citadel wall. Friendly casualties were high; twenty-five were killed and over one hundred were wounded.[4]

A U.S. tactical air ban went into effect the following morning. President Thieu decreed that Quang Tri would be recaptured without U.S. assistance. The president was upset by press reports claiming airpower saved An Loc and Kontum. He wanted to prove that the ARVN and VNAF could take Quang Tri. Over Lieutenant General Truong's objections, an imaginary circle was drawn around the city; all U.S. airstrikes were prohibited within the area. President Thieu and the JGS had an inflated assessment of VNAF capabilities. South Vietnam's air force lacked the flying skills and fortitude to provide 2nd Brigade sustained air support.

My counterpart viewed the air restrictions as a conspiracy fostered by the United States. That these restrictions were implemented by his president was an empty argument. More than once I tried to explain this. When he got on a tirade, Dinh also railed on the United States about lack of support during the 1971 fight in Laos. My response to his rants was that more than a hundred American helicopters and many flight crews were lost. U.S. casualties in Laos were actually 219 KIA, 919 WIA, and 38 MIA.[5] After a futile attempt to explain that the U.S. military obeyed the congressional restrictions specified in the Cooper-Church Amendment, I stopped trying to justify the absence of U.S. advisors during Lam Son 719. Dinh went so far as to say that the South Vietnamese were victims in a war started and prosecuted by Americans. We were beyond the point of logical, rational conversations. Laos was the source of Dinh's rancor toward the United States and U.S. advisors. The retreat from An Loc in April and the current fight in Quang Tri were simply accelerants thrown on a smoldering fire. Colonel Dinh was consumed by anti-Americanism and there was nothing that would change his outlook.

Bob Riddell described our conversations with the battalion commander with an inelegance of speech that no one could match. His comment after one of the sessions was, "Sir, talking to that fuckin' guy is like trying to converse with the fuckin' wall." Bob used the word as the fourth article: "a," "an," "the" and "fuckin'." My response was, "Riddell, how in the world did you ever pass English at West Point?"

The only visitor throughout our time in Quang Tri City was a CBS reporter, Bruce Dunning. We never saw Colonel Lich, the brigade commander, or anyone from the division staff. One morning, amid the artillery fire, Dunning showed up at the CP. Advisors had been cautioned not to give interviews to reporters since the MACV commander wanted the media to focus on the ARVN. The spin was that they were defeating the NVA, not U.S. airpower. A gag rule was implemented in April when General Abrams told Major General Hollingsworth to "zip it." During the battle of An Loc, Danger 79 appeared on U.S. TV networks saying, "we are goin' to kick their asses all the way back into Cambodia." The interview moratorium worked its way down the chain. We told Dunning that we could not comment on the fighting. During the course of the conversation, we asked if he had any cigarettes. He produced a carton of Marlboros which triggered an in-depth interview, based on the assurance of anonymity and our retention of his smokes. The war reduced us to a primitive level; we could be bought by a carton of U.S. cigarettes.

———

Airborne troops pressed forward but with only minor gains. Friendly casualties were mounting. Unlike An Loc, medical personnel were able to evacuate the patients in trucks that brought supplies and occasional replacements. When vehicles had additional space, dead paratroopers were taken to the division's morgue at LZ Sally. Still the North Vietnamese were able to replace their losses faster than the ARVN. They employed nighttime ferries across the Thach Han River to shuttle men and equipment into the battle. Failure to isolate Quang Tri City, the enemy's strength advantage, and the ban on U.S. air support were game changers.

Incoming artillery increased in volume and inflicted more and more casualties. We could hear the NVA tubes fire and in a few seconds, some unit in the 2nd Airborne Brigade would be on the receiving end. Most devastating were the 130mm rounds that packed more than 70 pounds of high explosives and sounded like freight trains roaring in. We could tell by the initial report if it was headed our way or the 5th or the 11th were going to catch hell. When the 130s cranked up, our FACs looked for muzzle flashes but had little success. Artillery spotting was poor utilization of a well-trained FAC, who was better employed outside the prohibited area.

Riddell and I were concerned about the battalion's exposed flanks. On the left, the 6th Battalion was not in physical contact with the 11th Battalion. Five hundred meters separated the two units. Woody Furrow told me via secure radio that Major Me was sending out patrols and setting up listening posts (LP) to protect his battalion. Bob and I sketched the situation to Dinh and with great discretion recommended similar actions. Dinh gave us a look that radiated disdain and venom, as if we suggested surrender. His response was recorded in my journal: "I don't need Americans to tell me about combat."[6] The gap problem was about to bite us in the ass.

Part of the NVA defensive plan encompassed spoiling attacks to stymie any attempts to coordinate operations. On July 19, a large NVA force hit the 5th Battalion. Earl Isabell reported his counterpart, LTC Nguyen Chi Hieu, was withdrawing the TOC in the face of a determined attack. Listening on the radio, we were afraid that Earl was going to be killed or captured. Not realizing how close they were to routing the 5th Battalion, the NVA broke off the attack just when success was within their grasp.

Two days later, an enemy force infiltrated the area between the 6th and 11th Battalions. We were an easy target because no LPs were posted. The pre-dawn attack began with a "130" prep, causing us to crouch against the wall as concrete splinters flew around the building. The situation was touch-and-go because NVA were all around the battalion CP. Riddell, Phelps, and I took our weapons off safe and prepared to defend ourselves. When the NVA finally withdrew, forty enemy bodies were found outside the building. A prisoner said that his battalion had moved out of the Citadel at 0400 on July 21 and assembled in the gap. Their knowledge of ARVN dispositions indicated the thoroughness of their battlefield preparation and amplified a major security problem in the 6th Airborne Battalion.[7] After the incident, I realized that nothing I did would change Colonel Dinh or make our relationship more cooperative. Americans could only provide him with things and when we could not, he had no use for us. Our presence in the 6th Airborne Battalion was to serve as the conduit for U.S. firepower, and when there was no air, we had no role. Our three-man team was a waste of U.S. manpower.

Sending Bob Riddell and Bill Phelps back to the rear was an option. With no mission to perform, I was concerned one or the other would be wounded or worse. The incident on the early morning of July 21 showed that being taken prisoner was not a remote possibility. It was one thing to be a fighter but quite another to be excess baggage, a strap hanger. Right now our only function was self-defense. I had to be there, but the presence of two other Americans was needless exposure. Second Brigade advisor, MAJ John Hadjis, and Colonel Hyatt, both at the end of their tours, would deny such a request. Major Hadjis, normally the G4 advisor, was a quartermaster officer who was filling in until an infantry lieutenant colonel arrived. Naturally, he shied away from anything controversial. If I sent Riddell or Phelps back, I would not ask permission but beg forgiveness after it was a *fait accompli*. On the other hand, the presence of other Americans offset the effects of Dinh's ill-humor. I had experienced a sense of isolation back in May when I joined the 6th Battalion. Having them present allowed me to maintain a level of psychological balance. In the end, the situation was partially resolved by Staff Sergeant Phelps's medical evacuation. He had an earlier wound that needed tending, plus his DEROS was just a few weeks away. After three years in Vietnam, it was time for him to go. Phelps sought out the battalion commander to say farewell. Colonel Dinh simply looked at him and turned away, unaffected by the man's departure.

Quang Tri's meat grinder had taken the 2nd Brigade's strength down to 60 percent. Only a few replacements arrived as the ARVN personnel system was struggling to keep pace with friendly losses. The brigade commander was going to make one more attempt to take the Citadel; this time the main attack was reinforced. Two companies of the 81st Airborne Ranger Group, plus a tank platoon, were attached to the 5th Battalion. President Thieu lifted the U.S. air restriction allowing a USAF aircraft to drop a 1,000-pound laser-guided bomb (LGB) on the Citadel wall. The LGB breached the northeast ramparts and, on the night of July 23, 51st, 52nd and 53rd Companies crossed the moat and entered the fortress. When daylight came, the U.S. tac air restrictions were again imposed. VNAF was called in to help expand the penetration. A South Vietnamese aircraft mistakenly dropped three MK 82 500-pound bombs among the paratroopers, killing forty-five and wounding twice that number. The tenuous hold on the Citadel was lost. By late morning the NVA were again in complete control of the position. The stalemate continued.

The Airborne troops had to be relieved by Vietnamese Marines. On July 26, the VNMC battalion commander and his USMC advisors came to the CP to coordinate the details for a relief-in-place. As the two commanders talked, I took my U.S. Marine colleague for a quick tour of the AO. As we threaded our way through a debris-littered street, there was a large explosion that knocked me to the ground. My first thought was I had walked into a wall. In fact, I had been hit by shrapnel from either an artillery or mortar round. Fortunately my flak vest had absorbed the bulk of the blast, but fragments were lodged in my right arm, cheek, and leg. My Marine colleague helped me to my feet and with adrenaline pumping hard we weaved our way back to the CP. The Vietnamese battalion surgeon removed some of the metal shards and wrapped my arm and leg. All U.S. personnel carried emergency aid kits containing morphine and drugs to combat infection, so I self-medicated. We were being relieved in a day, so I would get treatment at the 85th Evacuation Hospital in

Phu Bai, just south of Hue. Until then, I could hang in and depart with the battalion.

The fight decimated all three airborne battalions. The 5th (ninety-eight killed and 400 wounded) and 6th (seventy-one killed and 350 wounded) were hit the hardest and were no longer combat effective. It was the second time in three months that the units were practically destroyed.

Four advisors were wounded: Earl Isabell, Woody Furrow, SFC John Olesh (11th Battalion), and me.[8] Woody, Earl, and I ended up in the hospital together. A U.S. doctor dressed our wounds, dug out the remaining shrapnel, and loaded us up with tetanus serum and penicillin. The three of us stayed overnight at the 85th, slept in a bed with clean sheets, ate a hot American meal, and took a shower. The next day I was back to duty, telling Riddell that life was pretty good down the road in Phu Bai but I did not want a repeat visit there.

Earl Isabell said that his counterpart, Lieutenant Colonel Hieu, was difficult to work with. Hieu also blamed Isabell for the restrictions on U.S. air support and would not give him the time of day. I was not aware of CPT Mike McDermott's issues with the same man during the hard fighting in An Loc. I thought my experiences with Colonel Dinh were unique and was surprised another advisor was having problems with his counterpart. Earl and I knew better than to make an issue of it. In accordance with the prevailing philosophy, there were no advisor-counterpart problems and if there were, you damn sure kept it to yourself.

———

A new division senior advisor, COL Marcus W. Hansen, arrived in early August. I had served with him in the 1st Battalion, 327th Infantry at Fort Campbell. He was an intense man who would leave no stone unturned to improve the Vietnamese Airborne Division. Yet he would not pamper our ally, saying "No" when it was required. Hansen was the antithesis of his predecessor, and the division would be better for it.

Vietnamese Marines were fighting to capture the Citadel in Quang Tri while the Airborne Division continued to eliminate enemy forces west of QL 1. On August 17, MACV Team 162 lost 1LT Grady Triplett, the third ADAT man killed during the Easter Offensive. Grady, serving with the 3rd Airborne Battalion, was hit by enemy artillery fire, probably a 130mm round.

Two days later, Phelps's replacement, SSG Raymond Mayes, joined the 6th Airborne Battalion. Mayes arrived at LZ Sally the day of Triplett's death and was shaken by it. One look at him and you knew that the U.S. Army was scrapping the bottom of the human resources barrel, another manifestation of Vietnamization. His appearance signified that the days were long gone when the NCO advisors in the Airborne Division were the "pick of the litter." With a florid complexion and overweight, Mayes resembled the Pillsbury Doughboy. He was not ready for field duty.

First impressions proved right. When he arrived, Staff Sergeant Mayes was missing some of his equipment. He had left his flak vest at the brigade firebase. The first thing he said was he could not eat Vietnamese food. His dietary issues were secondary to his general lack of awareness. Both Bob Riddell and I were amazed, because we were having enough trouble with a modern-day mandarin and did not need a dysfunctional NCO added to the mix.

Mayes made no attempt to be part of the team. When Riddell and I showed him how to key the secure radio set, he was inattentive. Bob Riddell was so exasperated that he threw up his hands and said, "Mayes doesn't realize this is serious shit." A few days later, I sent Mayes to the 2nd Brigade to pick up supplies. When he came back, his helmet was missing, left at the 2nd Brigade CP. The problem was immediately clear. . . . Mayes was an intentional screw-up. He wanted out of the Airborne Division and was using rookie mistakes to write his ticket to a rear area assignment. While both Riddell and I hated to see someone like Mayes get a soft job, he was a liability and needed to go. I kept a log on the man and provided the brigade senior advisor with a written evaluation. Within three weeks of his arrival, Mayes feigned sickness and ended up on light duty at LZ Sally. Colonel Hansen had the man reassigned. Mayes got what he wanted, a sham position in the rear. In addition to an adverse NCO Efficiency Report, I wrote an official letter documenting his issues. A Reduction in Force (RIF) was imminent and the man needed to be swept up in it.

During the Mayes dilemma, the 6th Battalion was ordered to push farther westward. Progress was slow because the VNMC received priority for U.S. tac air. President Thieu's air restrictions were lifted in Quang Tri, and the Marines were making great use of American firepower. The 6th was mopping up stay-behind units that could attack the Marine's flank. Dinh was very frustrated that there was no tac air to eliminate the enemy units and their fortified positions. He again complained that the United States was not supporting the ARVN and again explanations of prioritization fell on deaf ears.

Bob Riddell was the first to notice an increase in self-inflicted wounds (SIW). Every day soldiers were brought to the battalion aid station with foot and hand wounds. Numbers were included in our daily report to the 2nd Brigade senior advisor. I mentioned this to both the battalion commander and the battalion executive officer. Major Tung, the XO, did not share Dinh's anti-American views but he could not appear too cozy with the U.S. advisors. He sought me out and asked for my observations and numbers. I gave him a count from the past few days. While neither Tung nor Dinh acknowledged the SIW problem, both started visiting the battalion aid station. Several men with hand wounds were treated, punished, and sent back into the line. Self-inflicted wounds were signs of slipping morale and a source of concern to all of us.

Naval gunfire (NGF) was used to offset the lack of close air support. As the Division worked its way westward, the 6th Airborne Battalion was at the extreme range of NGF. A U.S. Navy lieutenant junior grade, the equivalent of an Army first lieutenant, joined us as the naval gunfire spotter. The man was a reluctant warrior, not excited about being in the field. I asked him to show us how his radios worked and how to use his code books. He questioned why and was told that we needed to know in the event he was a casualty. The reality of an advisor's life in the Airborne Division did little to improve his morale.

Colonel Dinh readily agreed to the use of NGF. Bob and I watched our Navy colleague closely and saw that the technique was similar to adjusting artillery and airstrikes. The targets were NVA bunkers which, given the flat shell trajectory of the ships' guns, were difficult to hit. I decided it was worth a try. On my first Vietnam tour one of the NCOs said that no shot in the direction of the enemy is ever wasted! The big rounds reminded the NVA that airstrikes were not the only weapon in our bag of tricks. Even firing at an extended range, we managed to destroy several emplacements.

Our Navy lad, like Staff Sergeant Mayes, had a weak constitution. He developed several maladies, more imagined than real, and asked to be medically evacuated. Initially, I was hesitant but Bob interceded saying, "Sir, the son-of-bitch is worthless anyway! We know how to use naval gunfire as well as he does." Riddell's assessment convinced me to call for a medical evacuation. We were able to get a U.S. helicopter to fly the mission. As the man was getting his gear ready, we decided the U.S. Navy's radios were mission essential and therefore were to remain in the field. I told the lieutenant that the radios were staying; he could remain with us and keep the radios or get on the chopper without them. He decided that leaving the area was more important than his Navy property. After his departure, the USS *Newport News*, a cruiser, became our asset, the naval term for firing platform. The combat control center aboard the ship acknowledged me and asked why I used the suffix Alpha in my call sign. I told them that I was the alternate NGF officer because the primary "had the shits and got out of Dodge." Naval personnel were not used to colorful radio procedure. Riddell and I had no idea our transmissions were broadcast throughout the ship. We went into great detail describing what was happening on the ground. It established an excellent rapport with the *Newport News* personnel, who often called to see if we needed fire. Unfortunately, our relationship ended because the battalion moved out of range. We later heard that there was an explosion aboard the *Newport News* but could not ascertain the extent of the damage. We hoped there were no casualties because we had grown fond of the ship and its crew. Later reports stated that nineteen sailors were killed and ten were injured.

Little headway was made against the scattered forces left to delay us. It was not unusual for one NVA bunker to hold up the entire battalion. We were unable to get an airstrike or a nighttime Spectre to knock it out. The battalion commander insisted he lacked the capability to eliminate it by fire and maneuver but we saw few attempts to try. I suggested we bring up one of the recently issued TOW weapons systems and take out the bunker with a guided missile. The aperture made a great aiming point. Vegetation was light, so there was no chance that the wires directing the missile would get foiled. Dinh thought for a moment and then said, "TOW is much money. Five thousand dollars each!" My comeback was that an airstrike cost more and it would be better to fire a TOW now than wait for the USAF. Plus, I pointed to Riddell and said, "The *dai-uy* (Vietnamese for captain) and I have already paid for those TOW missiles. Let's use 'em!" My humor concerning the portion of our taxes that went toward defense spending was lost on our counterpart. Like other recommendations, Dinh disregarded it. The enemy remained in place . . . and so did the 6th Airborne Battalion.

CHAPTER 11

Chia Tay, Vietnam (Farewell, Vietnam)

Paris, Jan. 27—The Vietnam ceasefire agreement was signed here today in eerie silence, without a word or gesture to express the world's relief that the years of war were officially ending.
                                                                —*NEW YORK TIMES*[1]

ON SEPTEMBER 16, VIETNAMESE MARINES DROVE THE NVA OUT of the Quang Tri Citadel. They had relieved the Airborne Division on July 27 and had been fighting continually since then. When U.S. air support restrictions were lifted, VNMC used the opportunity to blast the NVA out of their deep bunkers. The old fortress and the town were destroyed, but recapturing the province capital caused great rejoicing. Authorities considered it a huge morale victory. Given the total destruction of the city and friendly casualties, the victory appeared to be a Pyrrhic one. All provincial seats were now held by the Thieu administration, although the NVA still occupied much of the territory gained at the outset of the Easter Offensive. In our part of I Corps, South Vietnam's troops only controlled Quang Tri City and the rolling hills to the west. Everything north of the Thach Han River, including the district town of Dong Ha, remained Indian Country.

Two days later, Colonel Hansen broke a long-standing precedent . . . he pulled Riddell and me out of the 6th Airborne Battalion and did not replace us. His action took courage because conventional wisdom prevailed that the Americans provided support to the South Vietnamese regardless of the conduct of a particular ARVN commander. To my knowledge, it was a first in Team 162. Colonel Hansen instituted a new way of doing business and everyone noticed.

In mid-September, 6th Battalion moved to a secure area for rest and refitting. The battalion headquarters settled into a multi-story house just off the main highway. A wealthy landowner had abandoned the residence during the May fighting. Colonel Dinh directed Bob Riddell and me to a small shed behind the building. "*Co van house*," he said. Calling the place a house was a misuse of terminology, because livestock had been kept there in the not too distant past. We took this in stride and moved our equipment into the place, which smelled like the previous residents. We adhered to the adage, "If you are given lemons, make lemonade," and began cleaning up. Dinh took satisfaction watching a U.S. major and captain stripped to the waist shoveling waste.

Colonel Hansen's unannounced visit occurred on the afternoon of September 18. The senior advisor walked into the command post and spoke briefly to the battalion commander, who was reclining in his hammock. Hansen's next stop was the livestock shed where Bob Riddell and I were in the throes of making some home improvements. Colonel Hansen looked at the conditions, including a hole in the roof, and in a terse statement said: "Pack your gear." Dinh figured something was amiss and walked over in his T-shirt, drawers, and flip-flops, his usual attire when the battalion was not in the field. Hansen stated that Major Howard and Captain Riddell were leaving and would not return, nor would other advisors be assigned. Dinh was startled; he was finally being taken to task for his intemperate behavior. Colonel Hansen stated that Dinh should treat Americans better, especially since they were trying to help him and his countrymen. Upon returning to LZ Sally, Hansen briefed the division commander. His position was that advisors were professional partners assisting the South Vietnamese, and he would not tolerate them being treated as whipping boys by a testy commander.

The next day, I was transferred to the 11th Airborne Battalion, replacing CPT Woody Furrow. Bob Riddell was reassigned as deputy to the new 2nd Brigade advisor, LTC Rex Bramlette. I met MAJ Le Van Me, CO of the 11th, when Lam Son 72 kicked off at the end of June. His reputation was excellent then and it continued to flourish. Me knew about the problems with Colonel Dinh and assured me that we would not have similar issues. Both of us were determined to make things work. Several bonds of commonality strengthened the new relationship; we were the same age, the same rank, and both commissioned in 1964, Me from the Vietnamese Military Academy and me from West Point. The most striking difference between the 6th and 11th Battalion was being included in all discussions. As the unit prepared to occupy a new sector, Le Van Me showed me the map, sketched out the plan, and asked, "John, what do you think?" It was the first time an ARVN officer posed that question to me or addressed me by my Christian name.

When he was not wearing a helmet or a red beret, Le Van Me wore a paratrooper cap popularized by the French hero of Indochina and Algeria, GEN Marcel Bigeard. Called a "Bigeard hat" or "lizard cap," it gave him a rakish look. Me had taken over the 11th Airborne Battalion in April 1972 when the battalion commander was killed during the heavy fighting in the Central Highlands along a mountainous spine known as Rocket Ridge. He rallied the troops and with the help of some timely airstrikes was able to lead them off a firebase before it was overrun. General Dong recognized he had a good man and kept Major Me in command.

Not long after my arrival, Me discussed the Airborne Division's experience during Lam Son 719. His observations were unsolicited and part of a normal conversation. Laos undermined the confidence of the airborne leaders and the paratroopers. Frustrations mounted when they encountered problems calling for U.S. air support. U.S.

FACs and helicopter pilots had difficulty understanding the men on the ground who were under great stress. Coupled with lapses in procedural knowledge, it was a painful reminder that the South Vietnamese were not prepared to go it alone. Tactics compounded problems. A permanent firebase invited disaster because once the NVA located it, artillery, mortars, and rockets targeted it. The noose was further tightened when AAA was emplaced around the firebase preventing resupply by helicopters. In short order a firebase became isolated and untenable.

Sixth Airborne Battalion was cut up badly on its first mission. The unit was sent on a reconnaissance-in-force to eliminate enemy artillery batteries that were pounding the division's firebases. U.S. helicopters were hit by heavy ground fire during the initial assault so subsequent lifts were diverted to alternate LZs. Companies were spread out, unable to support each other. North Vietnamese attacked them one after the other, taking prisoners and inflicting heavy losses. The battalion had to retreat leaving some of their twenty-eight dead behind, unheard of in the Airborne Division. Nguyen Van Dinh was never the same after Lam Son 719.

Not far away FSB 31, occupied by a brigade headquarters and the 3rd Battalion, was under siege. It was established to protect the northern flank of the advance along Highway 9, the only thoroughfare in the area but little more than an unimproved dirt road. In addition to stopping westward movement along QL 9, North Vietnamese were intent on destroying FSB 31. U.S. airstrikes kept the enemy away from the perimeter. When a USAF F4 Phantom was shot down, all air support was shifted to assist the rescue of the crew. The pause reenergized the NVA assault and in short order FSB 31 was overrun. That day, February 25, 1971, the commander of the 3rd Airborne Brigade, Colonel Nguyen Van Tho, was captured, the highest-ranking paratrooper to become a POW. Further humiliation occurred when Tho made radio broadcasts encouraging ARVN soldiers to lay down their arms.

Lieutenant General Dong was very vocal in his criticism of U.S. support and priorities. One of his complaints alleged that the U.S. Air Force viewed a pilot and his weapons officer as more important than Vietnamese soldiers. Dong's inflammatory comments created a festering sore within the division. In early March 1971, as the number of dead, missing, and wounded mounted, President Thieu insisted that the operation be terminated. When Lam Son 719 ended, the Airborne Division began retraining in I Corps rather than returning to Saigon. The president, chairman of JGS, and the division commander did not want the citizens of the capital hearing about the Laotian disaster from returning soldiers.

Major Me was providing some rationale for the behavior of Colonel Dinh and others. He was not justifying it, simply giving some background on the origin of the foul atmosphere I experienced. Me said that the decrease in U.S. air support, compared to what was seen at the outset of the Easter Offensive, was apparent to everyone and a source of concern. Continued American disengagement would resurrect tensions that General Dong stirred up a year before. I wrote a synopsis of Me's assessment and forwarded it to my boss so he could alert senior leaders to the growing animosity, another product of Vietnamization.

—◦—

Meals with Major Me and his staff were enjoyable because discussions were lively, with Me translating the comments of officers who were less fluent in English. The food was far superior to what I subsisted on earlier. We ate family style . . . a plate of pork, chicken, or water buffalo, some greens and a pot of rice were placed in the center of a makeshift table. Nuoc mam, fermented fish sauce, was our primary condiment. Chopsticks were used to take food from the communal plates to our individual rice bowls. By that time, I was quite adept at eating with chopsticks and acquired a taste for nuoc mam. You held your rice bowl to your mouth and used the chopsticks to shovel the food in.

When chicken was prepared, the soldier/cook chopped the bird up with a machete and threw it in the pot. Bone fragments were part of the meal so everyone chewed carefully. Lulls in the fighting allowed us to send men to the markets in Hue to procure baguettes and other food. When villages along QL 1 were selling fresh seafood, I bought bushels of crabs to change the dietary pace. Special occasions meant other delicacies might be served. One of the favorites was Duck's Blood Pudding. The cook slit the throat of a duck or two and let the blood drain into a large bowl. When it coagulated, peanuts were sprinkled on top of it and that was the main course for the evening. The other culinary delight was "Bird." Recent hatchlings were steamed and eaten whole. I forced myself to eat Duck's Blood Pudding but just could not bring myself to "do Bird." I apologized to Major Me, but he was fine with that digestive limitation.

While I was basking in the civility shown by my new counterpart, other battalion advisors were seeing fault lines develop in ties that were previously viewed as unbreakable. Over the years the "airborne brotherhood" was viewed as an indestructible union between Vietnamese and U.S. paratroopers but was becoming more illusionary than anyone wished to believe. For years ARVN commanders maintained strong bonds with the U.S. advisors. The Americans were the source of many things . . . U.S. helicopters, massive artillery fire, tactical air support, medical evacuations, immediate equipment replacement, Marlboros, Courvoisier, and occasionally a truckload of building material. As air squadrons returned to their home stations and the logistical infrastructure dismantled, all that was left was the advisors' counsel. It came as a shock to the men who had previously served with the Airborne Division that their advice was considered far more valuable when it was bundled with other U.S. things.

CPT Jack Jacobs, who won the Medal of Honor in 1968, was senior advisor with the 1st Airborne Battalion. Jack spoke Vietnamese and knew the culture. His previous tour in the Mekong Delta with the 9th ARVN Division gave him keen insights. He noticed a change in the attitude of his counterpart, Major Hong, as the effects of the drawdown hit. Even though Jack was a great tactician, the battalion commander was not interested in his advice. One of his reports echoed what was thought by many of us but few MACV officers in the grade of colonel or above wanted to hear:

"Although I speak Vietnamese fairly well, my rapport with counterparts is superb . . . we really do little advising here . . . I believe the Airborne Division Assistance team has outlived its usefulness . . . our main reason for existence is to talk to American FAC's . . . the continued existence of the Battalion Combat Advisory Team . . . performing limited functions and higher levels existing to support the battalions is ludicrous. . . ."[2]

Art Taylor also weighed in. He was the only brigade senior advisor to do so. LTC Rex Bramlette, the 2nd Brigade SA, had not been in ADAT long enough to have an opinion and withheld comment. The senior advisor to the 3rd Airborne Brigade was on his second tour with the Airborne Division and thus did not acknowledge there was a problem. Lieutenant Colonel Taylor did not mince words:

"I still believe that the battalion advisory teams can be eliminated. . . . The only function of the U.S. battalion advisor remains controlling and directing a reduced number of U.S. airstrikes. This is a waste of talent for a Major or a Captain and it is not surprising that so many of our battalion advisors are frustrated."[3]

At the end of October, Henry Kissinger announced "peace is at hand." None of the American advisors knew what this meant, although the North Vietnamese negotiators released the full text of the tentative agreement. Colonel Hansen wanted no discussion about it since our personal observations would only muddy an already cloudy situation. Senior ARVN officers were greatly concerned that Americans were about to pull up stakes, leave Vietnam, and never look back. Their feelings were somewhat mollified on November 7, 1972 when President Nixon won a landslide election victory over Senator George

McGovern, the Democratic antiwar candidate. But, the seeds of suspicion were already planted and further nourished by speculation in the Vietnamese press.

The ceasefire provision allowing NVA troops to remain in South Vietnam and cuts in U.S. strength increased tensions between advisors and counterparts. In November 1972 U.S. troop strength dropped to 27,000, causing carefully nurtured relationships to rupture.[4] Mike Flynn, the quintessential military intelligence officer and advisor, was shocked when he was rebuked by his counterpart. "The advisor cannot teach me anything. You should not attempt to make recommendations because you are only a major and junior to me, so you do not know as much or have as much experience as I."[5]

That attitude was prevalent in most of the infantry battalions. MAJ Hugh Walker, with the 3rd Airborne Battalion, noticed an abrupt change and reported that his counterpart, Major Dong, suddenly made a point of ignoring him. Walker was totally alienated and shut off from information, so much so that he had to query his boss, the brigade senior advisor, to get the 3rd Battalion's SITREPs.

"Little or no information on Bn activities or missions is freely offered. . . . Acceptance of advice or suggestions is neither requested nor so far accepted if offered. Discussing of Bn tactics, ie, that of deploying companies in the attacks instead of platoons and squads, are received almost as insults or disbelief."[6]

The rupture of the partnership veneer in the 5th and 6th Airborne Battalions was now spreading throughout the Airborne Division like a running windshield crack. No one should have been surprised by the backlash experienced by Mike Flynn, Hugh Walker, and others. The departure of the U.S. military was creating life and death uncertainty within the ARVN. If our fellow citizens in the United States were unable to differentiate between the policymakers and those far down the chain who were the face of the policy, why should we expect our allies to be any different, especially when so much was at risk?

Assuming the United States would leave RVN high and dry, some staff officers and commanders exhibited blatant animosity toward the co vans. Major Me was just the opposite; he continued to include me in all discussions and never once showed any sign of rancor. Our talks covered a wide range of subjects, from operational issues to events outside Southeast Asia. His intellectual curiosity and interest in technology was another source of amazement. He was fascinated by reports of Apollo 17, a topic I was "ho hum" about since it was the sixth lunar landing. Politics of peace and the recent Nixon landslide did not grab his attention like the lunar rover vehicle and the moon walks.

Neither the ARVN nor the NVA showed any enthusiasm for renewing the offensive. There was periodic incoming fire, but nothing like the volume that was encountered in July and August. With the stalemate continuing, I elected to take a "7 & 7" leave over Christmas. I had been in country for eight months so it was an ideal time to go. The operational tempo was the lowest of the year and intelligence reports did not indicate any impending uptick in enemy activity. Seven & Seven was a program instituted to allow service members to take R & R, normally seven days, and then add on seven days of leave. The U.S. military flew you to Hawaii; from there, you purchased a ticket back to the mainland. A round-trip from Honolulu to Maryland was on my dime. One of my fellow advisors believed a ceasefire agreement would be reached in my absence. Since the North Vietnamese negotiators, Le Duc Tho and Xuan Thuy, had terminated the peace talks on December 13, that seemed unlikely. Five days later, the 18th, I wished all Merry Christmas and boarded a Pan Am 747 headed to Guam, Hawaii, and then on to Salisbury, Maryland.

Recent events in Paris were perceived as another example of "*dan va danh*," talking while fighting, an age-old communist strategy. It was the DRV's way to prolong the process, play upon America's war weariness, and reap good publicity in the sympathetic western press. Behind the scenes emissaries from Washington were in continuous dialogue with President Thieu about the tentative provisions of a peace settlement. A deadlock occurred; Thieu refused to accept that North Vietnamese forces would remain in Vietnam after a cease-fire, while North Vietnam was equally opposed to withdrawal of the NVA and restoring the DMZ as the demarcation between North and South.

President Nixon had to do something to end the impasse, so he ordered the full-scale bombing of North Vietnam. To everyone's surprise, B-52s attacked military sites in Hanoi, Haiphong, and other major cities. For the first time, bombers hit targets in down-town Hanoi, strikes the Joint Chiefs of Staff had advocated for years. When our commercial flight landed at Guam the evening of December 18, we could see lines of B-52s at the adjacent Andersen AFB. Raids that night were the beginning of eleven days of bombing DRV. The North's leaders knew leaving Paris would prompt a reaction but did not anticipate the extent of it, specifically the use of B-52s against targets in urban areas. Again, they misread Nixon.

Linebacker II was the biggest air campaign of the Vietnam War. U.S. airmen encountered the most formidable air defense (AD) system in the world, which included 300 Russian SA 2 surface-to-air missile (SAM) sites and a variety of 57mm, 85mm, and 100mm AAA weapons. The accuracy of AAA was enhanced because the 57mm and larger guns were integrated into target acquisition radars that controlled the SAMs. Smaller-caliber weapons, the more mobile 23mm and 37mm guns, were also seeded around critical installations and depots. Hanoi and Haiphong were the most heavily defended. President Johnson's 1968 bombing halt gave the North Vietnamese ample time to acquire the most sophisticated AD weaponry, accompanied by thousands of advisors from the USSR and PRC to train and assist operators.

December weather was notoriously bad because it was the height of the winter monsoon season. Low ceilings inhibited U.S.

fighter-bombers that were dependent on visual target identifica-tion. AAA was most lethal when aircraft made low-level bomb runs. This was a source of comfort to Hanoi's leaders who discounted the probability of B-52s attacking military targets in large cities. The air offensive also coincided with the U.S. Congress's Christmas recess, so House and Senate doves could voice their disapproval but not take any legislative action to stop it. Some representatives and senators never realized they were being played by the North Vietnamese. Through-out the war they became dependable Politburo allies whose actions encouraged our enemy, resulting in more U.S. combat casualties.

As expected, reaction to what the media called the Christmas bombing was particularly harsh. President Nixon was vilified in the newspapers, on TV and by congressional carpers. When I arrived home, the anti-Nixon campaign was shrill. Even Salisbury, Mary-land, a conservative town, was not immune to criticism of the bomb-ing. During his Christmas Eve sermon, my parents' minister called the bombing "madness."

Two Delmarva men were Linebacker II casualties. CPT Dick Cooper, a B-52 navigator-bombardier from Salisbury, was shot down on the first night's mission and listed as MIA. Several days later (December 26), my cousin, N. J. Wimbrow, who hailed from a nearby town, was aboard a bomber that was lost. N. J. was an elec-tronic counter-measures officer on a B-52D destroyed by an SA 2 missile. His name was added to the growing number of missing men. Both men were ultimately declared dead and their remains were later returned to the United States for burial.

On December 26, Hanoi notified Washington its negotiators were ready to return to Paris, but President Nixon continued Line-backer II for three more days. The bombing took a severe toll on North Vietnam's infrastructure; railroads were interdicted, petroleum reserves were depleted, and 80 percent of power production capabil-ity was destroyed. When several bombs inadvertently hit a civilian hospital in Hanoi, the U.S. antiwar faction and North Vietnamese claimed the USAF employed carpet bombing as a terror tactic. This fabrication played well in worldwide media, but in fact U.S. bombing was more accurate than any in the history of air warfare. An excess of caution exposed aircraft to unnecessary risks. Telford Taylor, an acclaimed American jurist and outspoken critic of the Vietnam War, was in Hanoi over Christmas 1972. He remarked: "Despite the enormous weight of bombs that were dropped, I rapidly became convinced that we were making no effort to destroy Hanoi. The city remained largely intact and it seemed quite apparent that if there were an effort to destroy Hanoi it could have been done readily in two or three nights."[7]

B-52s flew 741 sorties and lost fifteen bombers; thirty-three crew members were KIA and another thirty-three became POWs. The leadership in Hanoi claimed twice the number of bombers were downed. The USAF, Navy, and Marine Corps lost twelve aircraft flying suppression and rescue missions. Twelve aviators on those flights were killed and eight were taken prisoner. "Horrific US losses" cited by the North Vietnamese and some U.S. reporters did not occur.[8]

When I returned to LZ Sally, Colonel Hansen reassigned me as the division G3 advisor. MAJ Paul DeVries, who had held the position since August, was leaving. Paul came to ADAT after assisting in the deactivation of the last elements of the 1st Cav. He was well versed in the art of conventional warfare and possessed a wealth of patience, much-needed attributes for advisory duty in 1972. Paul left a great legacy and was a hard act to follow. However my time in the G3 job would be short-lived.

With resumption of the Paris Peace Talks, we expected a ceasefire announcement any day. Our parent headquarters, Army Advisory Group (AAG), had directed development of contingency plans, including what would happen on "X Day," the day the ceasefire began. Colonel Hansen kept Brigadier General Luong, the new division commander, fully apprised of the preparations. Although Luong understood U.S. political realities, he was unhappy about it. In most cases the division staff totally rejected the fact that the United States was leaving. Disbelief permeated all ranks.

In the meantime, operations continued. On January 8, 1973, a routine US resupply mission was scheduled. MAJ Bill Deane, G1 advisor and head of the rear detachment at Tan Son Nhut, was at LZ Sally for a visit. He asked to fly on the helicopter that would take SSG Elbert Bush, NCO advisor with the 8th Airborne Battalion, back to the field. A U.S. Huey, call sign Sahara 27, flew into LZ Sally for a mission briefing. Warrant Officer 1 (WO1—equivalent of a second lieutenant in the warrant officer ranks) Mickey A. Wilson was the commander; the co-pilot was WO1 Richard A. Knutson. Both had limited flying hours since they had been on flight status less than twelve months. Knutson had only been in Vietnam since December 3, 1972. Two inexperienced aviators in the same cockpit was against normal aviation procedure but was overlooked because of shortages in experienced pilots, a ripple effect of the drawdown.

The flight route was planned along easily identifiable terrain features, north along QL 1, then a southwest turn upon reaching Quang Tri City. Following these prominent landmarks ensured the aircraft would remain in friendly airspace. The LZ where Staff Sergeant Bush was to be dropped off was not far from the turn point. The helicopter lifted off from LZ Sally at 1430 and field locations were notified that the mission was "a go." The ETA at the first destination was 1445-1450. After forty-five minutes, everyone was concerned since Sahara 27 was not responding to radio calls. A VNMC unit reported seeing a Huey crossing the Thach Han River, heading due north. We were sure it was ours. The pilots must have become disoriented and missed the turn point. Apparently, the Huey was taken under fire and downed but aerial searches were unable to find any wreckage. Two pilots, Wilson and Knutson, a crew chief, SP5 Manuel A. Lauterio, a door gunner, SP5 William S. Stinson, Bill Deane, and Elbert Bush were listed as MIA. Their remains were recovered years later not far from the search area. After identification, all except Lauterio were interred at Arlington Cemetery twenty-seven years after they were lost. Deane and Bush were the last casualties suffered by MACV. Team 162.[9]

A week later, January 15, President Nixon announced that all offensive air operations in North Vietnam were suspended, another indicator something was about to happen. The U.S. government still had to persuade President Thieu to agree to the draft accords. Even though a strong U.S. response was promised if the North Vietnamese attacked again, the South Vietnamese president balked. When Thieu was told that the United States would go it alone if he continued to disagree, he reluctantly gave his assent. Nixon announced a ceasefire would take effect on January 28 at 8:00 A.M. local time. That evening Colonel Hansen talked about the president's announcement. He was not sanguine about the long-term prospects for cessation of hostilities. His comment was, "They'll try again another day."

X Day plans required determining if the fighting had actually stopped and getting thirty-four advisors out of their field sites. A small team was designated to remain at LZ Sally as a liaison party between the Airborne Division and First Regional Assistance Command. For a few weeks, they would be the honest brokers in the reporting system. All U.S. personnel, other than a small military detachment at the embassy, had to be out of Vietnam in 60 days, referred to by all as "X + 60."

On the night of January 27, artillery fired back and forth across the Thach Han River. It was heaviest in the early morning hours but near the specified time, the guns were silent. MAJ Roberto Eaton recorded the following:

"The artillery ceased firing at approx. 0815 hrs, 28 Jan 73. When this happened, the NVA crossed the river all along the front & planted flags on the shore. Leaving their weapons on the shore, they walked up to the friendly unit. The South VN would not shoot because they were unarmed. They formed circles of NVA & SVA and had pleasant chats."[10]

The scene along the Thach Han River was calm compared to other locations where fierce fighting raged. We received reports of pitch battles for control of small hamlets, towns, and even individual rice fields, called "land-grabbing." All over South Vietnam, flags of the National Liberation Front and South Vietnam were planted to show ownership. NVA used the blue, red, and yellow flag of the NLF, not the red flag of North Vietnam. The communists were maintaining the façade of an insurgency, the NLF versus the "puppets and imperialists." The battle of the flags continued after Americans left Vietnam.[11]

Advisors departed quietly. In some battalions, Vietnamese counterparts made no pretense of civility. Several refused to say farewell or shake hands, which made departure easier. When all were accounted for, they were loaded aboard a C-130 bound for Tan Son Nhut. I managed to visit MAJ Le Van Me before it was time to go. He presented me with an 11th Airborne Battalion plaque and I gave him my CAR 15. He had coveted the weapon since we first met at the outset of Lam Son 72. Major Me admitted he had the plaque made in October when rumors were rife about "peace is at hand." To Le Van Me the withdrawal of U.S. personnel was a foregone conclusion, so he was devoid of the ill will that affected other commanders. I was touched; we had established a firm bond from September to December 1972. His professionalism and demeanor renewed my faith in the Airborne Division and its officer corps.

On February 6, 1973, a memorial service was held at Tan Son Nhut on the Airborne Division Parade Field. After years of continuous service ADAT, now only forty men, was holding its last formation. GEN Fred C. Weyand, the commander of USMACV, MG William Coleman, AAG commander, and BG John McGiffert, now MACV J3, were present. No senior South Vietnamese officers from JGS and the Airborne Division attended. They were registering their displeasure with the ceasefire agreement by snubbing the team. At LZ Sally, the snubs were far from subtle. The tension between the U.S. liaison team and the Vietnamese paratroopers was palpable. Interaction between U.S. personnel and the Vietnamese was minimal and gleaning any meaningful information was impossible. The shock of severing the U.S. umbilical cord was too much to digest. Consequently, the liaison mission was terminated earlier than planned.

Colonel Hansen was leaving for an assignment at Nakhon Phanom (NKP) Air Base in Thailand. Because the peace agreement limited the number of U.S. personnel who could remain in Vietnam, a headquarters was sent to Thailand to monitor activity in the war zone. Over dinner the night before he left for NKP, Colonel Hansen was philosophical about the events of the past six months. He had been in contact with other division senior advisors and was told of incidents where Americans were subjected to overt hostility. The situation in the Airborne Division was not an isolated phenomenon. He made the comment: "Dinh and you were in some tough fights. Too bad you were not always on the same side." As the evening ended, Colonel Hansen summed up the entire experience when he said, "We have just witnessed the ragged edge of Vietnamization."[12]

I was tasked to ensure all Team 162 administrative work was completed prior to X + 60. Final reports had to be rendered, detachment files purged, and remaining property turned over to the Vietnamese. In one of the cabinets I found paperwork approving an award for the former division commander, Lieutenant General Dong. He was presented a Silver Star for gallantry during Lam Son 719. The citation did not tally with the after-action reports I read. Pressure from Washington to show the Laos incursion in a good light was intense and U.S. decorations for South Vietnamese commanders were part of the success story. Dong's citation prompted me to think of the recommendation I submitted for Colonel Dinh after An Lôc. All of us, from the MACV commander down to battalion advisors, were doing our part in the name of Vietnamization.

By the end of February, all that was left to do was turn off the lights. Within a few days, I was instructed to report to the Tan Son Nhut for my return home. LTC Art Taylor, who had been transferred to MACV headquarters in October, was on the same aircraft. We arrived at Travis AFB where it all began, signed the required forms, and went to San Francisco International Airport. An airport bar was a welcomed oasis as we awaited our flights to the East Coast. We struck up a conversation with two businessmen who were also killing time. They were interested in Vietnam and, unlike many Americans in 1973, were friendly toward men in uniform. Their generosity was expressed by buying the drinks the moment we sat down. Many topics were discussed, some funny and others serious. One of the men asked what we would have done differently if either of us had been in charge. I deferred to Colonel Taylor. Art told them that nothing was simple, and in Vietnam, even if it appeared simple the issue was incredibly complex. With that caveat, he said that we, the United States, should have focused on improving the South Vietnamese armed forces much earlier in the war. But as the U.S. buildup gained momentum, our U.S. military leadership was intent on taking the fight to the enemy . . . so the war was Americanized. Teaming with the ARVN and improving its capability came later. Vietnamization was a way for the United States to exit honorably, although we spent enormous sums providing modern equipment to the South Vietnamese armed forces. Throughout the American experience in Vietnam, we never tried to exercise any meaningful influence over our ally. Graft and corruption flourished within the South Vietnamese officer corps where political ties in the senior ranks won out over military competence. Consequently, inept senior commanders were retained and disasters followed. Colonel Taylor cited the Easter Offensive when Lieutenant General Lam was finally relieved and Lieutenant General Truong was brought in to turn things around. He was emphatic about tough days ahead and the requirement for U.S. air support when the communists struck again. It was a given that the NVA would go another round. One of the men said, "Well at least we are out of there and that damn war is over." Art responded, "Yes, it is for the United States, but it will be with us for a long, long time."

⌒

Americans celebrated the return of the POWs and accorded them a welcome no other Vietnam veterans received. A collective sigh of relief seemed to engulf the country. It was short-lived because Hanoi's Politburo used the time to rearm its force. Allowing North Vietnamese units to remain in South Vietnam placed the Saigon government at a tremendous disadvantage. However, the nation's death knell sounded when Congress passed the Case-Church Amendment. The 1973 legislation banned all military operations in Southeast Asia, denying RVN the air support it would desperately need if North Vietnam struck again. In January 1975 NVA conducted probing attacks to test U.S. response and launched a major offensive when there was none. The Watergate scandal and a hostile Congress negated any attempts to help South Vietnam. Without U.S. assistance, ARVN crumbled. Pictures of soldiers fighting to get on departing aircraft, the plight of refugees escaping the communist advance, and Khmer Rouge terror in Cambodia were enduring images of that time.

When the South was overwhelmed on April 30, 1975, scholars and journalists wrote volumes of opinions and recriminations. Vietnam became a syndrome as well as a war. Almost forgotten were the two million of our generation who answered John F. Kennedy's challenge. His call still resonated in the summer of 1965 but over time its tone muted. As the war continued and casualties mounted, our nation changed. Those who did their duty in Southeast Asia had their judgment questioned and were not readily accepted in mainstream America. Hollywood was fond of characterizing Vietnam veterans as meltdown cases and borderline psychotics. Lawmakers and government agencies, particularly the Veterans Administration, appeared indifferent toward those who needed help. Vets were the nation's red-headed stepchildren, often shunted aside, an embarrassing reminder of a failed policy. Those who had borne the burden, paid the price, and endured the hardships were let down. Many agreed with the historian, Geoffrey Perret, who remarked we served our country better than our country served us.

Although five decades have passed since those days, they are never far from my thoughts. Consequently, I have not said, "*Chia Tay* . . . Farewell, Vietnam." Most of my recollections are good ones . . . of Dave Hackworth, Art Taylor, Harry Godwin, Doc Benjamin, Bob Riddell, and Woody Furrow. Debilitating memories, regrets, and remorse are offset by the knowledge we did our best and fought the good fight in what a U.S. president later called "a noble cause." Still, mourning the casualties and victims is a lifelong journey. Unlike some of my brethren, I have not been burdened by questions of the morality of that conflict and whether or not we should have been there in the first place. My ambition to be a soldier, kindled long ago, was molded, tempered, and tested in that war. The unseen price was the loss of my innocence and idealism. Like lost comrades, they will never be reclaimed.

EPILOGUE

"When were you in Vietnam?" "Last night," the veteran replied.

THE VIETNAM WAR CLAIMED THE LIVES OF MORE THAN 58,000 Americans. Three hundred thirty-four graduates of the U.S. Military Academy were among them. Two hundred ninety-one were killed in action; forty-three were classified as "non-combat" casualties, many from helicopter crashes. Death visited all ranks of the Long Gray Line, from general to second lieutenant.[1] Six graduates and two ex-cadets, men who attended USMA but did not graduate, were awarded the Medal of Honor; only three of the eight recipients lived to be presented the award.

Within a year of our graduation from West Point, members of the Class of 1964 were in combat. Charlie Hutchinson was killed on May 10, 1965 leading an infantry platoon in the Dominican Republic. Twenty-three classmates died in Vietnam and scores were wounded. The first were Claire Thurston and Dave Ugland, killed on November 8, 1965. Both were second lieutenants in the 173rd Airborne Brigade. Forty-nine Americans perished that day on an obscure piece of terrain in War Zone D called Hill 65. The battle was memorialized in a 2005 Big & Rich song, "8th of November."

Two-thirds of the Class of 1964 made the military their career. With a few exceptions, all served in Vietnam. Fifteen were promoted to general officer from the Regular Army; four more were given honorary promotions after spending the bulk of their service teaching at West Point. Five classmates were promoted to general from the reserve components, either the National Guard or the Army/ Air Force Reserve. From the Regular ranks, two, Barry McCaffrey and Dave Bramlett, became four-star generals. Four were lieutenant generals, three were major generals, and six were brigadier generals. Barry was our senior soldier and the most highly decorated. During the Vietnam War, he was awarded two Distinguished Service Crosses, two Silver Stars, and three Purple Hearts. Upon retirement, he served as the drug czar in the Clinton Administration and then became a regular commentator for NBC News. His insights have educated untold numbers of Americans.

West Point laid the foundation for the profession I came to love. Attending the institution was one of the most fortunate things to happen to me. Under today's standards, I probably would not be admitted. Without the U.S. Military Academy, my path in life would have been entirely different. Still, unpleasant memories of times at West Point outweigh the good ones.

———

Disease felled Dave Hackworth; it did what the North Koreans, Chinese Communists, and North Vietnamese had been unable to do in combat. He suffered from cancer and was in Mexico seeking alternative treatment when he died. He retired from the Army in 1971 under a cloud of allegations. Dave returned to Vietnam in early 1969 and commanded a battalion in the 9th Infantry Division, was deputy senior advisor in the Vietnamese Airborne Division, and served in the Mekong Delta's 44th Special Tactical Zone. He did not go quietly into the night. He was featured in an ABC TV special on misdirection of the war. Rather than prosecute him, the Army allowed him to retire. Many of us thought that he had been in Vietnam too long. My comment at the time was, "Dave Hackworth 'died' in the service of his country."[2]

Hack immigrated to Australia and made a fortune running a duck farm and a high-end restaurant. He became active in the antinuclear scene and orchestrated a media event when he threw away his many medals. He was always one for a grand gesture. Dave came in from the cold in 1989 when he published his autobiography, *About Face*, a bestseller that went through multiple printings. During his rehabilitation, he decided he wanted his medals back. His heroism in Korea and Vietnam gave him great credibility, and he used it to burnish his new literary career. After much deliberation, the Department of the Army reluctantly reissued the awards. His website later proclaimed that he was America's most highly decorated living soldier. Hack was not the first to make that claim.

On May 30, 2005, David H. Hackworth was buried with full military honors in Arlington. There was standing room only in the Fort Myer chapel with more people attending the graveside ceremony. Doc Benjamin, Don Hilbert, Ben Willis, and I were among the pallbearers who carried Hack to his final resting place. Dave and I reflected on our forty years together a month before his death. His counsel and his guidance when I was a young officer were responsible for me staying in the Army and started me on a successful track. I loved him then and still do today.

Art Taylor retired from the U.S. Army in June 1982; he had been in uniform for thirty years. After we returned from Vietnam, he was promoted to colonel and served in a variety of jobs including the U.S. Army Recruiting Command (USAREC). We saw each other often. His last assignment was command of an ROTC region. There was no one in the U.S. Army better suited to advise aspiring cadets. Following retirement, Art and his wife, Elaine, settled in Columbia, South Carolina, where he served in the state government as emergency preparedness coordinator. He died of a heart attack on March 21, 1994. Elaine, his bride of forty-two years, was at his side at the end. Art was an invaluable source of support when I was struggling with my Vietnamese counterpart in the 6th Airborne Battalion. Had it not been for him, I would have been fed to the wolves by those who consistently apologized for ARVN shortcomings. I continue to mourn his passing.

CPT Bob Riddell left the Army in 1974. During his tour in Vietnam, he was awarded the Silver Star, two Bronze Stars, and the Purple Heart. Always the good soldier, Bob made bad days with Colonel Dinh bearable. He retired from U.S. civil service in June 2014. A well-earned retirement in St. Augustine, Florida, was cut short by his death on December 8, 2014. Robert C. Riddell II was sixty-eight years old.

Jerry F. Metcalfe retired as a lieutenant colonel after commanding an infantry battalion in the 82nd Airborne Division. Prior to retirement, he was diagnosed with multiple sclerosis. Jerry fought the disease for years, finally succumbing on July 25, 2014. His tenacity in the face of adversity, whether in combat or fighting his debilitating illness, never wavered.

Gail Woodrow Furrow retired from the Army in 1980. Ten years of enlisted service prior to commissioning allowed him to leave the military at a relatively young age. He became a successful businessman. Furrow bought a large farm in Kentucky and raised Angus cattle. Woody died on December 19, 2016, at the age of seventy-seven.

Both my commanders in the 1st Battalion (Airborne), 327th Infantry, LTC Joe Rogers and LTC Walter Meinzen, have passed away. So have the two men who served as senior advisors to the Vietnamese Airborne Division in 1972-1973. I worked for COL Marcus Hansen in USAREC at Fort Sheridan, Illinois in 1974 and 1975. The draft had ended and the Volunteer Army was making its first shaky steps. USAREC was barely making its goals, so it was a stressful environment. Following a tour in Turkey, Colonel Hansen retired after more than thirty years of service. He died in 1991 while I was in Pakistan. I did not learn of his death until a year later.

Don Hilbert had a distinguished military career. He went back to Vietnam in 1970 and commanded the 1st Battalion, 327th Infantry. Don retired in 1990 as a major general. After serving thirty-five years in the Army, he headed the Old Soldiers' Home and then was the director of a retirement community. He helped mold me into a soldier.

Doc Benjamin left active duty when he returned from Vietnam. He completed his residency in radiology at Baylor College of Medicine and enjoyed a successful thirty-year practice in Santa Fe, New Mexico. Karen and Doc raised three children and celebrated their fiftieth wedding anniversary in 2012. Retirement in 2004 allowed him to devote time to a variety of charities, including the Vietnam Project. He has returned to Vietnam on numerous occasions. R. J. Benjamin was one of a handful of Medical Corps officers decorated four times for bravery. In addition to the Silver Star, he also received two Bronze Star medals and the Army Commendation Medal, all three with "V" devices for heroism.

Time has also taken its toll on the NCOs of ABU. First Sergeant Finley and three of the four platoon sergeants are gone. John T. Humphries, who retired as a first sergeant, died on April 26, 2007. His son in Japan, who John financially supported for years, never acknowledged his assistance. Only Bob Press is left. He retired as a sergeant major in 1974. I had the opportunity to meet with him over the last few years. Although age has slowed him down a step, he is still every inch a soldier and, like the legendary Basil Plumley of *We Were Soldiers Once . . . and Young* fame, he is a lion in the winter.[3]

SSG Travis Martin was wounded twice. In March 1966, he was evacuated from Vietnam with heart problems. The ailment claimed his life. Rocky Ryan, my RTO, spent over a year in the hospital recovering from the wound he received on September 10, 1965. His leg was saved but he suffered permanent disability, unable to work because of its severity. Originally a Yankee, he now lives in North Carolina and is still a tough guy.

Charlie Loustaunau recovered from his wounds and completed his Vietnam tour with ABU Company. He left the Army when he returned to the U.S.A. Charlie used the GI Bill to earn a degree from San Jose State University, even though he had never finished high school. He enjoyed a successful career with the U.S. Postal Service and is retired in Carmichael, California.

LTC Nguyen Van Dinh was promoted to full colonel and commanded the 1st Brigade of the Airborne Division. He was captured by the North Vietnamese in April 1975 and spent thirteen years in a re-education camp. After his release in 1988, Dinh immigrated to Portland, Oregon. The North Vietnamese jailers convinced him that Americans were not so bad after all.

MAJ Le Van Me managed to escape from Vietnam just before its fall. He moved to the United States and was employed in Silicon Valley. He became a model citizen in his adopted country. His interest in technology was a stepping stone to a new, productive life. Me is now retired and lives in San Jose, California.

＊＊＊

In 2011, my wife and I flew on Vietnam Airlines from Paris to Ho Chi Minh City, still called Saigon by everyone except government officials. We were aboard a new Boeing aircraft. Like the rest of the Socialist Republic of Vietnam, renamed after unification, the national airline has embraced *"Doi Moi,"* the new economy. The purser asked if I had ever visited his country. When I said I had been there a long time ago, he remarked I would see many changes. He was right, more than I anticipated.

An ultra-modern international terminal at Tan Son Nhut had replaced the small building I first saw in June 1965. Half-moon concrete revetments that protected U.S. jet fighters were now storage areas. Outside, the roads were filled with traffic and cars competing for the right of way with thousands of motor scooters, the preferred mode of transportation. U.S. facilities that once dominated the old base had been torn down and replaced with gleaming office buildings. Signs touted a mind-boggling array of international companies cashing in on Vietnam's economic expansion. Capitalism and communism have become comfortable bedfellows.

Flags are a staple of Vietnamese life. The red flag superimposed with the gold star, the North Vietnamese standard in our day, flew on every building. After unification in 1976, the National Liberation Front flag was quietly replaced. Officials of the NLF were shoved aside too. The Politburo in Hanoi no longer needed the pretense of a local revolution to exert total power. The southern resistance movement was sent down the river . . . literally, the Mekong River.

We stayed in the Caravelle Hotel, a symbol of wartime luxury. Remodeled, it continues to be one of Saigon's best. The hotel is located on Dong Khoi Street, meaning "uprising," an event that never occurred. When I was there, it was called Tu Do (Independence) Street and was the site of seedy bars. Brand-name shops like Louis Vuitton and Versace had replaced dives that featured ladies of the evening and watered drinks. From the top floor of the Caravelle, I could see old landmarks: city hall, the opera house, and the famed Continental Hotel.

Other French colonial buildings were still prominent. Notre Dame Cathedral and the Central Post Office were as imposing in 2011 as they were in yesteryear. The contrast between those edifices and what the United States built is startling. The French came to Indochina to stay and their imprint remains. MACV headquarters at Tan Son Nhut, called "Pentagon East," was the largest structure erected by the United States. Made of prefabricated sheet metal, it was meant to be temporary and is long gone, leveled when the last Americans evacuated in April 1975.

Guided tours are big business and the tunnels of Cu Chi, not far from Saigon, are a favorite attraction. They held no interest for me. Instead, we hired a driver and interpreter to take us up QL 13 to An Loc, 60 miles north. A new, dual-lane highway has replaced "Thunder Road" where the 101st Airborne Division encountered its first command-detonated mines in December 1965. It was difficult to get my bearings even though I had a hand-held GPS and my military maps. At Lai Khe, I found remnants of the old airfield but there was no trace of the U.S. 1st Infantry Division base. When the two Vietnams were unified, the new government was intent on ridding the country of any vestiges of U.S. presence.

Badly needed infrastructure was torn down simply because it was constructed by Americans.

An Loc was destroyed during the Easter Offensive. The town was rebuilt and commercial enterprise flourishes. You would never know anything of consequence, let alone a climactic struggle, occurred there. The communist government left no evidence of the battle. Several "martyr" cemeteries, each with a large statue commemorating the freedom fighters, are located just south of the town. Interred are the remains of NVA soldiers killed in 1972. These shrines are a reminder of the devastating effect of U.S. airpower. After the communists took over in 1975, they desecrated the 81st Airborne Ranger cemetery that the people of An Loc meticulously tended when the battle ended. There is no trace of it today. Similar acts of vandalism occurred at the National Military Cemetery at Bien Hoa, South Vietnam's Arlington. Many of the 20,000 graves, including the Tomb of the Unknown Soldier, were destroyed.

The Politburo opted for a harsh peace. Re-education camps, agricultural collectivization, and forced resettlement into new economic zones were part of a concerted plan to reform the South. The area around An Loc received more than its share of reformation activity. The old revolutionaries in Hanoi wanted to create a socialist utopia. Instead, they created famine and ushered in what became known as the Dark Years. A "brain drain" occurred, as people escaped from Vietnam, were incarcerated in camps, or were forced to resettle in inhospitable areas. When governmental incompetency was coupled with U.S. economic sanctions, Vietnam became a lost frontier. The invasion of Cambodia on Christmas Day 1978 added to misguided socialism's litany of woes. Except for its alliance with the Soviet Union, Vietnam was internationally isolated. The country of the early 1980s was close to being a failed state. Only after younger men replaced the old guard did saner foreign policy and free market initiatives begin to turn the flailing economy around.

Thanks to Doi Moi, the rubber industry around An Loc was thriving in 2011 and the stands of trees were being actively harvested. Tanker trucks collecting raw latex lined the road. The pace of the activity shows that entrepreneurial spirit was not eradicated by the doctrinaire brand of socialism imposed when the war ended.

Nowhere were the signs of economic growth more prevalent than in the seaside town of Nha Trang. Well-heeled tourists fly into the former U.S. air base at Cam Ranh Bay and then drive north to the city along a new coastal highway. The pristine shore was lined with luxury hotels. Several resort complexes featured beachfront bungalows renting for $400 or $500 a night. I found the site of the 8th Field Hospital where I was a patient in May 1966. Like other American facilities, it was torn down and replaced by shoddy Soviet construction. The buildings were crumbling and in dire need of replacement, illustrating the short-lived Vietnamese-USSR relationship.

Our final stop was Quang Tri, the last place I served in Vietnam. We stayed in Hue's Saigon Morin Hotel. First opened in 1901, it later housed Hue University. U.S. Marines fought hard to recapture it during the 1968 Tet Offensive. The Saigon Morin was renovated and has recovered the charm of the French era.

Again, we hired a vehicle to take us farther north. The town of Quang Tri was rehabilitated in the late 1970s. During its reconstruction, the Communist Party secretary, Le Duan, designated it a "heroic revolutionary city." One structure, Long Hung Catholic Church, was left in its destroyed state. The authorities use it for a photo opportunity to remind everyone of their ultimate victory. Called a relic of war, the church is lauded as a 1972 defensive position that "helped protect the Quang Tri Old Citadel [sic] for 81 days and nights of history." Reflecting the spirit of triumphalism that is seen on most war memorials, the sign in English and Vietnamese makes questionable assertions.

Quang Tri's Citadel is now a vast memorial park dedicated to the North Vietnamese victory over the "Saigon regime and its imperialist allies." Destruction of the old fortress is attributed to indiscriminate U.S. airstrikes. Accounts of the battle conveniently omit that the North captured the Citadel and the South Vietnamese successfully recovered it. It is a popular venue for local and foreign tourists. An English-speaking tour group was raptly listening to an earnest young guide expound on the tonnage of American bombs dropped in the summer of 1972. The guide called it wanton desecration. I had the urge to tell the tourists they were hearing BS but I refrained. Winners get to rewrite history and airbrush uncomfortable blemishes.

Being so close, I could not resist traveling to the former DMZ. The demarcation line between North and South ran along the Ben Hai River. When the 1954 Geneva Accords were signed, French soldiers assembled a bridge to allow refugees to migrate south. The repaired bridge now parallels QL 1 and is flanked by two more victory monuments. I paid 20,000 dong, one U.S. dollar, for the privilege of walking across it. I had vowed to relieve myself in the Ben Hai River but an ounce of judgment and partial dehydration saved me from myself.

After ten days it was time to return home because I had seen enough. The trip was a bucket list item. Closure, whatever that is, was not on the agenda. My war would not be tucked away nor forgotten. "Old Vietnam" would always be with me because it had been a defining moment in my life. Nevertheless, I had my own modest epiphany. I found no emotional connection, no nostalgia, at any location visited . . . they were just places from my past. I saw nothing to take me back in time, back to the bad old days. Perhaps that was healthy too. The Vietnam of my memory was not the same one just visited and I needed to let them both stay that way.

Rain came down in torrents the night we left. I remembered similar deluges. As our Air France A340 taxied toward Tan Son

Nhut's active runway, the concrete revetments that once protected U.S. jet fighters were plainly visible. These wartime structures were a reminder of all the sacrifices and losses in Vietnam. As they faded from view, the revetments were the only evidence I saw that two-plus million Americans had ever been here. I leaned back in the seat, closed my eyes, and for a moment the Vietnam War was very near. Dave Hackworth and I were peering at a map in the midst of a monsoon downpour, and we were both young men again.

Abbreviations/Glossary

1LT: First Lieutenant.

1SG: First Sergeant.

AAA: Antiaircraft Artillery.

AAG: Army Advisory Group. AAG was the parent U.S. Army headquarters of the Airborne Division Advisory Team. In 1972, AAG was commanded by MG William Coleman.

AAR: After-Action Report.

AD: Air Defense.

ADAT: Airborne Division Assistance Team. ADAT was the official designation of the division combat assistance team that advised the South Vietnamese Airborne Division. It was also referred to as MACV Team 162.

AFB: Air Force Base.

AFVN: Armed Forces Vietnam Network. A U.S. radio station that broadcast throughout Vietnam.

AO: Area of Operations.

AP: Associated Press.

ARVN: Army of the Republic of Vietnam

BCAT: Battalion Combat Assistance Team.

BCT: Basic Combat Training. Initial entry training for a new soldier.

BOQ: Bachelor Officer Quarters.

BG: Brigadier General

CDC: Combat Developments Command. U.S. Army command that was charged with overseeing research and development efforts from the 1960s to the 1980s.

COL: Colonel

CP: Command Post.

CPT: Captain.

DCAT: Division Combat Advisory Team.

DEROS: Date Eligible Return from Overseas.

DMZ: Demilitarized Zone—both in Korea and Vietnam.

DPRK: Democratic Republic of Korea, the official name of North Korea.

DRV: Democratic Republic of Vietnam, North Vietnam. Once North and South Vietnam were united in 1976, the country received a new name: Socialist Republic of Vietnam.

DSA: Deputy Senior Advisor.

DZ: Drop Zone. The designated landing area for paratroopers.

FAC: Forward Air Controller. A USAF spotter in a small, propeller-driven aircraft. FACs were the interface between advisors on the ground and the U.S. jet fighters.

FSB: Fire Support Base.

FTX: Field Training Exercise.

GEN: General

IOAC: Infantry Officers Advanced Course. A nine-month course at Fort Benning, Georgia, aimed at providing professional education to Infantry captains and majors.

JGS: South Vietnam's Joint General Staff. Equivalent of the U.S. Joint Chiefs of Staff.

KATUSA: Korean Augmentation to the U.S. Army.

KIA: Killed in Action.

KPA: Korean Peoples' Army, army of North Korea.

LGB: Laser Guided Bomb. Commonly referred to as a "Smart Bomb" because of its accuracy.

LT: Lieutenant.

LTC: Lieutenant Colonel.

LTG: Lieutenant General.

LWA: Light Weapons Advisor. Title given to NCO advisors in the Vietnamese Airborne Division.

LZ: Landing Zone. Usually given a name, the LZ is a designated area where helicopters land.

MAAG: Military Assistance Advisory Group. MAAG was established to distribute aid to the French; it remained in existence until it was replaced by Military Assistance Command Vietnam (MACV).

MACV: U.S. Military Assistance Command Vietnam. MACV commanded U.S. military units in Vietnam and the U.S. advisory effort.

MAJ: Major

MDL: Military Demarcation Line, showing the boundary between North and South Korea.

MG: Major General.

MPC: Military Payment Certificate.

MR: Military Region. A term used interchangeably to denote the geographical regions in Vietnam that the four corps encompassed. MR I was the northern region of South Vietnam, usually called I Corps.

NATO: North Atlantic Treaty Organization.

NCO: Noncommissioned Officer.

NCOCC: Noncommissioned Officer Candidate Course.

NDP: Night Defensive Position.

NGF: Naval Gun Fire.

NLF: National Liberation Front.

NPS: Naval Postgraduate School, Monterey, California.

NVA: North Vietnamese Army.

OCS: Officer Candidate School

OER: Officer Efficiency Report, an officer's "report card."

ORSA: Operations Research/Systems Analysis.

PCS: Permanent Change of Station. The term given when a military man receives orders for a new assignment.

PRC: People's Republic of China.

PRG: Provisional Revolutionary Government.

PX: Post Exchange, a military store.

PZ: Pickup zone, where helicopters land to pick up troops and supplies.

QL: Quoc Lo, National Highway in Vietnam.

QRF: Quick Reaction Force.

RCT: Regimental Combat Team.

REMF: Rear Echelon Motherfucker.

RIF: Reduction in Force, an action taken by U.S. officials to involuntarily release soldiers from active duty to reduce the size of the military. Following, the Vietnam War there was a large-scale RIF.

ROK: Republic of Korea, commonly called South Korea.

RPG: Rocket-Propelled Grenade.

RTO: Radio Telephone Operator.

RVN: Republic of Vietnam, South Vietnam.

SA: Senior Advisor.

SFC: Sergeant First Class.

SGT: Sergeant.

SITREP: Situation Report.

SIW: Self-Inflicted Wound.

SP4: Specialist Fourth Class.

SP7: Specialist Seventh Class.

SRV: Socialist Republic of Vietnam. The official name of Vietnam after the 1976 unification.

SSG: Staff Sergeant.

TIC: Troops in Contact.

TOC: Tactical Operations Center

TOW: Tube Launched, Optically Tracked, Wire Guided Missile.

TRAC: Third Regional Assistance Command. The U.S. headquarters that provided the advisory effort for the ARVN III Corps, the area around Saigon. MG James Hollingsworth was the senior advisor to the III Corps Commander during the battle of An Loc.

TRUST: Trieste U.S. Troops, a U.S. occupation force in the disputed territory of Trieste, Italy.

UH1: Utility helicopter known as the "Huey." Made by Bell Helicopter, this aircraft was the workhorse of the U.S. rotary wing fleet. It had a distinctive sound that most Vietnam veterans can identify to this day.

UI: Unidentified Infiltrator. Term given to an individual from North Korea who either breached or attempted to breach the barrier fence along the DMZ.

UNC: United Nations Command in Korea.

USATC: U.S. Army Training Center.

USCC: U.S. Corps of Cadets.

USFK: U.S. Forces Korea.

USMA: United States Military Academy.

USSR: United Soviet Socialist Republics, also known as the Soviet Union.

VNAF: Vietnamese Air Force. All Vietnamese aircraft, including helicopters, were part of VNAF. This structure increased coordination problems with ARVN.

WIA: Wounded in Action.

XO: Executive Officer, the #2 in command of a company, battalion, or brigade.

NOTES

PREFACE

1. E. J. Dionne Jr., "Murtha and the Mudslingers," *Washington Post*, January 17, 2006.
2. Lawrence M. Baskir and William A. Strauss, *Chance and Circumstance: The Draft, the War and the Vietnam Generation* (New York: Vintage Books, Random House, 1978), 33.
3. U.S. Government Archives, www.archives.gov/research/military/ vietnam-war/casualty-statistics.
4. James H. Webb Jr., Memo from the Assistant Secretary of Defense for Reserve Affairs to the Secretary of the Army, the Honorable John O. Marsh, dated August 26, 1986, 3–4, in author's possession.

CHAPTER 1: THE WAR WE CAME TO FIGHT

1. Vo Nguyen Giap, *People's War, People's Army: The Viet Cong Insurrection Manual for Underdeveloped Countries* (New York: Praeger Books, 1967), xxxvii.
2. David Fulghum and Terrence Maitland, *The Vietnam Experience: South Vietnam on Trial* (Boston: Boston Publishing Company, 1984), 151.
3. Peter Braestrup, "The South Vietnamese Army—Commanders and Soldiers 1972," in *Reporting Vietnam: American Journalism 1959–1975* (New York: Library Classics of America, 1998–2000), 614.
4. USACGSC RB 100-2, Volume I, "Selected Readings in Tactics (Chapter 7—1972 Vietnam Counteroffensive)," U.S. Army Command and General Staff College, Fort Leavenworth, KS, April 1974, 7-4–7-8.
5. Tonly Clifton, "Another Ordeal Looms for Hue," *Newsweek*, May 15, 1972, 22–23.
6. USACGSC RB 100-2, Volume I, Op. cit. 7-9 and 7-3.

7. Ronald H. Spector, *The US Army in Vietnam: Advice and Support—The Early Years 1941–1960* (Washington, DC: U.S. Army Center for Military History, 1983), 105–10.

8. Dave R. Palmer, *Summons of the Trumpet: U.S.-Vietnam in Perspective* (San Rafael, CA: Presidio Press, 1978), 18–21.

9. Edward Doyle and Samuel Lipsman, *The Vietnam Experience: America Takes Over 1965–1967* (Boston: Boston Publishing Company, 1982), 18–19.

10. Robert Pisor, *The End of the Line: The Siege of Khe Sanh* (New York: Ballantine Books, 1982), 160.

11. Andrew Wiest, *Essential Histories: The Vietnam War 1965–1975* (Long Island City, NY: Osprey Publishing, 2002), 13.

12. Graham A. Cosmas, *The US Army in Vietnam: MACV—The Joint Command in the Years of Withdrawal, 1968–1973* (Washington, DC: U.S. Army Center for Military History, 2007), 273.

13. Jeffrey J. Clarke, *The US Army in Vietnam: Advice and Support—The Final Years* (Washington, DC: U.S. Army Center for Military History, 1988), 542.

14. Fulghum and Maitland, Op. cit., 128.

15. MAJ John D. Howard, "The War We Came to Fight: A Study of the Battle of An Loc, April–June 1972," Student Research Report, Command & General Staff College, Fort Leavenworth, KS, June 1974, 2.

CHAPTER 2: EDUCATION, THE ARMY WAY

1. "Official Register of Officers and Cadets," United States Military Academy, West Point, NY, June 7, 1961, 148–50.

2. Stanley Karnow, *Vietnam: A History* (New York: Viking Press, 1983), 395.

3. *Cross of Lorraine: A Combat History of the 79th Infantry Division, June 1942–December 1945.* (Nashville, TN: Battery Press, reprinted in 1986), 4, 110.

4. David H. Hackworth and Julie Sherman, *About Face: Odyssey of an American Warrior* (New York: Touchstone Books/Simon & Schuster, 1990), 460.

CHAPTER 3: A FAR COUNTRY

1. This poem was in a newspaper published in Vietnam in the fall of 1965; it was sent back to the U.S.A. where my parents kept it. A copy was furnished to Dave Hackworth and used in his book, *About Face.*

2. Michael Casey, Clark Dougan, Samuel Lipsman, Jack Sweetman, and Stephen Weiss, *The Vietnam Experience: Flags into Battle* (Boston: Boston Publishing Company, 1986), 146.

3. *The Observer: Published Weekly for U.S. Forces in Vietnam*, August 21, 1965.
4. "Vietnam Humidity Ruins G.I.'s Boots in 6 Weeks," *New York Times*, September 15, 1965.
5. Hackworth and Sherman, Op. cit., 471–73.

CHAPTER 4: STEEL 5

1. John M. Carland, *US Army in Vietnam: Stemming the Tide—May 1965 to October 1966* (Washington, DC: U.S. Army Center for Military History, 2000), 80–81, 88.
2. Ibid., 185.

CHAPTER 5: THE TIGER FORCE

1. Michael Sallah and Mitch Weiss, *Tiger Force: A True Story of Men at War* (New York and Boston: Little, Brown and Company, 2006), 23.
2. Hackworth and Sherman, Op. cit., 144.
3. CPT John D. Howard, "Recon—Combat Notes from Vietnam." *Infantry*, 1968, 66.
4. Bernard B. Fall, *Street Without Joy* (Harrisburg, PA: The Stackpole Company, 1967), 146.
5. Dennis Foley, *Special Men: A LRP's Recollections* (New York: Ivy Books, 1994), 183–90.
6. Carland, Op. cit., 188.
7. Shelby L. Stanton, *Rangers at War: Combat Recon in Vietnam* (New York: Orion Books, 1992), 164. An extensive search of the Library of Congress POW/MIA digitized database on SGT Newton and PFC Wills corroborates Stanton's information.
8. Hackworth and Sherman, Op. cit., 519.
9. Ibid., 520–21.
10. Interview with Command Sergeant Major (Retired) Robert A. Press on August 15, 2012, in Nashville, TN, during the 101st Airborne Division Reunion, August 14–18, 2012.
11. Letter dated October 9, 2012 from Command Sergeant Major (Retired) Robert A. Press, in author's possession.
12. Carland, Op. cit., 192.
13. Interview with Press on August 16, 2012 in Nashville.
14. Carland, Op. cit., 193.
15. DA Form 67-5, Officer Efficiency Report dated June 15, 1966, in author's possession.

CHAPTER 6: SECOND KOREAN CONFLICT

1. Daniel P. Bolger. "Scenes from an Unfinished War: Low Intensity Conflict in Korea, 1966–1969," U.S. Army Command & General Staff College, Combat Studies Institute, Fort Leavenworth, KS, Leavenworth Paper #19, xiv.
2. Ibid., 46–49.
3. Richard K. Kolb, "Fighting Brush Fires on Korea's DMZ," *VFW*, March 1992, 28.
4. Bolger, Op. cit., 69–70.
5. John S. Bowman, ed., *The Vietnam War: An Almanac* (New York: World Almanac Publications, 1985), 218.
6. Bolger, Op. cit., 86–87.

CHAPTER 7: VIETNAM REDUX: MAY 1972

1. James H. Willbanks, ed., *Vietnam War: The Essential Reference Guide* (Santa Barbara, CA: ABC-CLIO, 2013), 53.
2. Willard J. Webb and Walter S. Poole, *The Joint Chiefs of Staff and the War in Vietnam*, Office of Joint History for the Chairman of the Joint Chiefs of Staff, (Washington, DC: Government Printing Office, 2007), 168.
3. Fulghum and Maitland, Op. cit., 23.
4. BG John D. Howard, U.S.A., "First In, Last Out: A Short History of the Vietnamese Airborne Division Advisory Team (MACV Team 162), 1955–1973" in Michael Martin, ed., *Angels in Red Hats—Paratroopers of the Second Indochina War* (Louisville, KY: Harmony House Publishers, 1995), 17–18.
5. Department of the Army General Orders #23, "Presidential Unit Citation," Washington, DC, April 16, 1969; Department of the Army General Orders #82, "Presidential Unit Citation," Washington, DC, December 9, 1969.
6. Clarke, Op. cit., 416.
7. 1LT Ross S. Kelly, Untitled Report Covering the Period April 14–21, 1972, 1–6, in author's possession.

CHAPTER 8: AN LOC I: APRIL–MAY 1972

1. Lewis Sorley, *Vietnam Chronicles: The Abrams Tapes, 1968–1972* (Lubbock: Texas Tech University Press, 2004), 833.
2. LTC Arthur E. Taylor Jr., Headquarters 1st Airborne Brigade Combat Assistance Team, APO 96307, "Combat Operations After Action Report, 1st Airborne Brigade," July 22, 1972, 2–3.

3. MAJ A. J. C. Lavalle, ed., *Airpower and the 1972 Spring Invasion* (Washington, DC: USAF Southeast Asia Monograph Series, Volume II, Monograph 3), 86–91.

4. Terrence Maitland and Peter McInerney, *The Vietnam Experience: A Contagion of War* (Boston: Boston Publishing Company, 1983), 91.

5. Mike McDermott, *True Faith and Allegiance: An American Paratrooper and the 1972 Battle for An Loc* (Tuscaloosa: University of Alabama Press, 2012), 135, 142.

CHAPTER 9: AN LOC II: JUNE 1972

1. Rudolph Rauch, "A Record of Sheer Endurance," *Time*, June 26, 1972, 26.

2. Ray L. Bowers, *The United States Air Force in Southeast Asia: Tactical Airlift* (Washington, DC: Office of Air Force History, 1983), 555.

3. Dale Andrade, *America's Last Vietnam Battle: Halting Hanoi's 1972 Easter Offensive* (Lawrence: University of Kansas Press, 2001), 424.

4. James H. Willbanks, *Battle of An Loc* (Bloomington: Indiana University Press, 2005), 149.

5. LTC James H. Willbanks, "Thiet Giap! The Battle of An Loc, April 1972," Combat Studies Institute, Fort Leavenworth, KS, 1993, 58–59.

6. Willbanks, Op cit., 175.

7. Taylor. Op. cit. Annex A. This annex lists all U.S. advisors who participated in the battle of An Loc, April 7–June 25, 1972. Not all the Airborne advisors were at the ceremony on June 23, 1972. Many had already DEROS'd or been med-evac'd.

8. SP4 Allen Schaefer (S&S Staff Correspondent), "Out of An Loc—Dead or Alive," *Pacific Stars & Stripes*, June 23, 1972, 6.

CHAPTER 10: QUANG TRI: JULY–SEPTEMBER 1972

1. LTG Ngo Quang Truong, *Indochina Monographs: The Easter Offensive of 1972* (Washington, DC: U.S. Army Center for Military History, 1980), 67.

2. MAJ John D. Howard, "The Vietnamese Airborne Division's Attempt to Retake Quang Tri City, 10–28 July 1972," unpublished paper written at Command & General Staff College, May 20, 1974, 3–4. This paper was incorporated into CGSC Publication RB 100-2, Volume I, Chapter 7. A copy of the original paper is in the author's possession.

3. Erik Villard, *The 1968 Tet Offensive Battles of Quang Tri City and Hue* (Fort McNair, Washington, DC: U.S. Army Center for Military History, 2008), 17–18.

4. Letter, dated December 17, 1973, from Captain Earl Isabell describing the 5th Airborne Battalion's attack in July 1972, in the author's possession.

5. Keith William Nolan, *Into Laos: The Story of Dewey Canyon II/Lam Son 719* (Novato, CA: Presidio Press, 1986), 358.

6. MAJ John D. Howard, Airborne Advisory Team 162, "Daily Log," 22, unpublished daily journal in author's possession.

7. Howard, "The Vietnamese Airborne Division's Attempt to Retake Quang Tri City, 10–28 July 1972," Op. cit., 5.

8. Ibid., 6–7.

CHAPTER 11: *CHIA TAY, VIETNAM*
(FAREWELL, VIETNAM)

1. Flora Lewis, "Vietnam Peace Pacts Signed; America's Longest War Halts," *New York Times*, January 28, 1973.

2. CPT Jack Jacobs, "After Action Report from the SA, 1st Airborne Battalion," Headquarters Airborne Division Assistance Team, APO SF 96243, dated August 20, 1972.

3. LTC Arthur E. Taylor Jr., "Combat Operations After-Action Report, 1st Airborne Brigade 23 July–19 September 1972," Airborne Division Assistance Team, APO SF 96243, October 27, 1972, 4.

4. Clarke, Op. cit., 524.

5. "After Action Report of the Airborne Division Assistance Team," Headquarters Airborne Division Assistance Team, APO SF 96243, dated February 15, 1973, 2–5.

6. MAJ Hugh D. Walker, "Evaluation of Counterpart Relations in 3rd BN, Airborne Division," Headquarters Airborne Division Assistance Team #162, APO SF, dated December 17, 1972, 1.

7. John Morrocco, *The Vietnam Experience: Rain of Fire—Air War, 1969–1973* (Boston: Boston Publishing Company, 1985), 157.

8. Marshall L. Michel III, *Eleven Days of Christmas: America's Last Vietnam Battle* (San Francisco: Encounter Books, 2002), 239–42.

9. Report from the Joint Task Force—Full Accounting: "Information paper for case 1978-0-04 and 1978-0-05 (SFC Elbert Wayne Bush and LTC William Lawrence Deane)" dated March 22, 2000, 1.

10. Handwritten memo for record by MAJ Roberto Eaton, Senior Advisor 3rd Airborne Battalion, "Ceasefire Observations," dated February 2, 1973, in author's possession.

11. Samuel Lipsman and Stephen Weiss, *The Vietnam Experience—The False Peace 1972–74* (Boston: Boston Publishing Company, 1985), 35–37.

12. MAJ John D. Howard, Op. cit., "Daily Log." 41, in author's possession.

EPILOGUE

1. Information furnished in an e-mail from the West Point Association of Graduates on March 31, 2014, is in author's possession. The West Point magazine, *Assembly*, published by the Association of Graduates (December 1988), lists 291 Academy men killed in action or died of wounds. Forty-three died in non-combat-related incidents.

2. James H. Webb Jr. "Can He Come Home Again?" *Parade*, April 2, 1989, 7.

3. LTG Harold G. Moore, U.S.A. (Ret.) and Joseph L. Galloway, *We Were Soldiers Once . . . and Young* (New York: Random House, 1992), 360.

BIBLIOGRAPHY

BOOKS/MONOGRAPHS

101st Airborne Division Association. *Vietnam Odyssey: The Story of the 1st Brigade, 101st Airborne Division in Vietnam.* Texarkana, TX: Southwest Printers and Publishers, Inc., 1967.

Andrade, Dale. *America's Last Battle: Halting Hanoi's 1972 Easter Offensive.* Lawrence: University Press of Kansas. 2001.

Baskir, Lawrence M., and William A. Strauss. *Chance and Circumstance: The Draft, the War and the Vietnam Generation.* New York: Vintage Books, Random House, 1978.

Boston Publishing Company, eds. *The American Experience in Vietnam: Reflections on an Era.* Minneapolis: Zenith Press, 2014.

Bowers, Ray L. *The United States Air Force in Southeast Asia: Tactical Airlift.* Washington, DC: Office of Air Force History, 1983.

Bowman, John S., ed. *The Vietnam War: An Almanac.* New York: World Almanac Publications, 1985.

Carland, John M. *US Army in Vietnam: Stemming the Tide—May 1965 to October 1966.* Washington, DC: Center for Military History, 2000.

Casey, Michael, Clark Douglas, Samuel Lipsman, Jack Sweetman and Stephen Weiss. *The Vietnam Experience: Flags into Battle.* Boston: Boston Publishing Company, 1986.

Clarke, Jeffrey J. *US Army in Vietnam: Advice and Support—The Final Years.* Washington, DC: Center for Military History, 1988.

Cross of Lorraine: A Combat History of the 79th Infantry Division, June 1942—December 1945. Nashville, TN: Reprinted by the Battery Press, 1986.

Cosmas, Graham A. *US Army in Vietnam: MACV—The Joint Command in the Years of Withdrawal, 1968–1973.* Washington, DC: Center for Military History, 2007.

Doyle, Edward, and Samuel Lipsman. *The Vietnam Experience: America Takes Over 1965–1967.* Boston: Boston Publishing Company, 1982.

Ethell, Jeffrey, and Alfred Price. *One Day in a Long War: May 10, 1972—Air War, North Vietnam*. New York: Random House, 1989.

Fall, Bernard B. *Street Without Joy*. Harrisburg, PA: Stackpole Company, 1967.

Foley, Dennis. *Special Men: A LRP's Recollections*. New York: Ivy Books, 1994.

Fulghum, David, and Terrence Maitland. *The Vietnam Experience: South Vietnam on Trial*. Boston: Boston Publishing Company, 1984.

Giap, Nguyen Vo. *People's War, People's Army: The Viet Cong Insurrection Manual for Underdeveloped Countries*. New York: Praeger Books. 1967.

Hackworth, David H., and Julie Sherman. *About Face: Odyssey of an American Warrior*. New York: Touchstone Books/Simon & Schuster, 1989.

Karnow, Stanley. *Vietnam: A History*. New York: Viking Press, 1983.

Lavalle, Major A. J. C., ed. *Airpower and the 1972 Spring Offensive*. Washington, DC: USAF Southeast Asia Monograph Series, Volume II, Monograph 3.

Lipsman, Samuel, and Stephen Weiss. *The Vietnam Experience: The False Peace 1972–1974*. Boston: Boston Publishing Company, 1985.

Maitland, Terrence, and Peter McInerney. *The Vietnam Experience: A Contagion of War*. Boston: Boston Publishing Company, 1983.

Martin, Michael, ed. *Angels in Red Hats—Paratroopers of the Second Indochina War*. Louisville, KY: Harmony House Publishers, 1995.

McDermott, Mike. *True Faith and Allegiance: An American Paratrooper and the 1972 Battle for An Loc*. Tuscaloosa: University of Alabama Press, 2012.

McKenna, Thomas P. *Kontum: The Battle to Save South Vietnam*. Lexington: University Press of Kentucky, 2011.

Michel, Marshall L., III. *Eleven Days of Christmas: America's Last Vietnam Battle*. San Francisco: Encounter Books, 2002.

Moore, LTG Harold G., and Joseph L. Galloway. *We Were Soldiers Once . . . and Young*. New York: Random House, 1992.

Morrocco, John. *The Vietnam Experience: Rain of Fire—Air War, 1969–1973*. Boston: Boston Publishing Company, 1985.

Nhut, GEN Tran Van, with Christian L. Arevian. *An Loc: An Unfinished War*. Lubbock: Texas Tech University Press, 2009.

Nolan, Keith William. *Into Laos: The Story of Dewey Canyon II/Lam Son 719*. Novato, CA: Presidio Press, 1986.

Palmer, Dave R. *Summons of the Trumpet: U.S.-Vietnam in Perspective*. San Rafael, CA: Presidio Press, 1978.

Pisor, Robert. *The End of the Line: The Siege of Khe Sanh*. New York: Ballantine Books, 1982.

Randolph, Stephen R. *Powerful and Brutal Weapons: Nixon, Kissinger and the Easter Offensive*. Cambridge, MA: Harvard University Press, 2007.

Sallah, Michael, and Mitch Weiss. *Tiger Force: A True Story of Men at War.* New York and Boston: Little, Brown & Company, 2006.

Sorley, Louis. *Vietnam Chronicles: The Abrams Tapes 1968–1972.* Lubbock: Texas Tech University Press, 2004.

Spector, Ronald H. *US Army in Vietnam: Advice and Support—The Early Years.* Washington, DC: Center for Military History, 1983.

Stanton, Shelby L. *Rangers at War: Combat Recon in Vietnam.* New York: Orion Books, 1992.

Thi, Lam Quang. *Hell in An Loc: The 1972 Easter Invasion and the Battle that Saved South Vietnam.* Denton: University of North Texas Press, 2009.

Truong, LTG Ngo Quang. *Indochina Monographs: The Easter Offensive of 1972.* Washington, DC: U.S. Army Center of Military History, 1980.

Turley, Colonel G. H. *The Easter Offensive Vietnam—1972.* Novato, CA: Presidio Press, 1985.

Vien, GEN Cao Van et al. *Indochina Monographs: The US Adviser.* Washington, DC: U.S. Army Center of Military History, 1980.

Villard, Erik. *The 1968 Tet Offensive Battles of Quang Tri City and Hue.* Washington, DC: U.S. Army Center of Military History, 2008.

Webb, James. *I Heard My Country Calling: A Memoir.* New York: Simon & Schuster, 2014.

Webb, Willard J., and Walter S. Poole. *The Joint Chiefs of Staff and the War in Vietnam 1971–1973.* Washington, DC: Office of Joint History for the Chairman of the Joint Chiefs of Staff, Government Printing Office, 2007.

Weist, Andrew. *Essential Histories: The Vietnam War 1965–1975.* Long Island City, NY: Osprey Publishing, 2002.

Willbanks, James H. *Abandoning Vietnam: How America Left and Vietnam Lost Its War.* Lawrence: University Press of Kansas, 2004.

Willbanks, James H. *A Raid Too Far: Operation Lam Son 719 and Vietnamization in Laos.* College Station: Texas A&M University Press, 2014.

Willbanks, James H. *Battle of An Loc.* Bloomington: Indiana University Press, 2005.

Willbanks, LTC James H. "Thiet Giap! The Battle of An Loc, April 1972." Combat Studies Institute, Fort Leavenworth, KS, 1993.

Willbanks, James H., ed. *Vietnam War: The Essential Reference Guide.* Santa Barbara, CA: ABC-CLIO, 2013.

Willbanks, James H. *Vietnam War Almanac.* New York: Checkmate Books, 2010.

OTHER GOVERNMENT PUBLICATIONS

Bolger, Daniel P. "Scenes from an Unfinished War: Low Intensity Conflict in Korea, 1966–1969." Combat Studies Institute, Fort Leavenworth, KS, Leavenworth Paper #19, 1991.

Department of the Army General Orders #23 and #82. Washington, DC, 1969.

HQDA Circular 624-59. "Recommended Lists for Temporary Promotion to Major, Army, Chaplain, Women's Army Corps and Army Medical Department." Washington, DC, Headquarters Department of the Army, October 18, 1968.

Mann, CPT David K. "The 1972 Invasion of Military Region I: Fall of Quang Tri and the Defense of Hue." Directorate Operations Analysis, CHECO/ CORONA HARVEST Division. HQ Pacific Air Forces, March 15, 1973.

"Official Register of Officers and Cadets." West Point, NY: United States Military Academy, June 1961.

"Official Register of Officers and Cadets." West Point, NY: United States Military Academy, June 1962.

"Official Register of Officers and Cadets." West Point, NY: United States Military Academy, June 1963.

"Official Register of Officers and Cadets." West Point, NY: United States Military Academy, June 1964.

Ringenbach, MAJ Paul T., and CPT Peter J. Kelly. "The Battle of An Loc 5 April–26 June 1972." Directorate Operations Analysis CHECO/ CORONA HARVEST Division, HQ Pacific Air Forces, January 31, 1973.

USACGSC RB 100-2, Volume I. "Selected Readings in Tactics." Command and General Staff College, Fort Leavenworth, KS, 1974.

PERIODICALS

Bauch, Rudolph. "A Record of Sheer Endurance." *Time*, June 26, 1972.

Clarke, Phillip C. "The Battle That Saved Saigon." *Reader's Digest*, March 1973.

Clifton, Tonly. "Another Ordeal Looms for Hue." *Newsweek*, May 15, 1972.

"COMUSMACV Pins Infantry Badges on Paratroopers." *The Observer: Published Weekly for U.S. Forces in Vietnam*, August 21, 1965.

Dionne, E. J. "Murtha and the Mudslingers." *Washington Post*, January 17, 2006.

Howard, CPT John D. "Recon—Combat Notes from Vietnam." *Infantry*, 1968.

Howard, MAJ John D. "An Lòc: A Study of US Power." *Army*, September 1975.

Howard, MAJ John D. "They Were Good Ol' Boys: An Infantryman Remembers An Loc and the Air Force." *Air University Review*, January–February 1975.

Kelly, LT Ross S. "Offensive and Counteroffensive: New Lessons in an Old War." *Infantry*, January–February 1973.

Kolb, Richard K. "Fighting Brush Fires on Korea's DMZ." *VFW*, March 1992.

Kolb, Richard K. "GI's Leave Behind the Vietnam War in 1973." *VFW*, February 2013.

Lewis, Flora. "Vietnam Peace Pact Signed; America's Longest War Halts." *New York Times*, January 28, 1973.

Schaefer, SP4 Allen. "Out of An Loc—Dead or Alive." *Pacific Stars & Stripes*, June 23, 1972.

Ulmer, COL Walter P. "Notes on Enemy Armor in An Loc." *Armor*, January–February 1973.

"Vietnam Humidity Ruins GI's Boots in 6 Weeks." *New York Times*, September 15, 1965.

Webb, James H., Jr. "Can He Come Home Again?" *Parade*, April 2, 1989.

UNPUBLISHED SOURCES

Chandler, LTC F. H. "After Action Report of Sapper Attack on Camp Evans 7 Sept 72." Airborne Division Assistance Team 162, Undated.

Eaton, MAJ Roberto. "Memorandum for Record—Cease Fire Observations." Handwritten note dated February 2, 1973.

Hansen, COL Marcus. "After Action Report of the Airborne Division Assistance Team." Headquarters Airborne Division Assistance Team, APO SF 96243, February 15, 1973.

Howard, MAJ John D. "The War We Came to Fight." Student Research Report for U.S. Army Command and General Staff College, Fort Leavenworth, KS, June 1974.

Howard, MAJ John D. Daily Log—6th Airborne Battalion, Airborne Division Advisory Team 162. Unpublished daily journal in author's possession.

Isabell, CPT Earl. Letter describing 5th Airborne Battalion's attack on Quang Tri City in July 1972. December 17, 1973, in author's possession.

Jacobs, CPT Jack. "After Action Report from SA, 1st Airborne Battalion." Headquarters Airborne Division Assistance Team, APO SF 96243, August 20, 1972.

Kelly, 1LT Ross S. Untitled Report Covering the Period, April 14–21, 1972, in author's possession.

Metcalfe, CPT Jerry F. Letter dated September 11, 1973 regarding the 8th Airborne Battalion's attack on FSB Barbara, October 1972, in author's possession.

Press, Sergeant Major (Retired) Robert A. Letter dated October 9, 2012, in author's possession.

Taylor, LTC Arthur E., Jr. "Combat Operations After Action Report, 1st Airborne Brigade." Headquarters 1st Airborne Brigade Combat Assistance Team, APO SF 96243, July 22, 1972.

Walker, MAJ Hugh D. "Evaluation of Counterpart Relations in 3rd Battalion, Airborne Division." Airborne Division Assistance Team 162, December 17, 1972.

Webb, James H., Jr. Memo from the Assistant Secretary of Defense for Reserve Affairs to the Secretary of the Army, August 26, 1986.

INTERVIEWS WITH FORMER MEMBERS OF ABU/1-327TH INFANTRY

CPT (later MAJ) Donald C. Hilbert: commander of A Company, 1-327th Infantry until August 1965. He became the operations officer (S3) of the battalion.

SP4 Charles Loustaunau: A rifleman in the 3rd Platoon, A/1-327th Infantry. He was wounded in September 1965 and returned to the platoon in 1966.

SP4 Galen Mitchell: grenadier in the 3rd Platoon. Wounded in April 1966. Retired from the U.S. Army as a first sergeant.

SFC Robert A. Press: platoon sergeant, 1st Platoon, A/1-327th Infantry. Press was promoted and became the first sergeant of A Company in 1966. He retired from the U.S. Army as a sergeant major.

SSG Billy Robbins: weapons squad leader, 3rd Platoon, A/1-327th Infantry, 1965–1966.

SP4 Raymond Ryan: My radio operator (RTO) in 1965. He was seriously wounded on September 10, 1965 and was medically evacuated to the United States.

SGT Frank Trezbuckowski: team leader in 3rd Platoon. His enlistment was up after we arrived in Vietnam and he returned to the United States to become a civilian.

The men cited above were members of A Company/1-327th Infantry and deployed to Vietnam from Fort Campbell in July 1965. They were interviewed in Nashville, Tennessee, during a reunion of the 101st Airborne

Division, August 14–18, 2012. Follow-up interviews were conducted at Fort Campbell, Kentucky (September 26–29, 2013) with Press, Mitchell, Robbins, Ryan, and Trezbuckowski.

AIRBORNE DIVISION ADVISORY TEAM

Correspondence with USMA classmates Barry McCaffrey, Jim Carson, and Chuck Jackson, all former advisors with the Vietnamese Airborne Division, provided a wealth of detail about advisory duty during the period 1966–1969.

Index